CHILDREN'S
MENTAL
HEALTH
SERVICES

CHILDREN'S MENTAL HEALTH SERVICES

The mental health needs of children have concerned policymakers and professionals for nearly a century. These concerns have intensified in recent years with increasing documentation on the magnitude of the problem and the extent to which children's mental health needs continue to be unmet. Sage's **Children's Mental Health Services Series** is aimed at addressing this need for systematic scholarly analysis of children's mental health needs and the policies and programs that serve them. Through involvement in constructing policy to system development to evaluation design, the esteemed authors of these volumes represent pioneers in the development of systems of care. It is our hope that these contributions will provide a rich basis for thought, discussion, and action.

In this series:

CHILDREN'S MENTAL HEALTH SERVICES

Research, Policy, and Evaluation

Leonard Bickman and Debra J. Rog
Editors

CMHS Children's Mental Health Services, Volume 1

SAGE Publications
International Educational and Professional Publisher
Thousand Oaks   London   New Delhi

For information address:

SAGE Publications, Inc.
2455 Teller Road
Thousand Oaks, California 91320
E-mail: order@sagepub.com

SAGE Publications Ltd.
6 Bonhill Street
London EC2A 4PU
United Kingdom

SAGE Publications India Pvt. Ltd.
M-32 Market
Greater Kailash I
New Delhi 110 048 India

Printed in the United States of America

Library of Congress Cataloging-in-Publication Data

Bickman, Leonard, 1941–
    Children's mental health services: Research, policy, and
evaluation / Leonard Bickman, Debra J. Rog, editors
        p. cm. — (Sage's Children's mental health services series; v. 1)
    Includes bibliographical references and index.
    ISBN 0-8039-7348-9 (c : alk. paper). — ISBN
0-8039-7349-7 (p : alk. paper)
    1. Child mental health services—United States. 2. Child mental
health services—Government policy—United States. 3. Child mental
health services—United States—Evaluation. I. Rog, Debra J.
II. Title. III. Series: Children's mental health series: v. 1.
RJ501.A2B53 1995
362.2'083—dc20   95-21948

This book is printed on acid-free paper.

95 96 97 98 99 10 9 8 7 6 5 4 3 2 1

Production Editor: Diane S. Foster   Typesetter: Christina Hill

Contents

Preface

We are very pleased to launch the Sage **Children's Mental Health Services Series.** We feel honored to have such an esteemed group of authors in this inaugural volume, all individuals who have been involved in one or more aspects of systems initiatives in the last decade. From involvement in constructing policy to system development to evaluation design, the authors represent pioneers in the development of systems of care. These contributions will hopefully provide a rich basis for thought, discussion, and action.

We are grateful to Sage Publications for sticking with us and encouraging us to edit this volume. C. Deborah Laughton, our Sage editor, was her tenacious, supportive self and helped to make the book a reality.

Corinne and John, our spouses, supported us in yet another editing collaboration, helping to stretch the hours in the day to bring the book to closure. They have our love.

Finally, we dedicate this book to Judith Gardner, a research associate at Brandeis University and one of the chapter authors. During the past 5 years, Judith worked tirelessly on the evaluation of the Mental Health Services Program for Youth and more recently as a key person on the Technical Assistance Center for Evaluation of Children's Mental Health Services, funded by the Center for Mental Health Services. Her untimely passing during the final stages of the editing of the book will be a loss to those of us who knew and worked with her and to all those who have benefited from her work.

Foreword

The initiation of the Sage **Children's Mental Health Services Series** comes at a critical point in the history of the children's mental health field. More important, this series comes at a critical point in the history of children and families in our country.

In 1982, in a book prepared for the Children's Defense Fund entitled *Unclaimed Children*, Jane Knitzer did a wonderful service for children and families by pointing out the deplorable status of services for children with emotional and/or behavioral disorders and their families around the country, and by mobilizing action to improve services. The introductory chapter in this book, by Debra Rog, offers a historical perspective on the years in which the need for effective mental health services for children and their families was ignored.

Since the publication of *Unclaimed Children*, there has been substantial progress in the children's mental health field in developing effective services. Individually, the leadership for this progress has come from many individuals, including Lenore Behar and Chris Koyanagi, whose work is included in this volume. Programmatically, the major source of leadership has been the Child and Adolescent Service System Program (CASSP), originally operated by the National Institute of Mental Health, and transferred to the Center for Mental Health Services in 1992.

A new paradigm for the children's mental health field was developed, which emphasizes the provision of individualized, family-focused, culturally competent, and strength-based services through an organized, multiagency, community-based system of care. New partnerships were developed between professionals and families, and increased emphasis was placed on strategies for promoting system accountability and conducting system-of-care research (Chapters 4, 9, 10, and 11). Large foundations such as the Robert Wood Johnson Foundation (Chapter 10) and the Annie E. Casey Foundation launched major children's mental health initiatives; the Department of Defense supported a major children's mental health demonstration project at Fort Bragg, North Carolina, in a unique state-federal partnership (Chapters 2 and 9); and the U.S. Congress passed and initiated the Children's Mental Health Services Program (Chapter 3), which provides funds for the development of community-based systems of care.

The Children's Mental Health Services Program, which in 1994 provided $60 million for improved services, was initially proposed by the National Mental Health Association, under the leadership of Chris Koyanagi, and was passed with active support from groups such as the Federation of Families for Children's Mental Health and the Children's Defense Fund. In recognition of the importance of multiagency system-building efforts, and in building on the efforts of CASSP, this new services program calls for strong collaborations at the local level between all of the major systems serving children and families with emotional and/or behavior disorders. Part III of this volume describes several of these systems (Chapter 5, primary health care; Chapter 7, schools; and Chapter 8, juvenile court). It also includes a chapter on one of the essential components within a system of care, the psychiatric hospital (Chapter 6). As the model of a system of care that my colleague Beth Stroul and I described in 1986 indicates, there are many other important system components, such as outpatient treatment, case management, home-based services, day treatment, therapeutic foster care, crisis care, and group care, and other important service system linkages, such as child welfare, substance abuse, economic supports, and recreation.

The progress that has been made in conceptualizing a new paradigm for children's mental health, in developing new service delivery models, in strengthening the research base, and even in securing additional service money represents the good news since the early 1980s.

The bad news is that despite the progress, the problems facing children and families seem to be getting worse. Whether we speak of

the prevalence of emotional and behavioral disorders, the age of onset for them, or their overall seriousness, every indication is that the
problems are not improving. And when we look at the incidence and
prevalence of many related conditions, such as substance abuse, delinquency, violence, physical abuse, and sexual abuse, we see similar
deteriorations in the well-being of our young people.

Although emotional and behavioral disorders, and all of the related problems affecting children, clearly occur in all socioeconomic
groups within our society, there is no doubt that one of the most
important risk factors is poverty. And more and more children and
families are in poverty. The 1994 KIDS Count report of the Annie E.
Casey Foundation, for example, reports that a quarter of all children
under the age of 6 in the United States live in poverty.

Our families, always the most important part of a child's life, have
undergone tremendous structural change, and are increasingly in
need of supports from extended family, the natural support systems
within neighborhoods, and our educational and service systems.
And yet at a time when such supports are so greatly needed, the
availability of natural supports within neighborhoods appears to be
diminishing, and educational and service systems are in great dis-
tress themselves.

The initiation of the Sage **Children's Mental Health Services
Series** at this particular point in time is therefore especially appropriate. We are at a time when we cannot spend too long congratulat-
ing ourselves on the progress in the field of children's mental health
since the early 1980s when there are so many indications that the pain
and suffering of children and families is increasing, and that therefore
the ability of young people to grow up to realize their potential and
make a contribution to our society is diminishing.

It is important that we carefully assess the changes that have been
made in recent years and learn both from our successes and our failures. It is also important that we study these successes and failures
in terms of their implications for both the field of children's mental
health and the overall well-being of children and families. The gains
that have been made and the learning that has taken place must be
examined and applied broadly to support and strengthen families,
to rebuild caring communities, and to reform systems. Otherwise,

despite limited successes, we will fail in our effort to improve the well-being of children and families.

I would like to congratulate Leonard Bickman and Debra Rog on the publication of this volume and the initiation of the Sage **Children's Mental Health Services Series.** I applaud their work in bringing together so many leaders in children's mental health to produce thoughtful and strategic analyses of the progress that has been made and the issues that remain to be addressed. I anticipate that this volume and entire series will make an important contribution to an understanding of where we have come from in developing effective service systems, where we still need to go to better support children and families, who our partners in this effort should be, and, perhaps most important strategically, how we should strive to move ahead.

ROBERT M. FRIEDMAN
Department of Child and Family Studies
Florida Mental Health Institute
University of South Florida

PART I

Introduction

The Status of
Children's Mental Health Services

An Overview

DEBRA J. ROG

The mental health needs of children have concerned policy makers and professionals for nearly a century. These concerns have intensified in recent years, with increasing documentation on the magnitude of the problem and the extent to which children's mental health needs continue to be unmet.

Prevalence rates of mental disorder from nine population surveys conducted in the 1980s (Anderson, Williams, McGee, & Silva, 1987; Bird et al., 1988; Connell, Irvine, & Rodney, 1982; Costello et al., 1988; Esser, Schmidt, & Woerner, 1990; Kashani, Orvaschel, Rosenberg, & Reid, 1989; McGee et al., 1990; Offord et al., 1987; Verhulst, Berden, & Sanders-Woudstra, 1985) indicate that 14% to 26% of children and youth under 18 years of age suffer from some type of behavioral, emotional, or developmental problem. These problems include both childhood-onset disorders and disorders that more often affect adults. The disorders evidenced in children cover a wide range, from emotional disorders, such as depression and anxiety disorders, to behavioral problems, such as conduct disorder, to developmental disorders, such as autism. Often diagnosis is difficult because children can have multiple disorders, often confounded by physical impairments, developmental stages, and adverse environmental factors, such as divorce, homelessness, and others (Institute of Medicine, 1989; Kazdin, 1989).

However, it is estimated that only 20% to 30% of those children identified to be in need of services actually receive any care (Office of Technology Assessment [OTA], 1986), much of which is considered to be inappropriate, typically overly restrictive care (National Mental Health Association, 1989; OTA, 1986). For example, Burns (1989) estimated that 70% of the funds available for children's mental health at that time were supporting institutional services. Institutional care has often been criticized as being overly used and more expensive than community care without demonstration that it is clinically more effective (Inouye, 1988).

Moreover, when they do receive services, children suffering from mental health disorders and their families often must contend with a disorganized, fragmented system of care, further complicated by the many nonmental health systems involved in the identification and treatment of children's mental disorders. These systems include the child welfare system, the educational system, the health care system, and the juvenile justice system (Horwitz, Leaf, Leventhal, Forsyth, & Speechley, 1992; Knitzer, 1989; Macro International Inc., 1992; Westendorp, Brink, Roberson, & Ortez, 1986).

This recognition of the enormous unmet need for mental health services among children, the overrestrictiveness of the care that is available, and the fragmentation of the system has led service providers, policy makers, advocates, and researchers alike to focus on the concept of a comprehensive community-based system of care for children and adolescents. This volume, the first in the **Sage Children's Mental Health Series,** presents the major current developments in the policy, service, and evaluation arenas that have implications for the development and refinement of comprehensive systems of services for children and adolescents with mental health needs.

This chapter provides an overview for the volume. A brief historical review of the area is first presented, followed by a status report on children's services and systems. Major initiatives are highlighted that have resulted or promise to result in major gains in policy development, service provision, or knowledge development. The chapter closes with a discussion of the current strengths and the continuing challenges in the field as it heads into the next century.

Historical Review:
Much Attention, Little Action

Almost every publication describing the state of children's mental health begins with an acknowledgment of the long history of attention to the topic. Reports, conferences, and consensus statements have been numerous, yet highly consistent: Millions of children are in need of mental health services but few receive them. This section reviews briefly some of the major events that have shaped current developments in the children's mental health arena.

Prior to 1969, the record shows that several White House conferences on children's issues were held. The 1909 White House Conference was the first meeting to bring national attention to the issues (Institute of Medicine, 1989). As a result of the attention, Congress established the Federal Children's Bureau in 1912 to manage all issues related to the welfare of children. A similar White House Conference was held in 1930, focusing on the dependent child and the child in need of special protection. In 1940, a third conference was held but broadened its focus to all aspects of child welfare. Despite these initiatives, the federal government continued to place little concerted effort on the emotional and mental health needs of children.

The report from the Joint Commission on the Mental Health of Children in 1969, however, signaled unprecedented attention to the issue. This congressionally established commission published an 800-page report detailing what was known about the needs of children, the lack of programs to meet these needs, and recommended initiatives that could be undertaken at the federal, state, and local levels to tackle the problem. This document, entitled *Crisis in Child Mental Health: Challenge for the 1970s* and considered a landmark publication, spawned two White House conferences in 1970 and 1971 to reinforce the recommendations, including initiatives that would foster a multitiered system of child advocacy, a comprehensive array of prevention and intervention services, research, and training efforts for professionals. However, despite the attention and activity brought about by the report, its recommendations, like those of earlier conferences, were not followed.

Attention to the issue continued at the federal level in the form of reports and documents (e.g., Salasin, Bregman, Entingh, Katz, & Thackston, 1977; Select Panel for the Promotion of Child Health, 1981), but no direct funding of services or research. Jane Knitzer's report in 1982, *Unclaimed Children*, highlighted the inaction at state and federal levels in both service provision and policy direction, and noted the lack of advocacy targeted toward the mental health needs of children. This report, sponsored by the Children's Defense Fund, repeated many of the findings of earlier documents but also highlighted some of the promise that was available in individual innovative project initiatives that were implemented in a limited way across the country. Knitzer called for public agencies to "reclaim" responsibility for children with serious emotional disturbances, with specific recommendations for state mental health agencies, other state agencies, the federal government, and advocates.

Knitzer's report served as a catalyst for the first concentrated attention to children's mental health at the federal level. In response to the report, the National Institute of Mental Health created the Child and Adolescent Service System Program (CASSP) in 1984. CASSP was created to assist states and communities in developing systems of care for children and youth with serious emotional problems and their families. The program began with the modest goal that every state have at least one mental health professional devoted to children's mental health. Since that time, the program has pushed, promoted, and facilitated the development of service systems in the states and legislation to support and mandate these developments.

The Concept of a System of Care

CASSP, in collaboration with the Office of Maternal and Child Health and the National Institute on Disability and Rehabilitation Research, has focused much of its activity on developing the concept of a "system of care" for children with mental health needs and their families (Stroul & Friedman, 1986). A system of care is defined as "a comprehensive spectrum of mental health and other necessary services which are organized into a coordinated network to meet the multiple and changing needs of severely emotionally disturbed children and adolescents" (Stroul & Friedman, 1986, p. 3).

Some of the hallmarks of the system of care are that it is community based, child centered, and driven by the needs of the child and the child's family. In addition, the system framework developed by Stroul and Friedman (1986, 1988a, 1988b) follows 10 guiding principles:

- That a full array of services be accessible to meet the comprehensive needs of children and their families, including emotional, physical, social, and educational needs
- That the services provided be individualized
- That services be provided in the least restrictive, most normative, clinically appropriate environment
- That families be provided full opportunity to be involved in the planning and delivery of services to their children
- That services be planned and delivered in an integrated fashion with services provided by other children's agencies
- That services be delivered in a coordinated and therapeutic manner, responsive to the changing needs of children and their families, through the use of either case management or other coordinating mechanisms
- That processes be in place for early identification of, and intervention with, children with emotional and behavioral needs
- That the system provide for smooth transition to adult services when a child ages out of the children's system
- That the system include mechanisms for protecting the rights of children and their families and provide for effective, active advocacy on behalf of families
- That services be provided in a manner that is responsive to cultural differences and special needs, and that does not discriminate on the basis of race, religion, national origin, sex, physical disability, or other characteristics

Following CASSP's lead, several initiatives have been designed to promote the development of systems of care within the states, albeit on a limited basis. In Chapter 2 of this book, for example, Lenore Behar describes the continued development of a system of care for children with mental health needs in the state of North Carolina. The

chapter describes the evolution of North Carolina's system, highlighting the importance of joint state and local planning, the importance of leadership by both professionals and parents in serving as
catalysts for changes in service delivery, and the need for continued
financing to support and promote systems change.

There also have been broader efforts, extending the efforts of
CASSP, that have supported and promoted the development of systems of care in the states. For example, the state mental health planning legislation (Pub. L. No. 99-660), now incorporated within the
state block grant administered through the Alcohol, Drug Abuse,
and Mental Health Administration (ADAMHA) Reorganization Act
of 1992 (Pub. L. No. 102-321), required states to restructure their services into an integrated community-based system of care. In addition, a recent demonstration effort funded by the Robert Wood
Johnson Foundation (RWJF) (see Saxe, Cross, Lovas, & Gardner,
Chapter 10 of this book) encouraged eight states to develop multiagency state community partnerships designed to improve services
for children and youth with serious mental illnesses. A major focus
of the RWJF program was to change financing policies to create more
support for community-based services. Finally, the military's insurer of civilian dependents, CHAMPUS, sponsored a major demonstration at Fort Bragg, North Carolina, designed to establish a
coordinated, community-based continuum of care for children (see
Bickman & Heflinger, Chapter 9 of this book).

Current Systems Initiatives

The Comprehensive Community Mental Health Services Program
for Children and Adolescents with Severe Emotional Disturbances
was signed into law on July 10, 1992, in Section 119 of the ADAMHA
Reorganization Act, and signals a new era for children's mental
health services. For the first time, children's mental health services
have received both congressional attention and a significant source
of funding for the provision of services and their integration. In 1994,
$35 million was distributed under this program for systems of care
in 38 different localities. More than any other development in the
history of children's mental health, this new program is likely to

accelerate the development of comprehensive services systems for children with serious emotional, behavioral, or mental disorders. Koyanagi, in Chapter 3 of this book, describes the developmental activities leading to this landmark legislation for children's mental health systems and highlights the importance of the parent advocacy movement in its creation. This sustained advocacy, through the Federation of Families for Children's Mental Health and other groups, had been a notable missing element in prior legislative attempts (Knitzer, 1982).

The program provides funding for a range of services and mandates that the states follow the principles of CASSP in developing their systems. Consequently, some of the key features of the intended system are a collaborative structure that involves multiple agencies; a coordinating mechanism to ensure services integration; and a range of community-based services that eliminate the typical barriers to access and provide care that is individualized, family focused, and culturally competent.

The overall purpose of the initiative is to enable states to develop coordinated systems of care that extend beyond the boundaries of the mental health system to include all systems in which children are identified or served. Thus, the multiagency structure of the system is to include child welfare, health, education, and juvenile justice. In Part III of this book, the chapters focus on several selected components of a multiagency system of care and note the strengths and contributions each can make in serving children with mental health needs and their families. Maloy, in her historical analysis of the juvenile justice system in Chapter 8, provides a convincing case for a pivotal role for the juvenile court in the system of care for children with mental health needs. Having played the role of gatekeeper to other agencies for troubled families and youth, the court has the power of the mandate to help promote comprehensive, integrated service delivery.

Two other components, primary care clinics and schools, share the advantage of being "natural," nonstigmatizing settings in which all aspects of a system—prevention, identification, diagnosis, and treatment—can occur. Wolraich, in Chapter 5 of this book, describes the current underutilization of the primary care setting for mental health intervention and the changes that are needed to increase its role in the system. Similarly, Ring-Kurtz, Sonnichsen, and Hoover-Dempsey in Chapter 7 describe the limited role that school-based mental health services have played and the barriers that continue to make it difficult to develop and implement mental health services in educational settings.

In Chapter 6, Nurcombe focuses on a renewed role for the psychiatric hospital, once a central element of mental health care, and now having a much more limited role. Nurcombe describes a model of ultrabrief hospitalization that would fill a crisis alleviation function within a comprehensive system of care for children with mental health needs and their families.

Current Services Initiatives

In addition to the attention focused on systems, there has been a focus on the services that are believed to be needed within a comprehensive system of service delivery (Rivera & Kutash, 1994). Among them are intensive home-based services (e.g., AuClaire & Schwartz, 1987; Hinckley & Ellis, 1985; Kinney, Madsen, Fleming, & Haapala, 1977; Stroul, 1988), therapeutic foster care (Hawkins, Meadowcroft, Trout, & Luster, 1985; Stroul, 1989), individualized wraparound services (e.g., Burchard & Clarke, 1990) and crisis services (Goldman, 1988). To date, data on the effectiveness of these services have come largely from program evaluation studies that have yielded promising, but not definitive, results (Burns & Friedman, 1990). More rigorous, controlled studies are needed that assess both the clinical and cost outcomes of these innovative services to develop a solid knowledge base on which to change and influence policy (Burns & Friedman, 1990).

Sondheimer and Evans, in Chapter 4 of this book, review federal efforts to develop a stronger knowledge base on effective system building as well as individual service strategies. The first major effort was the Request for Applications for the Child and Adolescent Mental Health Service System Research Demonstration Grants, initially published in 1990 and made a standing program announcement in 1991. This announcement was intended to stimulate rigorous investigator-initiated research demonstrations of state and local service systems for children and adolescents with serious mental disorders or at risk of serious mental disorders. Sondheimer and Evans review a few selected projects funded under this announcement.

Current Evaluation Initiatives

Evaluation of systems initiatives has recently begun (Bickman & Rog, 1992). Rog (1992) reviewed the challenges that evaluators face in evaluating children's mental health services and systems. Specific systems challenges identified include definitional issues concerning what constitutes a "system" and what constitutes "appropriate" care; problems in finding appropriate comparisons for statewide or city-wide systems; and tracking the implementation of systems at the system, treatment, and individual levels.

Three of the major current systems evaluations are described in this volume. Attkisson, Dresser, and Rosenblatt (Chapter 11) describe the design of their evaluation of the California System of Care Model for Children, initially implemented in Ventura County and disseminated to three additional counties in the state through enabling legislation. The evaluation is conducting a comprehensive examination of the three counties as they attempt to shift from service-agency-driven systems to client-driven systems.

Saxe, Cross, Loras, and Gardner (Chapter 10) describe the evaluation of the RWJF Mental Health Services Program for Youth, an eight-site demonstration focused on changing the organization and financing of services such that services provided will be more comprehensive, coordinated, and appropriate. A 5-year evaluation, the study is conducting a comparative, longitudinal analysis of the program to assess organization, financing, and treatment changes.

Bickman and Heflinger (Chapter 9) describe a third major evaluation effort, the Fort Bragg Evaluation. This study is examining a demonstration designed to test the theory that a comprehensive, integrated, and coordinated continuum of services is more cost-effective than a fragmented service system with a limited variety of services. The evaluation involves a quasi-experimental design in which the children and families receiving services in the Fort Bragg treatment site are compared to children and families receiving traditional services in two other army posts. The Fort Bragg study is unique in comprehensiveness and design. This evaluation not only focuses on system-level constructs through a network analysis but also collects clinical outcome data on close to 1,000 families in a longitudinal design.

Current Strengths and Continuing Challenges

Current Strengths

During the last decade, a number of activities have signaled an unprecedented time in the children's mental health area. In particular, the enthusiasm and development in the last 3 to 5 years in so many facets of the children's mental health field herald an age of dramatic and positive change for children with mental health needs. Assessment and research efforts, services development, and advocacy are three major hallmarks for future growth.

Assessment and Research

Advances in the diagnosis and assessment of children's mental disorders have improved identification efforts and, in turn, have provided an improved basis for epidemiological investigations and services research. The National Institute of Mental Health (NIMH), for example, is beginning to launch a major study of children's mental health service needs and use that would have not been possible 10 years ago. With improved research technology, NIMH is able to support a national, multisite study of mental heath service use, needs, outcomes, and costs in child and adolescent populations. Entitled "National Survey of Mental Health Service Needs of Youth" (UNO-CAP), the study will provide the first national rates of incidence and prevalence of mental disorders and rates of mental health service utilization. The study also will be able to provide an understanding of the barriers to service use and the costs, financing, and outcomes of services.

Services

There also has been a steady, though slow, growth in children's services, and an increase in state legislation supporting improvements in services. The promise of a solid source of funding for services through the Comprehensive Community Mental Health Services Program for Children and Adolescents with Severe Emotional Disturbances is likely to foster even more rapid development of comprehensive, community-based services for children with serious emotional, behavioral, or mental disorders.

Advocacy

Finally, since the late 1980s, advocacy efforts for children with mental health needs and their families have received new energy and attention. Friesen and Koroloff (1990) documented the growth in advocacy in this area, finding 50 of 350 parent groups representing families with severely emotionally disturbed children in 1988, compared to only 9 of 209 such groups just 3 years earlier.

As described in a brief historical analysis (see Rog, 1990), the lack of sustained advocacy in past efforts often has been noted as one factor that may, in part, account for the lack of progress in mental health services for children over the last century. However, the recent blossoming of parent advocacy groups has changed the advocacy landscape. Two major parent groups, Families as Allies and Parents as Allies, were started by the Portland, Oregon Research and Training Center, supported by NIMH's CASSP. Two additional groups have developed on their own. The National Alliance for the Mentally Ill, a parent-run organization typically for parents with grown children with mental illnesses, has developed a Child and Adolescent Network (referred to as NAMI-CAN) for parents of younger children with mental disorders (Flynn, 1989). Perhaps most key to the advocacy efforts for mental health service systems for children is the Federation of Families for Children's Mental Health. The federation is the first national parent-run organization focused solely on the needs of children and youth with emotional, behavioral, or mental disorders.

Continuing Challenges

The strengths identified above bode well for the future for children's mental health. However, there continue to be challenges that need to be recognized and addressed in order for the field to benefit from the strengths offered by research, policy, and practice developments. Two major challenges that thread across all three aspects are discussed below.

Maintaining Legislative Attention and Support

The recent children's program has been one of the most significant actions in the history of mental health services for children. It has provided a new source of funding and programmatic structure at the federal level. The program has grown out of the strong recent advocacy efforts, the leadership by CASSP, and other developments in the field. It would be tempting to believe that the major work on Capitol Hill has been accomplished and that efforts could now be devoted to building the systems and services in the communities.

However, the need to continue the focus on children's mental health in legislative arenas may be just as great as in past years. With shrinking resources, competing domestic priorities for these resources, and a new age of conservatism across the nation, pressures to demonstrate effectiveness and efficiency are strong at all levels of government. Rigorous research and evaluation data on both services and systems are essential to inform ways in which systems may be able to be streamlined and focused on those ingredients that are most cost-effective in improving the mental health outcomes of children.

Adapting and Changing With Knowledge

Saxe and his colleagues (Chapter 10) suggest that after years of talking about how to develop systems and eliminate fragmentation of services, it is time to put the rhetoric into action. This has begun; however, it is also time to examine, test, and modify the concepts on which the action is based. That is, as systems are developed and implemented, the field must be willing to change and restructure its actions and ideas on the basis of the evidence collected. In health and social service areas, programmatic directions are often made without the advantage of years of controlled study and evaluation. In contrast to some service areas, the children's mental health area has the advantage of being built upon a strong conceptual foundation (Stroul & Friedman, 1986). However, as evaluation and research findings become available on both systems and services effectiveness, it is important for the field to remain flexible in its orientation and to be responsive to the knowledge that is developed. Often in service areas in which practice traditions have been in place long before research has been developed, it is difficult to change direction in the light of significant scientific evidence. There is often the danger that customary practice will prevail despite the lack of evidence to support its continuing or even in the face of contradictory findings.

As we know from history even in the children's mental health field itself, the availability of knowledge alone is not enough to make action occur. As the OTA report stated in 1986, "We currently know more about how to prevent and treat children's mental health problems than is reflected in the care available" (p. 3). The field, therefore, must be careful not to repeat history. It will be essential for researchers and evaluators to make their findings available and accessible to all stakeholders in a timely and understandable fashion. In particular, when the family stakeholder perspective is included in the design, conduct, and reporting of an evaluation, it will have a much greater chance of developing results that are relevant to all interests. In turn, with informed and sustained advocacy, the chances are much greater that empirical knowledge will have a voice in improving the services and systems for children with mental health disorders.

References

ADAMHA Reorganization Act of 1992, Pub. L. No. 102-321, § 201(2), 106 Stat. 378 (1992).

Anderson, J. C., Williams, S., McGee, R., & Silva, P. A. (1987). DSM-III disorders in preadolescent children: Prevalence in a large sample from the general population. *Archives of General Psychiatry, 44,* 69-76.

AuClaire, P., & Schwartz, I. M. (1987, May-June). Are home-based services effective?: A public child welfare agency's experiment. *Children Today, 16,* 6-9.

Bickman, L., & Rog, D. J. (Eds.). (1992). *Evaluating mental health services for children.* San Francisco: Jossey-Bass.

Bird, H. R., Canino, G., Rubio-Stipec, M., Gould, M. S., Ribert, J., Sesman, M., Woodbury, M., Huertas-Goldman, S., Pagan, A., Sanches-Lacay, A., & Moscoso, M. (1988). Estimates of the prevalence of childhood maladjustment in a community survey in Puerto Rico. *Archives of General Psychiatry, 45,* 1120-1126.

Burchard, J. D., & Clarke, R. T. (1990). The role of individualized care in a service delivery system for children and adolescents with severely maladjusted behavior. *Journal of Mental Health Administration, 17,* 48-60.

Burns, B. J. (1989). Critical research directions for child mental health services. In A. Algarin, R. M. Friedman, A. J. Duchnowski, K. M. Kutash, S. E. Silver, & M. K. Johnson (Eds.), *Children's mental health services and policy: Building a research base. Second annual conference proceedings* (pp. 8-13). Tampa: Florida Mental Health Institute.

Burns, B. J., & Friedman, R. M. (1990). Examining the research base for child mental health services and policy. *Journal of Mental Health Administration, 17,* 87-98.

Connell, H. M., Irvine, L., & Rodney, J. (1982). Psychiatric disorder in Queensland primary school children. *Australian Pediatric Journal, 18,* 177-180.

Costello, E. J., Edelbrock, C., Costello, A. J., Dulcan, M. K., Burns, B. J., & Brent, D. (1988). Psychopathology in pediatric primary care: The new hidden morbidity. *Pediatrics, 82,* 415-424.

Esser, G., Schmidt, M. H., & Woerner, W. (1990). Epidemiology and causes of psychiatric disorders in school-age children: Results of a longitudinal study. *Journal of Child Psychology and Psychiatry, 31,* 243-263.

Flynn, L. (1989). The family phenomenon: The story of the National Alliance for the Mentally Ill. In R. M. Friedman, A. J. Duchnowski, & E. L. Henderson (Eds.), *Advocacy on behalf of children with serious emotional problems* (pp. 134-142). Springfield, IL: Charles C Thomas.

Friesen, B. F., & Koroloff, N. M. (1990). Family-centered services: Implications for mental health administration and research. *Journal of Mental Health Administration, 17,* 13-25.

Goldman, S. K. (1988). *Series on community-based services for children and adolescents who are severely emotionally disturbed: Vol. 2. Crisis services.* Washington, DC: Georgetown University Child Development Center.

Hawkins, R. P., Meadowcroft, P., Trout, B. A., & Luster, W. C. (1985). Foster family-based treatment. Special Issue: Mental Health Services to Children. *Journal of Clinical Child Psychiatry, 14,* 220-228.

Hinckley, E. C., & Ellis, W. F. (1985). An effective alternative to residential placement: Home-based services. *Journal of Clinical Child Psychology, 14,* 209-213.

Horwitz, S. M., Leaf, P. J., Leventhal, J. M., Forsyth, B., & Speechley, K. N. (1992). Identification and management of psychosocial and developmental problems in community-based primary care pediatric practices. *Pediatrics, 89,* 480-485.

Inouye, D. K. (1988). Children's mental health issues. *American Psychologist, 43,* 813-816.

Institute of Medicine. (1989). *Research on children and adolescents with mental, behavioral, and developmental disorders: Mobilizing a national initiative.* Washington, DC: National Academy Press.

Joint Commission on Mental Health of Children. (1969). *Crisis in child mental health: Challenge for the 1970s.* New York: Harper & Row.

Kashani, J. H., Orvaschel, H., Rosenberg, T., & Reid, J. (1989). Psychopathology among a community sample of children and adolescents: A developmental perspective. *Journal of the American Academy of Child and Adolescent Psychiatry, 28,* 701-706.

Kazdin, A. E. (1989). Developmental psychopathology: Current research, issues, and direction. *American Psychologist, 44,* 180-187.

Kinney, J., Madsen, B., Fleming, T., & Haapala, D. (1977). Homebuilders: Keeping families together. *Journal of Consulting and Clinical Psychology, 45,* 667-673.

Knitzer, J. (1982). *Unclaimed children: The failure of public responsibility to children and adolescents in need of mental health services.* Washington, DC: Children's Defense Fund.

Knitzer, J. (1989). Children's mental health: The advocacy challenge. In R. M. Friedman, A. J. Duchnowski, & E. L. Henderson (Eds.), *Advocacy on behalf of children with serious emotional problems* (pp. 15-27). Springfield, IL: Charles C Thomas.

Macro International Inc. (1992). *Final report: Community-based mental health services for children in the child welfare system* (Report #HHS-100-91-0016-01). Washington, DC: Department of Health and Human Services.

McGee, R., Feehan, M., Williams, S., Partridge, F., Silva, P. A., & Kelly, J. (1990). DSM-II disorders in a large sample of adolescents. *Journal of the American Academy of Child and Adolescent Psychiatry, 29,* 611-619.

National Mental Health Association. (1989). *Final report and recommendations of the Invisible Children Project.* Alexandria, VA: Author.

Office of Technology Assessment. (OTA). (1986). *Children's mental health: Problems and services.* Washington, DC: Author.

Offord, R., Boyle, H., Szatmari, P., Rae-Grant, I., Links, S., Cadman, T., Byles, J., Crawford, W., Blum, M., Byrne, C., Thomas, H., & Woodward, C. (1987). Ontario Child Health Study: Six-month prevalence of disorder and rates of service utilization. *Archives of General Psychiatry, 44,* 832-836.

Rivera, V. R., & Kutash, K. (1994). *Components of a system of care: What does the research say?* Tampa: University of South Florida, Florida Mental Health Institute.

Rog, D. J. (1990). *The status of children's mental health.* Alexandria, VA: National Mental Health Association.

Rog, D. J. (1992). Child and adolescent mental health services: Evaluation challenges. In L. Bickman & D. J. Rog (Eds.), *Evaluating children's mental health services: Methodological issues* (pp. 5-16). San Francisco: Jossey-Bass.

Salasin, J., Bregman, H., Entingh, D., Katz, R., & Thackston, K. (1977). *Challenges for children's mental health services.* McLean, VA: MITRE Corporation.

Select Panel for the Promotion of Child Health. (1981). *Better health for our children: A national strategy* (DHHS Publication No. PHS 79-550781). Washington, DC: Author.

Stroul, B. A. (1988). *Series on community-based services for children and adolescents who are severely emotionally disturbed: Vol. 1. Home-based services.* Washington, DC: Georgetown University Child Development Center.

Stroul, B. A. (1989). *Series on community-based services for children and adolescents who are severely emotionally disturbed: Vol. 3. Therapeutic foster care.* Washington, DC: Georgetown University Child Development Center.

Stroul, B. A., & Friedman, R. M. (1986). *A system of care for severely emotionally disturbed children and youth.* Washington, DC: Georgetown University, Child and Adolescent Service System Program Technical Assistance Center.

Stroul, B. A., & Friedman, R. M. (1988a, July-August). Principles for a system of care. *Children Today, 17,* 11-15.

Stroul, B. A., & Friedman, R. M. (1988b, July-August). Putting principles into practice. *Children Today, 17,* 15-17.

Verhulst, F., Berden, G., & Sanders-Woudstra, J. A. R. (1985). Mental health in Dutch children: The prevalence of psychiatric disorder and relationship between measures. *Acta Psychiatrica Scandinavica, 72*(Suppl.), 1-45.

Westendorp, F., Brink, K. L., Roberson, M. K., & Ortez, I. E. (1986). Variables which differentiate placement of adolescents into juvenile justice or mental health systems. *Adolescence, 21,* 23-37.

PART II

Encouraging Comprehensive Systems of Care:
State and Federal Policies

Numerous developments over the last 15 years at both the state and federal levels have paved the way for unparalleled progress for children's mental health services. As many of the authors of this volume note, the need for improved children's mental health services and the problems with delivery of these services have been well known for years. Only within the last decade, however, have real strides been made on both state and federal fronts to accelerate the development of services and the research to continue this acceleration.

In Chapter 2, Lenore B. Behar describes the continued development of a system of care for children with mental health needs in the state of North Carolina. A pioneer in the field, Behar has led the nation not only in building a continuum of care but in demonstrating ways of improving the financing of this continuum through the integration of a variety of funding streams. This chapter describes the evolution of North Carolina's system, highlighting the importance of joint state and local planning and leadership by both professionals and parents in serving as catalysts for changes in service delivery. The chapter points out that system change can only occur if financing mechanisms support this change in perspective.

Chris Koyanagi and Diane L. Sondheimer and Mary E. Evans describe recent developments at the federal level that are encouraging the development of systems of care. Koyanagi (Chapter 3) describes the behind-the-scenes activities that helped to shape the more visible activities on Capitol Hill leading to the landmark legislation for children's mental health systems. In detailing the events that have increased the momentum in the children's mental health services arena, Koyanagi notes, as did Behar, the importance of the growing leadership by parents and the joint efforts of professionals in several related areas such as special education for making changes that in past times have not been possible. In addition, Koyanagi chronicles the leadership by the Child and Adolescent Service System Program (CASSP) and its continued efforts to improve conditions within the states.

Sondheimer and Evans (Chapter 4) describe in detail the latest evolution of CASSP, involving more emphasis on further developing the knowledge base of services for children with special health needs. The authors describe the set of research demonstrations currently underway as well as the areas that continue to be in need of further research and investigation.

State-Level Policies
in Children's Mental Health

An Example of System Building and Refinancing

LENORE B. BEHAR

During the 1980s, major changes were initiated by the states in the delivery of mental health services to children and their families. These changes included (a) an emphasis on *community-based treatment services*, especially nonresidential services designed to keep children and families together; (b) a renewed enthusiasm to develop a *continuum of care* with improved availability of and access to services appropriate to the needs of the child and family; (c) an effort to *enhance family involvement* in the design and implementation of treatment, incorporating a major change regarding attitudes about the role of the family; (d) a recognition that services must be designed and delivered in ways that are *culturally and ethnically sensitive*; (e) a focus on *coordination of services* across agencies and practitioners, recognizing shared responsibility for clients and the need to combine resources; and (f) a *reassessment of financing mechanisms*, based on the recognition that existing resources could be better used. These changes reflect shifts in policies and practices resulting from the combined impact of professional experience that grew out of earlier successes and failures to improve services to children with emotional disturbance and to their families. Further, these changes were tightly tied to changes in other systems for children and adolescents. Although the stimuli for these changes came from many sources, the leadership for changes in the delivery of child mental health services was provided by professionals, primarily in the public sector, and by parents. The impact was that many forces converged, resulting in significant consensus across the country on how mental health services to children and families should best be delivered.

The Forces for Change

At the beginning of the last decade, there was no coherent public policy regarding services for children with mental health problems. There was little understanding among decision makers and the general public of what child mental health problems were or how they should be treated. And although the needs of children with emotional problems were felt intensely by their parents, their teachers, and the mental health professionals who provided diagnosis and treatment, there was little public recognition of the struggles of these children or their need for services. Planning for the development of services was virtually nonexistent in most states. Parents, mental health professionals, and other professionals who dealt with children struggled to identify treatment resources for these children.

Despite the efforts of Congress, during 1965 through 1969, to understand the needs of children through the Joint Commission on Mental Health of Children, there was little sustained focus on child mental health as a public policy issue some 10 years after the publication of their report in 1969 (Joint Commission on Mental Health of Children, 1969). And despite the efforts of subsequent commissions and studies, the plight of children with mental health problems was overshadowed within the mental health community by concerns regarding deinstitutionalization of adults with mental illness. Efforts and funding within the states were concentrated on the development of community support programs for adults with mental illness to decrease the populations of the state hospitals. In some state mental health agencies, there was virtually no ownership of the population of children with mental health problems; in other state mental health agencies, attention to children took the form of services within state hospitals and residential treatment centers; and in still other state mental health agencies, a commitment to children was apparent, even though the resources for services were slow to materialize (Knitzer, 1982).

Because of a lack of programs providing appropriate mental health treatment, children with mental health problems were often referred to the services of other public agencies, such as special education, child welfare, and juvenile justice. These agencies found that their capabilities to meet children's needs were compromised by the lack of available mental health services. However, their efforts were focused on improving their capacity to respond to their own mandates, not on seeking improvements in other systems.

During the early 1980s, state efforts focused primarily on the implementation of federal laws that mandated educational services and/or protections for children. Through Public Law 94-142, the Education of the Handicapped Act of 1975, now the Individuals With Disabilities Education Act of 1990 (IDEA), parents, educators, and advocates struggled to ensure that children with handicapping conditions received free and appropriate public education. Despite the federal mandate, special educational services for children with mental health problems varied from state to state, given each state's interpretation of the criteria for inclusion. Protests from parents and advocates and legal action against some states brought increases in educational services for this population, but the lack of clear criteria for inclusion, the lack of funding, and the lack of trained personnel left the educational needs unfulfilled for children with mental health problems in many states. In other states, school systems, in order to fulfill their mandate, either developed their own mental health services or purchased them from private providers.

Similarly during this time period, the child welfare system was addressing the problems of protective services and foster care, as required by Public Law 96-272, to ensure that all reasonable efforts were made to keep children within their families. As with the education systems, the juvenile justice and welfare systems had varied approaches to meeting the mental health needs of children in their care or custody: Some developed their own mental health services;

some purchased services; and others were unable to address the mental health problems of children in trouble with the law or children who were abused, neglected, or orphaned.

In those states that had made a commitment to serving children within their public mental health system, none could be described as exemplary. In some of those states, professionals in leadership positions were formulating plans about how to develop a continuum of mental health services that was responsive to the needs of the children and their families and that was organized in a systematic way. Such change required a blueprint, and the continuum of care delineated by the Joint Commission on Mental Health of Children served this purpose well. In addition to a plan or a vision, change required the leadership to articulate the vision and the support or infrastructure to put the vision in place. In some places, the time was more right for such change than in others. In North Carolina during the late 1970s, several of the necessary ingredients were in place for developing a continuum of child mental health services. The movement in this state contributed substantially to improving the service system for children over the next decade across the country. As North Carolina was moving forward with systems change, the National Institute of Mental Health initiated the Child and Adolescent Service System Program (CASSP). Using the experience in North Carolina and a few other states, the CASSP initiative provided opportunity for state-level child mental health professionals across the country to develop organized plans for how mental health services to children should be delivered.

The Foundation for a System

Two features of the mental health system in North Carolina provided a foundation on which to build a continuum of child mental health services. These features were (a) the structure of the relationship between state and local agencies and (b) the commitment to child mental health services as a part of the mental health system.

The first feature of a community-based system for children in North Carolina was the basic structure of community mental health centers, which provide services to three disability areas: mental health, developmental disabilities, and substance abuse. Legislation designated these centers as geopolitical entities with decision-making boards that operated the programs essentially as public non-profit agencies. The centers that encompassed more than one county were administered neither by the state nor by county government. However, the centers that chose to encompass a single county were closely overseen by the county government.

The role of the state agency, from the beginning, was to operate the state residential institutions and to facilitate the development of the local entities, called *area programs,* a term derived from the concept of catchment areas. With this structure came agreements that strengthened system development, such as the policy that all community mental health funds went to these local agencies either for the direct delivery of services or for services delivered through contracts with local providers. The state did not develop contracts with private providers; all responsibility for planning, developing, and delivering services rested with the area programs. Thus, all decisions about program and budget priorities, monitoring standards, financing mechanisms, and any other major policies were made jointly by the office staff and the directors of the area programs. To maintain a balanced relationship between state and local entities, mechanisms for ongoing communication were developed, involving monthly meetings of key people from both levels of the system. The state-local relationship has created the infrastructure to support a mental health system and thus the foundation for developing child mental health services.

The second important feature was that from the beginning, at both the local level and the state level, child mental health services were to be an integral part of North Carolina's system. The first set of statewide standards required generic state funds for community-based programs to be distributed between adult and child services according to the distribution of the population. The North Carolina General Assembly, through its Mental Health Study Commission, maintained a similar commitment to building services within the mental health, developmental disabilities, and substance abuse system for the children of the state.

Building the
Continuum of Mental Health Services

Most professionals considered the logic of the continuum-of-care concept to be sound and adhered to the goal of having a range of services of increasing intensity to meet the needs of children in the community. The belief was that within a community there were children with treatment needs for varying levels of service, and that for any given child, the treatment needs might change over time, hopefully based on improvement, so that a range of services decreasing in intensity would be used.

This concept has been the basis of planning in North Carolina since the creation of the Child Mental Health Office in 1970. However, during the early 1970s, the polar points of the continuum—outpatient and inpatient services—were the most visible services. Group homes, as residential treatment sites, and some day treatment programs were begun during this period. Although not sufficient to address the volume of need, the existence of these programs served to stimulate the demand for more programs distributed across the state. Despite a basic commitment to building a continuum of child mental health services in North Carolina, the legislative increases in state dollars provided for slow, piecemeal additions, suggesting that it would take decades until the continuum was completed. Toward the end of the 1970s, it became apparent not only that the continuum of care was developing slowly but that the needs of children were more visibly not being met. Waiting lists for community-based services were growing; more children needed treatment services that were not available at all or not available in sufficient quantities. In addition, a state law was passed in 1978 to protect minors who were voluntarily admitted to both public and private inpatient psychiatric settings, requiring judicial review of the appropriateness of the initial placement and of the continuation of placement. With judicial review came the assignment of an attorney to each child in a hospital, and through the attorneys came an interest in accelerating the development of the community-based child mental health system so that children were not inappropriately referred to hospitals or kept for an inappropriate length of time.

Although litigation was considered a force for bringing about change in the juvenile justice, education, and child welfare systems, the bases for litigation in the area of child mental health were less clear, given the absence of a legal mandate for states to provide mental health services. There was no legal entitlement for children to receive mental health services, except as part of their educational entitlement under Public Law 94-142 or their right to treatment in exchange for confinement. These somewhat tenuous links to legal entitlements provided a basis within North Carolina for concerned judges, attorneys, and mental health professionals to carefully construct a lawsuit on behalf of children in the state psychiatric hospitals that led to an expansion of the community mental health system as the settlement plan. This class action lawsuit on behalf of seriously disturbed and assaultive children, *Willie M. v. Hunt* (1980), led to major changes in the way mental health services to children were provided both in North Carolina and across the country.

Clarifying Responsibility

The state of North Carolina moved to settle the *Willie M.* lawsuit by naming the Division of Mental Health, Developmental Disabilities, and Substance Abuse Services as the lead agency, with the responsibility for the delivery of services managed locally by the area Mental Health, Developmental Disabilities, and Substance Abuse programs. Their responsibility was to identify the treatment or rehabilitation needs of the approximately 1,150 class members and to organize the array of individualized services appropriate for each class member. The North Carolina legislature appropriated substantial funds, $18 million in 1981, to develop a community-based system of services for the class members, and these funds have been increased as the needs have demanded.

Providing the services required under the settlement agreement, beginning in 1981, marked a change in responsibilities for the state and the area programs (Behar, 1985). Statewide case management services were implemented, and the concept of wraparound services (Behar, 1986) was developed. This concept later was adopted nationwide as the way to provide individualized services for children with serious emotional disturbance (Burchard & Clarke, 1990; VanDenBerg, 1993).

Within the state of North Carolina, the Willie M. program had a profound, but subtle, effect on the professionals providing services. Because the program required a "no eject, no reject" approach to clients, children who formerly would have been denied services on the basis of their being "untreatable" were now required to be served. Using intensive case management, wraparound services, and a full continuum of other treatment services, professionals found that many "untreatable" children responded to treatment. The lesson learned was that individualized treatment plans could be effective if the array of services was broad enough, if progress was monitored, and if plans were revised as needed.

The drawback of the Willie M. program as a model for implementing the continuum of services for other populations of children with emotional disturbance was the cost of serving this most difficult population. By the mid-1980s, the average cost per child served was approximately $30,000 per year. Although mental health professionals understood that for this population the cost was not inordinately high, legislators and other decision makers were shocked at the cost of mental health services and were reluctant to undertake further development of the mental health system for children for fear it would "break the bank." By the mid-1980s, the continuum-of-care/system-of-services model had become the foundation of CASSP (Stroul & Friedman, 1986); therefore, to demonstrate the effectiveness of this model, it was important to fund a system of care that addressed the needs of children with a wider range of emotional problems, including those less severely impaired than the Willie M. population. In 1987, the North Carolina legislature adopted a Child Mental Health Plan to provide for all children in need the range of mental health services available to the Willie M. population; it was projected that this plan would take 10 years to fully fund and implement.

Enhancing the Model

In 1989, the development of the Fort Bragg Child and Adolescent Mental Health Demonstration Project provided the opportunity, in one part of the state, to implement a fully funded, full continuum-of-care system of services for all children with mental health problems, not only those most seriously impaired (Behar, 1990). The project began in 1989 through a 57-month cost-reimbursement contract between the Department of the Army and the North Carolina Division of Mental Health, Developmental Disabilities, and Substance Abuse Services. Through the General James Rumbaugh, Jr., Clinic, the project provided a fully comprehensive organized system of mental health and substance abuse services to approximately 46,000 children under 18 years of age who were dependents of military personnel and who resided within the Fort Bragg catchment area. The approximate annual budget for clinical services was $18 million to serve approximately 3,250 children, or 7% of the eligible population. This demonstration project is an example of a seamless system or integrated services system that integrates services across levels of care and across all the agencies and providers involved with the children served.

The demonstration was designed to test the belief among mental health professionals that many children are unnecessarily hospitalized for mental health problems and paid for through health care programs that limit benefits to outpatient and inpatient care. Children under these plans are hospitalized for lack of appropriate alternatives when more than outpatient care is needed. This type of hospitalization is unnecessarily restrictive and expensive. It is believed that a significant portion of this type of hospitalization can be prevented and that length of stay for children who need hospitalization can be reduced through the use of a continuum of services that offers community-based alternatives to hospitalization as well as appropriate step-down services for earlier release from more restrictive levels of care. The benefits of such a service system are believed to be twofold: (a) Clients receive more appropriate care, and (b) such care is provided at a lower cost per child served.

The project offers a wider range of treatment services to provide alternatives to hospitalization and to serve as aftercare services for those who are hospitalized appropriately for acute care. Children enter the service system through a single portal of entry and are provided a comprehensive intake assessment to identify their mental health needs. Through multidisciplinary treatment teams and a case

management approach, the project mobilizes the community's resources and coordinates each child's care to make sure he or she
receives the right mix of needed services in a clinically appropriate
and cost-effective manner. Services are individually planned for each
child and are provided in the least restrictive setting possible. Families participate in the treatment planning process as well as in the
client's treatment. Treatment may be provided at the clinic, in the
home, at school, in therapeutic residential settings, or by contract
with hospitals and private service providers in the community, as
appropriate. Treatment is managed through the use of case managers
who review progress and ongoing need for treatment; thus, the project exemplifies managed care within a continuum of seamless services.

To study the effectiveness of the demonstration project on a number of levels, an independent evaluation was conducted by the Center for Mental Health Policy of the Institute for Public Policy Studies
at Vanderbilt University (see Bickman & Heflinger, Chapter 9 of this
book). Vanderbilt University compared the project's service delivery
system with the traditional system at two comparison sites: Fort
Campbell, Kentucky, and Fort Stewart, Georgia. The comparison
sites were selected because of similarities in military mission, population size and characteristics, and available community mental
health services. The evaluation examines four major areas: mental
health outcomes, costs of providing services, quality of services,
and implementation/replication issues (Bickman, Heflinger, Pion, &
Behar, 1992). The quality and implementation studies were completed on September 30, 1993. The outcomes and cost studies were
completed in September 1994.

Although conclusive evaluation results are not available at this
time, preliminary data (Bickman, Heflinger, & Brannon, 1992) reflect
very favorably on the implementation of the demonstration project
and the positive impact that the integrated continuum of community-based services is having on reducing inpatient psychiatric
hospital and residential treatment center utilization by using high-
quality, lower-cost, intermediate-level and outpatient services whenever clinically appropriate. Access to care has been improved by
increasing the number of mental health providers available and
making a wide range of mental health services available to military

families in a variety of settings throughout the community. Valuable information has been collected on service utilization and the distribution of clients across components of the continuum of care. The Department of the Army deserves credit for the leadership role it has taken and the contributions it has made to improving the delivery of children's mental health services by supporting this important national demonstration.

Focusing on Infants and Toddlers

The Division of Mental Health, Developmental Disabilities, and Substance Abuse Services chose not to apply for CASSP grants until 1988 because the major CASSP activities had already been completed within the state. However, in 1987, it seemed very desirable to seek a CASSP grant to develop an infrastructure for infant and toddler mental health services. The interest in this very young population of children with mental health problems or at risk for such grew out of the services to preschool children that had been a part of the mental health system since the early 1970s. Much of the original funding for these services came from Part F of the Community Mental Health Centers Act and was later supplemented by state allocations. A second source of interest in this population stemmed from the emerging implementation of Part H of the Individuals With Disabilities Education Act, which mandated the states to provide education and other services to handicapped or at-risk populations of children from birth to age 5. In North Carolina, the responsibility for services to 3- to 5-year-old children rested with the state education agency, as in most other states. However, responsibility for the birth to 3-year-old children was placed with the Division of Mental Health, Developmental Disabilities, and Substance Abuse Services, a unique decision on the part of North Carolina's governor. The importance of establishing a place for children needing mental health services could not be overestimated, given the earlier failures across the country to include this population in services provided under Public Law 94-142.

The CASSP project involved coordinating services with the already established in-home parent training services provided through the Developmental Disabilities Section within the same state agency. By adding a mental health professional to the in-home team, services were provided to infants and toddlers, and mental health support services were available to their parents.

A substantial change in state policy resulting from the early childhood mental health initiative was the decategorization of children under the age of 3. The impact of this change was that services designated for handicapped youngsters could be provided to infants and toddlers who did not have a specific diagnosis, but rather met the more broad definition of "atypical development" or "at risk for atypical development." The decategorization was in response to the recognition that diagnoses may be difficult to make in emerging conditions, and the need to label very young children was avoided.

A second CASSP grant funded a local demonstration that provided a concentrated in-home service with a research component that studied the pre-post impact on mother-child relationships. This grant also provided for training of community providers to better identify emerging mental health problems in this very young population. The service network for infants and toddlers was further enhanced by the use of crisis nursery demonstration funds for four projects from the Administration of Children, Youth, and Families (ACYF) in the federal Department of Health and Human Services. These federal funds became the stimulus for using state and local funds for services to infants, toddlers, and their families, and through the refinancing initiatives described below, Medicaid and Title IV-A (Emergency Assistance) funds also became sources of support for such activities.

An additional benefit of the infant and toddler programs has been the interagency emphasis of Public Law 99-457, which has expanded the networking and has provided a good model for services to older children. Parents who have participated in the infant and toddler services have become a strong core group in the development of parent involvement in the state's mental health system.

Integrating Services Across Agencies

Under the leadership of child mental health services, during the early years in the 1990s, North Carolina, like many other states, began moving toward more comprehensive plans for integrating the services of the children's agencies for those children with emotional or behavioral problems and those at risk for separation from their families through out-of-home placement. These children have been an important focus for such integration because they simultaneously receive services from and are frequently the legal responsibility of several public agencies, or because they move from one system to the next as their needs or legal status change. In addition, there has been recognition that appropriately addressing the needs of these children is critical; there is substantial risk that if they are treated inappropriately, their lives and the lives of their families can be seriously affected and the costs of their services will become a greater financial burden to the state.

In 1989, stimulated in part by the Willie M. program and the plans for the Fort Bragg project, the Robert Wood Johnson Foundation designated $24 million for grants to the state mental health agencies for local projects to focus on the development of innovative strategies to integrate services and to prevent out-of-home placement of children. The intent was that these local demonstrations would influence state-level policies regarding the delivery of services and the financing of services for children with mental health problems. From the 41 applicants, 12 states were awarded 1-year planning grants, and subsequently, 8 states—California, Kentucky, North Carolina, Ohio, Oregon, Pennsylvania, Vermont, and Wisconsin—were awarded implementation grants for a 4-year period.

The North Carolina Robert Wood Johnson Project, called the Children's Initiative, was located in the Blue Ridge and Smoky Mountain Area Programs, covering the 11 most western counties in one of the most rural parts of the state. The project was designed to serve children with the most serious mental health problems in community-based services, with the goal of minimizing the use of out-of-home placements. The primary focus was on children with mental health problems who were also receiving services from county departments of social services or the juvenile court. Both of the area programs had substantial parts of the continuum of mental health services in place; thus, the project expanded intensive case management services and in-home crisis stabilization services (family preservation services) to decrease the use of residential services. However, a new focus for the area programs was joint case planning with the other child-serving agencies. Through the use of interagency treatment teams, joint treatment plans were developed and progress was reviewed, resulting in realization of the project's goals to decrease out-of-home placements to residential mental health facilities, foster care, and juvenile justice training schools. The success of the interagency model is further recognized by Blue Ridge Center's receiving an award for the project from the National Council of Community Mental Health Services in 1993.

A second focus of the Robert Wood Johnson Children's Initiative was on the financing of services. Through this project, national consultants reviewed the state's use of Medicaid, resulting in a statewide increase of over 400% in 1993 in Medicaid reimbursements for child mental health services. Because these funds are received directly by area programs, they are used for support of continuing services or for service expansion.

Further study of entitlement programs through the Children's Initiative led the state to increase revenues in Title IV-E by approximately $15 million annually across the mental health, social service, and juvenile justice agencies. Using Title IV-E revenues, the Division of Mental Health, Developmental Disabilities, and Substance Abuse Services has essentially developed a revolving fund for training in child mental health of approximately $400,000 per year. In addition, a position has been funded at the University of North Carolina School of Social Work to implement a curriculum for case managers, both within the graduate education program and as in-service training for practitioners (Weil, Zipper, & Dedmon, 1995). The curriculum development has been funded by the Robert Wood Johnson and Annie E. Casey Foundations, CASSP, and Title IV-E revenues.

Additional opportunities have emerged to influence state policy through the Robert Wood Johnson Project. At the project site, a CASSP evaluation project is being conducted to assess the impact of designated case managers compared with team case service coordination (Behar, Morrissey, & Burns, 1991), and a major epidemiological study is underway to chart the development of mental health and substance abuse problems in children (Costello, Angold, & Burns, 1991).

Restructuring the Financing of Services

The improvements in Medicaid reimbursements for community-based services, generated by the Robert Wood Johnson Project, has led to a serious study of how such services are delivered statewide. Both the Division of Medical Assistance (i.e., the state Medicaid agency) and the Division of Mental Health, Developmental Disabilities, and Substance Abuse Services focused attention on the startling increase in the costs of psychiatric inpatient services for children and adolescents, an increase from $19 million to $35 million in the 2-year period between 1989 and 1991. To address the unbridled access to psychiatric hospital services, the two agencies have planned and implemented a Medicaid waiver program 1915(b) waiver that uses a single portal of entry into the mental health system through the area programs for children under age 18 with mental health or substance abuse problems. As in the Fort Bragg Demonstration Project and the Robert Wood Johnson Project, initial assessments are completed and treatment plans are developed by the area program jointly with the family and with other providers involved with the child and family; treatment is then provided either by the area program or through an organized network of private providers and public agencies. It is the area program's responsibility to authorize services, manage the care, and manage the Medicaid funds, which are prepaid on a capitated basis. The savings realized from decreasing the use of inpatient services are used to broaden the array of community-based services to provide alternatives to hospital services and to improve early access to services for the treatment of emerging problems.

The Medicaid waiver program, called Carolina Alternatives, has been initiated in 10 of the 41 area programs (30 of the state's 100 counties), and plans are to add groups of area programs over the next 3 years to be statewide by 1996. As with other major changes in service delivery in child mental health in the state, the planning for this initiative has been shared by the participating area programs and the state agencies. Over a 14-month period, the program was crafted to avoid pitfalls and to ensure the likelihood of success. The goals to improve access, to improve mental health and substance abuse services to children and families, and to curb inappropriate growth of hospital use were supported by efforts to ensure that sufficient funds and technical assistance were available. The Division of Mental Health, Developmental Disabilities, and Substance Abuse Services and the Division of Medical Assistance worked at the state level to effect changes in laws and policies that the planning group found important for successful implementation.

Although the formal evaluation of Carolina Alternatives has only recently begun, the area programs are requesting that the Division of Mental Health, Developmental Disabilities, and Substance Abuse Services implement a similar program for adults. The area directors believe that this method of organizing mental health and substance abuse services represents a major and positive approach to health care reform and carves out a clear role for the public mental health/ substance abuse agency as an organizer and manager of services across the public and private sectors.

In addition to the efforts to improve services for children who are eligible for Medicaid, and on the basis of the successes of the Fort Bragg Project, the CASSP infant and toddler projects, and the Robert Wood Johnson Project, North Carolina has worked to increase the sharing of other funding streams. These funding streams earlier were thought to be tied to a single agency's responsibilities. To maximize the service capacity of public agencies and to pay for these services with funds to which certain groups of children are entitled by nature of their demonstrated needs and status in life, North Carolina is in the process of restructuring the financing of children's services. Such restructuring has focused on the federal entitlement programs to determine how to access reimbursement for services provided and how to use the reimbursements to expand services.

As North Carolina has developed plans to improve the use of federal entitlement programs, several elements of planning and implementation have emerged as important to the success of these endeavors. Integrating services and funding streams and maximizing revenue are complicated tasks, especially in a state with a strong county government system and strong local agencies that are tied to county governments. The entitlement programs were initially difficult to comprehend and difficult to implement because they required attention to complicated federal requirements and because implementation required changes in functioning at many levels of state and local government. Such changes required an initial stimulus and an energizing and organizing mechanism that might best be termed *leadership*. This leadership has been provided initially by the interagency Oversight Committee for the Robert Wood Johnson Project. The members of the committee have gained much understanding of innovative financing mechanisms from nationally recognized consultants and through the financing workshops sponsored by the Georgetown CASSP Technical Assistance Center. However, their willingness and their ability to make strategic changes in financing are derived as much from their shared vision of services for children and their capacity to work together as from the increased knowledge of options.

On the surface, the major reason to restructure financing may appear to be for states to recover federal funds, which they have earned, in return for services provided to the children who have these entitlements. However, it has become clear that the goals of successful restructuring of financing mechanisms and of improved collection of revenues require a planned strategy. Some of the steps North Carolina is using to achieve these goals are as follows.

Shared Vision of Children's Services

To coordinate a multiagency strategy for refinancing, the agencies involved in the refinancing process have articulated similar or coordinated goals for the children and families they serve. Several of the agencies have involved parents in these efforts. Without coordinated goals, problems could arise. For example, if one agency places priority on residential services because its revenues are earned that way, whereas another agency places priority on nonresidential services for the same reason, conflict occurs and the revenue enhancement expectations of the state may be diluted, especially if these efforts cancel each other out or if the less "profitable" one prevails.

The professionals who are responsible for programs and services in North Carolina have shared the goals of keeping families together, providing services in the least restrictive setting, and keeping out-of-home services to a minimum length of time, all to the extent possible given the needs of the child, which are placed above the needs of the family. These goals have superseded the goal of revenue enhancement. Thus, it has been important to articulate these goals clearly at the beginning, lest revenue enhancement become the driving force.

A Collaborative or Integrated
Plan for Providing Services

As noted above, North Carolina is a state with strong local agencies, and it was recognized that (a) the strengths of these agencies had to be enhanced rather than totally reconfigured and (b) the planning needed to be integrated across the state and local levels rather than through a "top-down" approach. Although the sophisticated local counterparts of the state agencies have recognized the importance of planning together around the needs of children and their families, there has been no required collaboration at the local level around individual clients. As collaborative planning moved forward within the Robert Wood Johnson Project and the CASSP projects, consideration was given to mechanisms to ensure that joint case planning was occurring and that this case planning served as the vehicle through which both the service plan and the funding for the plan were developed.

An Organized Plan for
Shared Funding Streams

It is a major task to determine what the most advantageous reimbursement plans are for which services by which agencies. It is important also to look at the costs to the agency of restructuring financing. For example, the cost of using Medicaid for a service may be more than the cost of using Title IV-A (Emergency Assistance) because of the level of professional services required and/or the supervision required; the reimbursement through Medicaid is 15% higher than through IV-A, but the Medicaid reimbursement for each service is based on a statewide average that is below the actual cost of the service for many local programs. Another factor is the number of children that might be eligible under each entitlement. Title IV-A eligibility can be easily broadened to include more than the population eligible for Medicaid. Thus, the decision of which entitlement program to use needs to be guided by multiple factors on a case-by-case basis at the local level. Clearly, technical assistance by the state to the local agencies is a critical part of successful implementation. Equally important is the willingness and the capacity of the local agencies to integrate their planning for services around each shared child client and family; thus, successful financing strategies are based on the same elements for success as overall programming.

Another object of refinancing is the use of existing state and local funds as match so that the need for new state and local dollars is not increased, and the state agencies and their local counterparts in North Carolina appear to have substantial amounts of unmatched dollars available. As with all other aspects of service coordination, it takes careful coordination to identify matching funds across agencies.

Planning is underway for an integrated infrastructure that could assist in use of funding streams that require coordination to include the tracking of services delivered; methods for invoicing and record keeping; and time studies that may need to be done at the service sites to determine appropriate costs.

Commitment for Use of Funds

In restructuring financing, professionals in local agencies are asked to change the way they function in terms of joint case planning, record keeping, or reporting. They need to understand the value of change and to receive some incentives to do so. Overall, it is anticipated that they will respond well to increased availability of funds for "their" children. Thus, it is important to gain commitments, in advance, that increased revenues to the state will result in increased funding to service programs. This enhancement activity cannot be seen only as a way for the state to get federal funds for state dollars already paid out; it must be seen as a way to enhance the impoverished services that all three agencies are delivering. It seems that the failure to plow the funds back into the services is a major reason that revenue enhancement has not been effective in some states.

The above-discussed issues take time and patience to address. As North Carolina works toward the goals of successful restructuring of financing mechanisms and ultimate improved collection of revenues, an important balance needs to be achieved. Planning and processing of plans are frequently best achieved through the joint efforts of the planners and the implementers. In this case, those efforts would involve the state-level planners, including both the program and budget staff, and those at the local level who will be responsible for implementation of the new strategies. It does require time for all these state and local stakeholders to come to agreement and craft an acceptable course of action.

However, planning and processing can become delaying techniques in themselves. It takes secure and sophisticated participants to determine when it is time to stop planning and start doing. A review of the implementation of other major changes suggests that essentially planning never ends, even after implementation begins. Most important, then, to a new way of doing business is the built-in capacity to identify problems and to address them as the new programming and financing moves forward.

It is important to understand that financing cannot change the system out of context. Only when financing mechanisms are created that support the vision and the structure that follows from it can they reach their system change potential. System change can occur based on current funding patterns, or through new mechanisms that radically modify funding streams so that they directly reflect an integrated service vision.

State-Local Partnership

What is essential in making refinancing a successful effort in North Carolina is the maximal use of the state-local partnership to design and implement change. The partnership has worked well over the years to effect change within the mental health system; as that system joins with other child-serving state agencies, bringing together the local agency counterparts and the parents of the children they serve becomes essential. The tasks to be undertaken in system building and in refinancing of those systems require an ongoing back-and-forth communication, or synergy, to identify problems, clarify processes, recognize successes, and plan for needed changes. This synergy developed the foundation on which to build child mental health services, and it appears that each level of improvement and change is based on this synergy as well.

References

Behar, L. B. (1985). Changing patterns of state responsibility: A case study of North Carolina. *Journal of Clinical Child Psychology, 14*, 181-195.

Behar, L. B. (1986). A state model for child mental health services: The North Carolina experience. *Children Today, 15*(3), 16-22.

Behar, L. (1990). Fort Bragg Demonstration Project: Community mental health services for children and adolescents. *Child, Youth and Family Services Quarterly, 13*(2), 3-13.

Behar, L., Morrissey, J., & Burns, B. (1991). *Assessing coordinated care.* NIMH grant, 1991-1994.

Bickman, L., Heflinger, C., & Brannon, A. M. (1992). *Fort Bragg Child and Adolescent Demonstration Program: Interim report.* Nashville, TN: Vanderbilt University Institute for Public Policy.

Bickman, L. B., Heflinger, C. A., Pion, G., & Behar, L. B. (1992). Evaluation planning for an innovative children's mental health system. *Clinical Psychology Review, 12*, 853-865.

Burchard, J. D., & Clarke, R. T. (1990). The role of individualized care in a service delivery system for children and adolescents with severely maladjusted behavior. *Journal of Mental Health Administration, 17*, 48-60.

Costello, J., Angold, A., & Burns, B. (1991). *The Great Smoky Mountain study.* NIMH grant, 1991-1994.

Individuals With Disabilities Education Act (IDEA) of 1990, 20 U.S.C. 9 1400 *et seg.*

Joint Commission on Mental Health of Children. (1969). *Crisis in child mental health: Challenge for the 1970s.* New York: Harper & Row.

Knitzer, J. (1982). *Unclaimed children: The failure of public responsibility to children and adolescents in need of mental health services.* Washington, DC: Children's Defense Fund.

Stroul, B., & Friedman, R. (1986). *A system of care for severely emotionally disturbed children and youth.* Washington, DC: Georgetown University, Child and Adolescent Service System Program Technical Assistance Center.

VanDenBerg, J. E. (1993). Integration of individualized mental health services into the system of care for children and adolescents. *Administration and Policy in Mental Health, 20*, 247-257.

Weil, M., Zipper, I. N., & Dedmon, S. R. (1995). Training principles for child mental health case management. In B. Friesen (Ed.), *Service coordination in a system of care: Children's mental health case management* (pp. 211-238). Baltimore: Paul H. Brookes.

Willie M. v. Hunt, Civil No. C-C-79-284-M (W.D.N.C., 1980).

3

Systems Change

Moving Beyond Reports

CHRIS KOYANAGI

Over the past 20 years, a number of major studies on the status of children's mental health have yielded similar findings and similar recommendations (Tuma, 1989). Reports have been issued by the Joint Commission on the Mental Health of Children (1969), the President's Commission on Mental Health (1978), the Select Panel for the Promotion of Child Health (1981), the Children's Defense Fund (CDF; Knitzer, 1982), the Office of Technology Assessment (OTA; 1986), and the Institute of Medicine (1989).

The themes in these reports are well known among child advocates: that children need different services and modalities than adults, that most children in need of mental health care do not receive it, that those who are receiving care are often receiving inappropriate or inadequate care, and, more recently, that there is a lack of coordination across systems to meet the needs of these children. Other common concerns are the lack of a cadre of appropriately trained personnel and the need for earlier interventions.

For example, in 1969, the Joint Commission on the Mental Health of Children (1969) concluded that this population was grossly underserved or inappropriately served in more restrictive settings than were necessary. In 1978, the President's Commission on Mental Health identified emotionally disturbed children and adolescents as a critically underserved population. In 1982, Knitzer found that two thirds of the 3 million seriously disturbed children in America were not getting the services they needed, while countless others received inappropriate care.

More recently, the OTA (1986) pointed out the tragedy that we currently "know more about how to prevent and treat children's mental health problems than is reflected in the care available" (p. 3), and the Institute of Medicine (1989) described the population as grossly underserved or inappropriately served. In 1990, the Select Committee on Children, Youth, and Families of the U.S. House of Representatives summed up the situation by stating that there were too few resources and that too many of the services that did exist were uncoordinated, inefficient, and ultimately ineffective. The committee's report spoke of "agencies in crisis" and "services that are failing families and children" (p. 2) and called for a bolder and more sustained redesign and redirection of services for children and families.

In addition to stating the problem, these reports all made calls for reform, and the actions they recommended were depressingly alike. Nonetheless, despite agreement over more than two decades of study, and despite the development of new approaches and pockets of innovation in certain areas, little priority has been given to addressing the needs of children with serious emotional disturbance in federal public policy.

At present, as is clear from Rog's overview of the status of children's mental health services (see Chapter 1 of this book), the data continue to bear out the findings of these earlier reports, and the prospects of finding appropriate community mental health care for a child with a serious emotional disorder are little better now than they were in 1969 when the Joint Commission report issued its landmark study.

Some numbers that have changed, however, show that the problem may be getting worse. The population of children in need is growing. There are increases in the number of cases of child abuse and neglect, to the point that the U.S. Advisory Board on Child Abuse and Neglect (1990) concluded that child abuse and neglect in the United States at that time represented a national emergency. There has also been an alarming increase in the number of children born to drug-addicted or alcohol-addicted mothers, an increasing number of younger and younger children who are abusing and experimenting with alcohol and drugs themselves, and a higher rate of completed suicide among adolescents. In addition, data show a surprisingly early age of onset for some types of psychiatric disorders (Brandenburg, Friedman, & Silver, 1990). According to Marion Wright Edelman (1989), President of the CDF, "We have seen mounting social and economic pressures on many of America's families and children. . . . The emotional health of more and more of our children is in peril" (p. xii).

The picture is not totally bleak, of course. During the past decade, some important shifts have occurred in the concept of delivering mental health services to children and their families, and the 1980s have been a time of great creativity in the children's mental health field. New services have been designed, and new models of community-based systems of care have been developed. According to Friedman (1991), there are three main origins for this creativity: no money, no manpower, no way out. Yet despite the creativity in developing and testing new ideas, there has been very little replication of promising approaches, and there is still no real investment of resources to address the needs of children with serious emotional disturbance and their families.[1] According to Lourie and Katz-Leavy (1991), a patchwork system has developed that may work for children with simple service needs but that fails when the child and family's needs cut across agencies or when services are unavailable to them.

One of the most important steps toward changing the depressing state of affairs described in earlier reports was the creation in 1983 of the federal Child and Adolescent Service System Program (CASSP) within the National Institute of Mental Health (NIMH) and later moved to the Center for Mental Health Services in the Substance Abuse Mental Health Services Administration. CASSP has focused upon the need for improved public policies to encourage interagency services for children and youth with serious emotional disturbance. Though minimally funded, CASSP has had an impact across the country that far exceeds its small budget and the activities it directly funds.

CASSP facilitates change at the state level in order to focus more coordinated, interagency funding for a range of programs for children with mental health needs. The goal of CASSP is to improve the way in which children and adolescents with severe emotional disturbances and their families are offered multiagency services. It was presumed that this must occur first at the state level and then be replicated at the community level (Lourie & Katz-Leavy, 1991). CASSP funds have been used for system development, planning, and coordination. CASSP does not provide funds for direct services but has supported the establishment of state coordinators with the goal of improving the availability of a continuum of care for severely emotionally disturbed children and adolescents, improving the availability and access to appropriate services across child service systems, establishing coordination mechanisms, and ensuring family involvement. CASSP funds were intended to develop leadership capacity at the state level, and state CASSP directors had access to a range of technical assistance, including considerable new research and training conducted by federally funded CASSP research and training centers at the Florida Mental Health Institute and the University of Oregon, Portland, and a national technical assistance center at Georgetown University, Washington, D.C.

The first CASSP grants were awarded in 1984, when 10 states were selected from 44 that had applied for funds. Ira Lourie, director of CASSP for its first 6 years, described the initial goal of CASSP as promoting the establishment of a child mental health program in every state (Day & Roberts, 1991). Over time, all states received a CASSP grant.

Clearly, a major hope of CASSP designers was to make large-scale changes in the way services were delivered, and the program has clearly laid the groundwork for accomplishing this goal. By seeding child advocates in state systems and providing them with important and timely information, CASSP formed a focal point for individuals in all child-serving agencies that desired change but needed a means to accomplish that change. CASSP also facilitated and advanced the thinking in the field by directly supporting research and by providing many forums for new research to be presented and discussed (Day

& Roberts, 1991). It fostered a sense of hope and of movement that attracted more and more attention. Perhaps the greatest legacy from CASSP will be not what CASSP has directly funded—although that is extremely significant—but what it has spawned. Some of the activities that have spun off from CASSP are a major foundation initiative (the Robert Wood Johnson Child Mental Health Initiative) and a parent advocacy movement involving three national groups: the parent-run Federation of Families for Children's Mental Health, Mental Health Associations around the country, and the formation of a network for children within the otherwise adult-focused National Alliance for the Mentally Ill.

CASSP ideas also spawned two federal policy initiatives for children that are the major focus of this chapter: the formation of a coalition of mental health and special education groups that has had a major impact on Department of Education activities, and an important new federal grant initiative.

Special Education

The CASSP focus on multiagency services soon led mental health advocates to realize both the potential of the Education of the Handicapped Act (Pub. L. No. 94-142), now known as the Individuals With Disabilities Education Act of 1990 (IDEA), and the failure of that statute to live up to its promise for children and youth with serious emotional disturbance. The Department of Education's own studies reported that youngsters with serious emotional disturbance were the most underserved group of students with disabilities in the special education system.

What was to later become the Mental Health and Special Education (MHSE) Coalition began with a strategy meeting of advocates in the fall of 1986 to discuss how to improve this situation. Aware that there were considerable barriers to securing the rights of children with serious emotional disturbance under Public Law 94-142, the National Mental Health Association (NMHA) organized this meeting to discuss what changes might be needed to the federal law, as it was shortly coming up for review and revision in the U.S. Congress.

Meeting participants were well aware that the focus on interagency coordination in CASSP had led many state CASSP directors into conflicts with state and local education systems. The education system increasingly stood out as the most difficult to influence of all the child-serving systems. Part of the problem was that education, unlike mental health, child welfare, and juvenile justice, was very much a local responsibility. Another problem was that, for the most part, mental health advocates and policy makers knew little of education and special education systems, even though many of them were familiar with the rights prescribed under federal law.

The purpose of the September 1986 gathering, then, was to identify the problems in the implementation of Public Law 94-142 as it pertained to children with serious emotional disturbance. The group consisted primarily of individuals from the mental health system, including parents, advocates, professionals, researchers, and providers. They concluded that although there had been considerable progress in serving seriously emotionally disturbed children through Public Law 94-142, significant problems remained. Problems were identified that related to the law itself, the federal regulations, federal and state implementation policies and procedures, and lack of funding. The group organized these issues into six priority areas: coordination of services; identification and assessment; delivery of appropriate services; advocacy for children and parents, particularly those from minority backgrounds; training; and research and evaluation (NMHA, 1988). In addition to these problem areas, the group identified inadequacy of resources to implement Public Law 94-142 as a major impediment to securing appropriate services.

Because it was acknowledged that there will never be enough resources, the group then chose to focus on how fiscal resources might be better utilized or allocated to improve services to this population of children and youth and began to identify specific problems under each of the six priority issue areas.

Through publication of a report on this meeting, information was shared with other advocates concerned with Public Law 94-142. Importantly, along with the report of the meeting, some draft ideas for changes to the law were circulated. In fact, these ideas were not very practical and might well have proved ineffectual. However, working on their own, these mental health groups were not well enough versed in special education law, policies, and practices to develop the most strategic recommendations. For instance, several changes to the federal mandate concerning state plans were suggested in ignorance of the fact that this part of the law was unlikely to be reconsidered for fear of loss of children's current rights under Public Law 94-142. Even if those changes had been made, changing state plan requirements would almost certainly have had little real impact on local school practices.

The distribution of these somewhat off-target recommendations served one very important purpose, however. It brought the special education community to the table in quick order.

Educational groups, such as the Council for Exceptional Children (CEC) and the National Association of State Directors of Special Education (NASDSE), came to a follow-up meeting with a determination to prevent a series of inappropriate and potentially harmful amendments from being proposed in Congress. At this meeting, the group, now composed of both mental health and special education representatives, reexamined the issues discussed at the first meeting to determine how mental health and special education advocates could work collaboratively for appropriate change.

Thus, those who would soon become advocates of collaborative, cross-system working relationships began a similar process themselves. Like many collaborative ventures, this one progressed quite slowly. At first, the group clearly consisted of two "sides" (often seating themselves at different ends of the table), and there were communication difficulties. Different terminology divided the group. Some terms were used by both systems but could mean very different things (*assessment*, for example, had a specific meaning in special education that was very different from what a mental health clinician might intend). No one understood the laws, policies, and problems of the other system. Acronyms had to be explained. Parents complained about the lack of basic information and about being excluded and blamed for their children's difficulties, and federal special education advocates were frustrated by what they believed was the mental health system's lack of interest in the problems with which the schools were struggling.

To facilitate progress, a decision was made to focus on developing a Consensus Statement of Problems. The group pulled together a series of problem statements concerning special education for children with serious emotional disturbance, grouping them under the following categories: parent advocacy, identification and assessment, delivery of appropriate services, ethnic and culturally diverse children, coordination of multiple agencies, training, and research. For each of the categories, the group developed a summary statement of the problem and a more detailed list of specific issues. The summary statements for each category were as follows:

- *Parent Advocacy.* Many parents do not have the knowledge or skills to advocate effectively for their children's educational needs. Although Public Law 94-142 specifies parent involvement and consent in the planning of a child's special education program, parents of children with serious emotional disturbance often are not effectively involved. There is a serious lack of self-help or advocacy organizations directed at meeting the unique needs of parents of children with serious emotional disturbance.
- *Identification and Assessment.* There is no consistent definition of or set of eligibility criteria for "serious emotional disturbance." For this and other reasons, many children with serious emotional disturbance are never identified and consequently do not receive services they require. Other children who were determined eligible in one jurisdiction find themselves ineligible in another jurisdiction.
- *Delivery of Appropriate Services.* For those children identified by the school system as seriously emotionally disturbed, the services provided are too often inadequate and/or inappropriate.
- *Ethnic and Culturally Diverse Children.* The provision of appropriate services to ethnic and culturally diverse children with serious emotional disturbance is complicated by important cultural, social, economic, and historical differences as well as legal considerations. Patterns of under- and overrepresentation of some groups of ethnically diverse students in programs for children with serious emotional disturbance, inappropriate placements, services in conflict with the values and perceptions of particular cultural groups, low rates of parental involvement, and ethnic mismatches of children and service providers challenge our present delivery systems to provide improved services to these children and youth and their families.
- *Coordination of Multiple Agencies.* Problems in adequately identifying and serving children with serious emotional disturbance result from the

lack of coordination of the multiple agencies that have some responsibility for children with serious emotional disturbance and their
families. A coordinated, interagency response is required to meet the
complex needs of children who are severely emotionally disturbed, yet
there are significant barriers to achieving appropriate coordination.

- *Training.* The lack of adequate training (including preservice and in-
service training) and support for educators, parents, and mental health
professionals is a pervasive problem in serving children with serious
emotional disturbance.

- *Research.* Although there are methods for successfully serving children
with serious emotional disturbance that have a strong empirical base,
this knowledge is not sufficiently disseminated and applied in the service community. Further, there is a serious lack of federally supported
and other research and demonstration initiatives specifically related to
the population with serious emotional disturbance.

The resulting Consensus Statement of Problems was then circulated and eventually endorsed by 22 national organizations and state
parent groups (NMHA, 1988). It was later followed by a second consensus document, citing agreed-upon goals. Further documents concerning the federal role and specific legislative and policy proposals
for the federal establishment then followed. However, the later success of the coalition resulted less from the actual words on the pages
of these documents than from the process of their development. By
the time the problem statement had been haggled over so that the
three major constituencies within the group (parents, mental health,
and special education) were satisfied, considerable understanding existed in the room about what was wrong, why it was not being
corrected, the depth of the problems facing each system, and above
all, the overwhelming need to work together for the outcomes every-
one sought for children and their families.

The sponsoring organizations had thought that the development
of the consensus papers on problems and goals represented the task
of this group. However, the process was so energizing and hope pro-
voking that the participants were not prepared to stop. They insisted
on the formation of a formal coalition—the Mental Health and Special Education Coalition—and urged cochairmanship by the NMHA
and the CEC, both of which accepted.

This coalition was to make a considerable impact on federal education and mental health policy. Its success has clearly resulted from

the power of united advocacy, and thus, the coalition's early consensus-building activities were critical to its later success. Although sometimes painstakingly slow, and often frustrating to federal policy advocates who wanted to force change quickly, the internal work—building consensus among diverse groups; jointly identifying the problem; agreeing upon common terminology, goals, and objectives—had laid the basis for making systems change. With trust established, the coalition was able to focus on specific federal legislative and administrative actions that could benefit this population of children, and achieved swift and impressive success in a number of areas. Several legislative and policy successes followed in quick order:

- Medicaid law was amended to allow schools to bill Medicaid for any services covered under the state's Medicaid plan, even when that service is listed as a necessary special education/related service in the child's Individual Education Program (IEP). This ended a long-standing dispute as to which program was responsible to pay for these services and opened the door to reimbursement for important mental health services.

- Comprehensive testimony was presented to Congress on the lack of appropriate special education and related services for these children and youth, including a summary of "the state of practice in education for children and youth with serious emotional disturbance" that greatly enhanced awareness of key legislators and staff concerning these problems (Forness, 1989, p. 1).

- NIMH expanded its research agenda and funded services-related research activities suggested by the coalition, particularly research grants on education- and school-related issues and a study of state practices that require parents to give up custody of their children in order to receive services.

- A revised definition of *serious emotional disturbance* was developed, along with a proposal changing the terminology (to *emotional or behavioral disorder*). Several states adopted aspects of the coalition's definition, and federal action is now pending.

- A new federal discretionary program under IDEA was designed, and the coalition successfully lobbied for its enactment as a new section of law (Part C, Section 627). This section authorizes research and demonstration programs targeted specifically for children with serious emotional disturbance and their families.

New Education Program for Children
With Serious Emotional Disturbances (SED)

The MHSE Coalition spent considerable energy working for passage of this new section of IDEA and for its funding. Congress clearly agreed with the coalition on the need, as the proposal was swiftly adopted in its entirety. According to the House Committee, the "pervasive and deep-seated nature of the problem requires a concerted initiative within the Department of Education" (Committee on Education and Labor, 1990).

Following passage of the legislation authorizing the program, $2 million was immediately appropriated for spending in FY 1990, and this was increased to $4 million the following year. The program then continued to be level-funded at $4 million per year for the next several years, and federal funds were used to stimulate local schools-based systems of care and to fund research and technical assistance initiatives.

This program authorizes the Department of Education, with respect to children and youth with serious emotional disturbance, to

- Conduct studies to assess the present state of special education and related services
- Develop curricula to improve special education and related services
- Develop and demonstrate strategies to reduce the use of out-of-home placements
- Develop the knowledge and skills for effective collaboration among agencies
- Demonstrate innovative approaches to prevention and early intervention

A second part of the authority allowed the department to fund demonstration projects by local educational agencies, in collaboration with mental health entities, that would increase the availability, access, and quality of community services; improve working relationships among the agencies and with families; and target resources to school settings taking into account the needs of minority children and youth.

The Section 627 program has had a significant impact on the activities of the Office of Special Education Programs (OSEP). Well aware of the problems of these youngsters, OSEP Director Judy Schrag not only endorsed the new program, but encouraged the director of the Division on Innovation and Development in OSEP, Martin Kauffman, to go beyond that and develop a focus in OSEP on both children at risk of emotional disturbance and those already in need of special education services. As a result, the department is now engaged in developing policies that will ensure better mental health services for students and increase the integration of children and youth with serious emotional disturbance into regular classrooms. These changes should offer many of them more challenging curricula and help them develop better social skills.

OSEP has engaged in a broad agenda-developing process through the organization of focus groups involving all systems as well as parents to identify what would ensure better outcomes for children. Fundamental concepts, a mission statement, and a strategic focus have been developed. Through electronic town meetings, OSEP sought grassroots input into this process and made significant revisions in response to public comments. As a result, OSEP will focus activity on better results for children through systemic linking, family-friendly services, professional development and support, activities to counteract risk factors, integration, and authentic and positive learning experiences for children. According to Kauffman, the department will be working to develop a system that provides a full range of services from prevention/early intervention through intensive services, development of access to information for parents and support services for families, greater support for professionals (particularly teachers), interventions to prevent children from deteriorating, appropriate reunification after a residential placement, and authentic opportunities for children to practice what they need to learn, such as social skills (NMHA, 1991).

The MHSE Coalition saw this program as a way to develop models and new approaches for school-based services, both special education and related services. It will focus on developing the models for good programming, but it does not provide the resources to implement these models nationwide. Clearly there are limits to what the federal government can accomplish through a small, discretionary grant program.

Other activities of the MHSE Coalition were therefore conceived to have a broader impact. Although the new knowledge generated by the discretionary program and the increased research in both the Department of Education and NIMH would lead the way to improving the services that should be offered to these children, it was recognized that other changes would be needed to push the development of appropriate systemic change in the schools and in the mental health system.

A change in the federal definition of *serious emotional disturbance* was one strategy to begin to change the school systems' responses to the needs of these children and youth. With a more appropriate definition of the population, those children most in need of services would more readily be identified. Among the important changes the coalition's definition makes are the dropping of poorly defined and poorly understood terms (such as *social maladjustment,* five characteristics of children that are not supported by previous or current research on subtypes of children with emotional or behavioral disorders, and the word *seriously* in the description of the children to be covered). The coalition's definition, in contrast, emphasizes the types of behavioral difficulties these children have in school, such as inappropriate responses that affect their ability to learn academic, social, vocational, or personal skills, and that are consistently exhibited in more than one setting (Forness & Knitzer, 1992).

Development of the definition took years of work. Prior to the establishment of the coalition, the issue of both the terminology used to describe these children and the definition of their characteristics had been quite contentious. In the early 1980s, an attempt to enact legislation changing the terminology failed, resulting in the authorization of several studies to garner greater support for such a change. Through the coalition, however, both mental health and special education interests as well as parents could ensure that the wording of the proposed change was appropriate and acceptable to each constituency. CEC and NASDSE both contributed substantially to the success of this effort, as did representatives from key mental health groups, including especially the National Association of School Psychologists (NASP). After many, many versions of the definition had been drawn up, final agreement was reached, and 20 groups signed onto the change, representing an unprecedented level of consensus. With such a consensus, many states began to adopt elements of the proposed definition, and in September 1992, Congress passed legislation—the Rehabilitation Act Amendments of 1992, Public Law 102-569—that directed the federal Department of Education to seek public comment on whether the federal definition should be changed, and specifically to ask for comment on the coalition definition and the coalition recommendation that the term *serious emotional disturbance* be replaced with the term *emotional and behavioral disorders*.

Child Mental Health Services

With these activities underway to improve special education, mental health advocates next turned their attention to how to build upon CASSP so as to improve the mental health system. A major issue that had emerged in the MHSE Coalition discussions, and that was mentioned frequently in the national studies and reports cited above, was the imbalance of the service system and the general lack of community mental health services. In many communities, individual hours of psychotherapy are available, as is access to inpatient or residential treatment, but there is generally nothing in between. For disturbed children who need more than an hour or so a week of therapy, but who should not be forced into a residential setting, there are no alternative all-day, structured programs, no in-home services, no respite services for the family, and no programs open after school or during the summer break.

Aware of the research that showed the potential of targeting severely disturbed children for intensive, community, "wraparound" services, as demonstrated through the Willie M. program in the North Carolina, the Ventura County model and the Alaska Youth Initiative (Burchard & Clarke, 1990; Dowrick, 1988; Friedman, 1988; Greenbaum, Friedman, Duchnowski, Kutash, & Silver, 1988), the group quickly determined the basic needs: more funds to start up programs for these children, interagency collaboration for the delivery of the services, full involvement of parents/families in development and implementation of programs and services, emphasis on the promising new approaches to community treatment, and substantial sums of money to be available to communities to put these services into place. To begin to address those needs, the NMHA drew up plans for another coalition, consisting of mental health groups, child advocacy groups such as the CDF and the Child Welfare League (CWL), state directors of welfare programs, juvenile justice advocacy groups, and several of the special education groups that had participated in the MHSE Coalition.

Interestingly, at the same moment, the child welfare community was also planning to reach out to form a coalition with the mental health and juvenile justice communities. These two fledgling concepts were merged into a broad-based child welfare coalition under the leadership of the CDF and the CWL. A subcommittee of this new coalition, cochaired by the NMHA and CDF, then worked specifically on the development of a mental health initiative, while other subcommittees worked to improve the child welfare system's policies through changes to child welfare laws that would parallel the concepts in the mental health package. (These proposals were eventually enacted as part of the Omnibus Budget Reconciliation Act of 1993 Pub. L. No. 103-66).

The finding that children's services have traditionally been underfunded in state mental health systems and that states have generally not developed even the rudiments of a continuum of care for children formed the basis for the development of a proposed new federal initiative. Focusing on the fact that there have been major breakthroughs in understanding mental health problems in children as well as understanding how to provide effective, family-based services, the group set about trying to close the gap between current knowledge on prevention and treatment of children's mental problems and actual practice (OTA, 1986).

The subcommittee decided that the federal government should assist states in their efforts to build the systems of care, so lacking in most communities, for children with the most serious problems. The coalition believed that through a carefully designed program that would build on CASSP and that would fully involve parents and all relevant child-serving agencies, states could launch major new initiatives for community services for children with serious emotional disturbance.

This proposal, later adopted by the larger CDF-CWL coalition, became the Children's and Communities' Mental Health Systems Improvement Act, first introduced in 1990 by Congressman George Miller (D-CA). This legislation was reintroduced at the beginning of the 102nd Congress by Miller (as HR 1197) and by Senator Edward Kennedy (D-MA) (as S 924). Congressional committees heard testimony, some of it quite dramatic, from parents, states, and advocates concerning the need for such legislation, and the proposal quickly passed the Senate in 1991 as part of an omnibus mental health bill, S 1306. The House moved more slowly, but by spring of 1992 the legislation had been approved by a House committee. Final enactment was delayed for reasons unrelated to this program, but the legislation was finally signed into law by President Bush in July 1992 as Section 104 of the ADAMHA Reorganization Act (Pub. L. No. 102-321).

This legislation requires states to plan for a statewide system of care, identify unmet needs, and involve parents in the planning and implementation of the programs. States must follow CASSP principles in developing local systems of care, which must be child centered. CASSP principles that have been built into this proposal include the following:

- Services must be provided in the least restrictive appropriate environment for the child.
- Families must be full participants in planning and development of services.
- Services must be integrated among child-caring agencies.
- Case management must ensure that multiple services are coordinated.
- Services must promote early identification and intervention.
- Services should be sensitive and responsive to cultural differences and special needs.

Funds would be distributed to the states, and states would have to ensure that matching funds were available. The groups proposed that the federal government would pay 75% of costs and that state and local sources would pay 25%. The funds would then be passed through for local services, including

- Day treatment
- Case management
- Home-based child and family services
- Respite services
- Emergency services
- Outpatient services
- Foster family care
- Services in therapeutic group homes (but not room and board)
- Transition to adult services

No funds could be used for inpatient or residential services in facilities serving more than 8 to 10 children, although these services are a necessary part of the continuum. The issue of whether to pay for inpatient and residential treatment received considerable discussion in the subcommittee. However, the strongly held view of the overwhelming majority of the organizations was that the data showed an underutilization of alternatives to 24-hour-a-day services. The group was particularly concerned by data showing high utilization of restrictive placements. For example,

- Over 115,000 youth were admitted to psychiatric hospitals in 1986 (NIMH, 1990).
- Over 24,000 youth were in residential treatment centers (RTCs) in 1986 (NIMH, 1990).
- The number of children between the ages of 10 and 19 discharged from psychiatric units between 1980 and 1987 ballooned 43%, according to the National Center for Health Statistics. The figure is all the more striking because the size of that age group *decreased* 11% during that period.

Moreover, significant numbers of children are often sent far from home for such residential services. An NMHA survey of states found 4,000 children placed out of state in institutions (for an average annual cost of $52,300). Lengths of stay averaged 15.4 months, with 10 years being the longest reported stay (NMHA, 1986). Other studies show that states lack effective gatekeeping mechanisms to screen children before placing them in out-of-state institutions or in institutions in their own state that are often miles away from their families. There is little or no oversight of treatment, and rarely any planning for local services to which the child should return (Select Committee on Children, Youth, and Families, 1990).

Also of concern to the subcommittee were data suggesting that these placements are not more effective, even though they may be far more expensive. Research literature shows no efficacy research base and very little program evaluation to support the efficacy of hospital services, and research on RTCs does not demonstrate superior benefits in comparison to community alternatives (Burns & Friedman, 1990; Knitzer, 1982). It has also been estimated that 40% of hospital placements of children are inappropriate (Knitzer, 1982). Children placed in institutions, as a group, are not very different in terms of their intelligence, age of onset, or rates of schizophrenia or depression from children who are successfully treated in their own communities while living at home (Silver et al., 1992).

Despite this, the alternatives to residential placement are grossly underutilized, with only 14,000 children in day treatment/partial hospitalization compared with 115,000 in psychiatric hospitals and 21,000 in RTCs. There are only a handful of intensive in-home services, such as Washington State's Homebuilders program, and therapeutic foster care/therapeutic group homes are extremely scarce.

The coalition continued to make the case that these alternatives, as well as providing effective care and keeping children with their families, would result in significant cost savings. This was confirmed through a 1993 study of several systems of care for children and adolescents with severe emotional disturbances conducted through the CASSP Technical Assistance Center (Stroul, 1993). On the basis of a review of 20 communities with systems of care, Stroul found that "the data suggest that children served in such systems demonstrate improvements in functioning, that parents are more satisfied with services and supports, and that the costs of providing systems of care are less than for traditional service delivery patterns which rely more heavily on expensive treatment environments" (p. 1).

Other aspects of the legislation emphasized interagency collaboration. All relevant child-serving agencies would have to be involved in the implementation of these services at the local level, and services would have to be cooperatively delivered by at least two such agencies. The applicant for such funds could be any state agency (or a political subdivision), not necessarily the state mental health agency.

Funds would be available for 5-year periods. Grants would be awarded on a competitive basis, and it was hoped that those states that received funding under this program would be given significant resources.

The Children's and Communities' Mental Health Systems Improvement Act marks a historic shift in federal mental health public policy. It is the first piece of federal mental health legislation to authorize substantial resources for children's needs. By requiring interagency planning and delivery of services, it goes well beyond the normal federal requirements for mental health grants.

This bill also represents a shift from the past. In the 1980s, the federal government's mental health funds were distributed primarily through a block grant approach. In the 1960s and 1970s, the federal government, through various categorical programs to local communities, attempted to take over leadership responsibility for community mental health. In contrast, the Children's and Communities Mental Health Systems Improvement Act has a partnership approach. It requires a partnership between federal and state governments, as well as partnerships between the various human services agencies concerned about children with serious emotional disturbance. It puts the federal government in a joint policy leadership role with the states.

Building on research on program effectiveness, involving parents and families, and, most important, following through on the experience of the CASSP program, this initiative can break new ground. Sponsors hope that if it is adequately funded, it will lead to a new era in meeting the needs of children with serious emotional disturbance.

Summary

No single initiative, however, can be expected to solve such a complex problem. It is important to see this legislation as part of a broader strategy of federal child advocates to reform many systems in which children are served. For example, the efforts of the MHSE Coalition to make reforms in special education will be supportive of the activities funded through the new mental health bill, and vice versa. Federal initiatives must also be accompanied by greater state and local activities.

For long-term success, there must be ongoing commitment and strong political will. Fortunately, the necessary force for change is emerging. The organization into a national movement of parents of children with serious emotional disturbance holds the promise of strong future advocacy. Local and statewide parent support groups are springing up all around the country, and the formation of an organization devoted entirely to their concerns, the Federation of Families for Children's Mental Health, bodes well for the future.

Long-term child advocate Lenore Behar called the 1990s the best of times and the worst of times for children's mental health services. According to Behar (1991), over the past decade, the foundation has been laid for major shifts in attitude, philosophy, and policy that have begun to effect change in treatment strategies, although we still know more about what needs to be done and how to do it than we have been able to put in place. Behar stated that the task before us now is to implement fully the complex array of changes that are needed to broaden the availability of prevention and treatment services.

It is the objective of federal child advocates to accomplish this task: to finally move beyond the reports into implementation and action to ensure delivery of appropriate services that are widely available to children and families across America. We must end the situation in which families find that the most effective services for their children are those that are the least available. It is past time for the federal government to lead the way so that we implement what we already know from research and experience to be effective.

Note

1. In this chapter, the term *children with serious emotional disturbance* is used throughout, but is intended to include children and youth with mental, emotional, or behavioral disorders.

References

ADAMHA Reorganization Act of 1992, Pub. L. No. 102-321, § 201(2), 106 Stat. 378 (1992).

Behar, L. (1991, Fall). Child mental health services: Where have we been and where are we going? *Community News*, 6-7.

Brandenburg, N. A., Friedman, R. M., & Silver, S. E. (1990). Epidemiology of childhood psychiatric disorders: Prevalence findings from recent studies. *Journal of the American Academy of Child and Adolescent Psychiatry, 29*, 76-83.

Burchard, J. D., & Clarke, R. T. (1990). The role of individualized care in a service delivery system for children and adolescents with severely maladjusted behavior. *Journal of Mental Health Administration, 17*, 48-60.

Burns, B. J., & Friedman, R. M. (1990). Examining the research base for child mental health services and policy. *Journal of Mental Health Administration, 17*, 87-98.

Committee on Education and Labor, U.S. House of Representatives. (1990). *Report to accompany HR 1013, a bill to amend the Education of the Handicapped Act, June 18, 1990* (House Report 101-544). Washington, DC: Government Printing Office.

Costello, E. J. (1989). Developments in child psychiatric epidemiology. *Journal of the American Academy of Child and Adolescent Psychiatry, 28*, 836-841.

Day, C., & Roberts, M. C. (1991). Activities of the child and adolescent service system program for improving mental health services for children and families. *Journal of Clinical Child Psychology, 20*, 340-350.

Dowrick, P. W. (1988). Alaska youth initiative. In P. Greenbaum, R. M. Friedman, A. J. Duchnowski, K. M. Kutash, & S. E. Silver (Eds.), *Children's mental health services and policy: Building a research base. Conference proceedings* (pp. 59-61). Tampa: Florida Mental Health Institute.

Edelman, M. W. (1989). Foreword. In R. M. Friedman, A. J. Duchnowski, & E. L. Henderson (Eds.), *Advocacy on behalf of children with serious emotional problems* (p. xii). Springfield, IL: Charles C Thomas.

Forness, S. R. (1989). Testimony on the state of education. *NMHA speaks: Students with serious emotional disturbance underserved in special education* [Pamphlet]. Alexandria, VA: National Mental Health Association.

Forness, S. R., & Knitzer, J. (1992). A new proposed definition and terminology to replace "serious emotional disturbance" in Individuals With Disabilities Education Act. *School Psychology Review, 21*, 12-20.

Friedman, R. M. (1988). Individualizing services. *Update: Newsletter of the Research and Training Center, Florida Mental Health Institute, 3*, 10-12.

Friedman, R. M. (1991). *University-based preparation of students to work with students and families* (Paper #700). Tampa: University of South Florida, Florida Mental Health Institute.

Greenbaum, P., Friedman, R. M., Duchnowski, A. J., Kutash, K. M., & Silver, S. E. (Eds.). (1988). *Children's mental health services and policy: Building a research base. Conference proceedings*. Tampa: Florida Mental Health Institute.

Individuals With Disabilities Education Act of 1990 (IDEA), 20 U.S.C. § 1400 *et seq.*

Institute of Medicine. (1989). *Report of a study: Research on children and adolescents with mental, behavioral and developmental disorders*. Washington, DC: National Academy Press.

Joint Commission on the Mental Health of Children. (1969). *Crisis in child mental health: Challenge for the 1970s.* New York: Harper & Row.

Knitzer, J. (1982). *Unclaimed children: The failure of public responsibility to children and adolescents in need of mental health services.* Washington, DC: Children's Defense Fund.

Lourie, I. S., & Katz-Leavy, J. (1991, May). New directions for mental health services for families and children. *Families in Society: The Journal of Contemporary Human Services,* pp. 277-285.

National Institute of Mental Health (NIMH). (1990). *Mental health, United States, 1990* (DHHS Publication No. ADM 90-1708). Washington, DC: Government Printing Office.

National Mental Health Association (NIMH). (1986, September). *Severely emotionally disturbed children: Report of a meeting of education and mental health experts.* Alexandria, VA: Author.

National Mental Health Association (NIMH). (1988). *Meeting the needs of children with serious emotional disturbances through Education for Handicapped Children Act (PL 94-142): Statement of problems.* Alexandria, VA: Author.

National Mental Health Association (NIMH). (1991, October 1). *Minutes of a meeting of the Mental Health and Special Education Coalition.* Alexandria, VA: Author.

Office of Technology Assessment (OTA). (1986). *Children's mental health: Problems and services: Background paper* (OTA-BP-H-33). Washington, DC: Government Printing Office.

Omnibus Budget Reconciliation Act of 1993, Pub. L. No. 103-66, § 13711.

President's Commission on Mental Health. (1978). *Report to the president from the President's Commission on Mental Health* (Vols. 1 and 3). Washington, DC: Government Printing Office.

Rehabilitation Act Amendments of 1992, Pub. L. No. 102-569, § 912(b), 106 Stat. 4486 (1992).

Select Committee on Children, Youth, and Families, U.S. House of Representatives. (1990). *No place to call home: Discarded children in America* (House Report 101-395). Washington, DC: Government Printing Office.

Select Panel for the Promotion of Child Health. (1981). *Better health for our children: A national strategy. Report presented to the U.S. Congress and the Secretary of Health and Human Services.* Washington, DC: Author.

Silver, S. E., Starr, E., Duchnowski, A. J., Kutash, K., et al. (1992). A comparison of children with serious emotional disturbances served in residential and school settings. *Journal of Child and Family Studies, 1*(1), 43-59.

Stroul, B. A. (1993). *Systems of care for children and adolescents with severe emotional disturbances: What are the results?* Washington, DC: Georgetown University, Child and Adolescent Service System Program Technical Assistance Program.

Tuma, J. M. (1989). Mental health services for children: The state of the art. *American Psychologist, 44,* 188-198.

U.S. Advisory Board on Child Abuse and Neglect. (1990). *Child abuse and neglect: Critical first steps in response to a national emergency.* Washington, DC: Government Printing Office.

Developments in Children's Mental Health Services Research

An Overview of Current and Future Demonstration Directions

DIANE L. SONDHEIMER

MARY E. EVANS

Approaches to organizing, delivering, and financing mental health services for children and adolescents with or at risk for serious emotional, behavioral, and mental (including biological) disturbances and their families have shifted dramatically since the inception of the Child and Adolescent Service System Program (CASSP) in 1984. Traditional service practices for this population have been both inadequate and inappropriate, concentrated mainly on residential and overly restrictive settings, often referred to as "deep-end" services. Moreover, the human and fiscal capacity for states to provide the coordinated and comprehensive services necessary to serve the multiple and complex needs of these children and their families has been severely lacking. The increasing utilization of the CASSP "system-of-care" model has resulted in family-centered and community-based service innovations as more effective and less costly alternatives to residential treatment and in a more organized and culturally competent approach to service delivery for this population that crosses all child-serving agencies.

The focus of this chapter is to document the significant developments that have led to the recent movement toward examining and broadening the methodological capabilities necessary to rigorously test the effectiveness of these new models of care, utilizing demonstration research, the study of service interventions applied in actual service settings and systems. The Center for Mental Health Services (CMHS), through the *National Plan for Research on Child and Adolescent Mental Disorders* (National Advisory Mental Health Council, 1990, for the National Institute of Mental Health [NIMH]), has begun to implement a set of research recommendations designed to improve service delivery and systems of care for children and adolescents with or at risk for serious emotional and mental disorders. This chapter summarizes the extant literature and reviews relevant NIMH- and CMHS-supported service and system-of-care research as well as emphasizing areas that need further development. The importance of validated research as a crucial mechanism with which to influence public policy is emphasized.

Background

On the basis of a recent review of prevalence studies (Brandenburg, Friedman, & Silver, 1990), approximately 9 million to 13 million children and adolescents in the United States (14% to 20%) have a diagnosable mental, emotional, or behavioral disorder at any one point in time. About 5%, or 3.25 million, of these youngsters are estimated to have a serious emotional disorder, which is a diagnosable mental disorder accompanied by an inability to function in family, school, or community settings. Although all reports in this century have described the mental health system of care for children and adolescents as inadequate, recent estimates suggest that between 70% and 80% of children with serious emotional disturbances receive no intervention (Costello, Burns, Angold, & Leaf, 1993; Fisher et al., 1993; Tuma, 1989). More children are receiving needed services now than previously

(Roghmann, Zastowney, & Babigian, 1985), yet only between 2% and 6% of children receive some form of mental health service (Bickman, 1993; Burns, 1989, 1991; Stroul & Friedman, 1986).

Children with mental disorders receive mental health services through multiple sectors, including child welfare, education, juvenile justice, and general health, as well as the mental health care sector. Even though there has been a tremendous paradigmatic shift toward providing community-based services for children through integrated service systems and establishing linkages between mental health systems and other service sectors (Friedman & Kutash, 1992), when services are received, they tend to be inappropriate and overly restrictive (Stroul & Friedman, 1986). In fact, Kiesler and Simpkins (1991) reported an 8% increase in the number of general hospital inpatient episodes for youth (from 101,757 to 109,941) between 1980 and 1985. Also noteworthy is the shift from treatment in specialized facilities to general hospitals without psychiatric units, and the increase in average length of stay from 16.9 days to 18.9 days. Moreover, the overwhelming majority of out-of-home placements have been out of state and made by systems other than the child mental health system. For example, the National Mental Health Association national survey regarding children in out-of-state placements found that in 1987, 47.6% had been placed by a child welfare agency, 21.6% by an education agency, and 17.6% by a juvenile justice agency. Only 7.2% had been placed by a mental health agency (NMHA, 1988).

Services also tend to focus treatment only on the child, providing little support and guidance to parents, other family members, and other persons providing social supports (Goldfine et al., 1985; Knitzer, 1982). Consequently, there exists a high rate of stress as families struggle alone to cope with the special needs of the child with emotional disturbance (Friedman & Street, 1985). Since the development of the Homebuilders model of family preservation in 1974 (Fraser, Pecora, & Haapala, 1991), more than 30 states have implemented some type of intensive in-home, family-centered service designed to keep families together (Dugger, 1993). Such programs have been implemented in 14 states for mental health populations, although no published reports have yet appeared focused specifically on the outcomes experienced by children with mental health problems and their families. Preliminary estimates from the child welfare literature indicate that intensive home-based programs are less costly than out-of-home placement. For example, Vermont estimated that the cost of short-term family preservation services ranged from $2,500 to $4,500. In contrast, assuming that enrolled children would have been referred for out-of-home placement, the average foster care home placement would have cost $7,000; residential treatment center (RTC) placement cost would have been even greater (Johnson, 1987). Henggeler, Melton, and Smith's (1992) experience with multisystemic therapy (MST) with serious juvenile offenders showed that MST was more effective than usual services and was less costly. Youths receiving MST had fewer arrests on self-reported offenses and spent an average of 10 fewer weeks incarcerated. The cost of MST was about $2,800 per youth, whereas the average cost of a course of institutionalization in South Carolina was approximately $16,300. Furthermore, the recent grassroots movement by parents and families has enabled them to take a more active role in designing and implementing the individualized services that their children will receive.

Similarly, costs of mental health care have risen drastically, and a disproportionate amount of these costs is expended on the relatively small number of children and adolescents with severe emotional disturbance in expensive inpatient settings (Burns, 1989). The U.S. Department of Education's report to Congress (1984) stated that children with serious emotional disturbances had a three times' greater chance of being placed in a residential care program than children with mental retardation or learning disabilities. Since the Department of Education report, alternatives to residential treatment (e.g., community-based, family-centered services) have become more prevalent across the states, yet fiscal, political, and philosophical constraints continue to plague the ability of many states to make significant progress in this area.

The Child and
Adolescent Service System Program

In 1982, Jane Knitzer published a landmark study, *Unclaimed Children*, that documented the state-level system inadequacies across the country in serving the needs of children with serious emotional disturbances and their families. In response to this study, in 1984 NIMH launched CASSP to assist states and communities in developing community-based systems of care for this underserved population.

CASSP's mission is to give children and youth with serious emotional disorders the full range of services necessary to enable them to function successfully within their family, school, and community. The overall goal of CASSP is to increase the accessibility, availability, and quality of services for the child and family across all child-serving systems.

In the past decade, a consensus has emerged that a comprehensive array of services is the most effective and efficient approach to serving children with serious emotional disturbance and their families. Services need to be managed in an organized system of care with the flexibility to meet individual needs (Stroul & Friedman, 1986). Important elements of these systems include

- Early identification and intervention
- A comprehensive continuum of services
- Development and monitoring of individualized treatment plans
- Services provided in the least restrictive environment
- Involvement of families in treatment planning and delivery, and support for families as primary caregivers
- Coordination of services across multiple providers and systems
- Case management
- Services that are responsive to cultural, racial, and ethnic differences

Once new models of care are developed, improved, and expanded, demonstration or evaluation studies are necessary to determine their effectiveness. Over the past decade, several states have experimented with alternatives to residential treatment in both the public welfare and the child mental health service systems. An initial body of research suggests that these services offer a promising alternative as part of a community system of care for children. To date, there has been a lack of controlled research demonstrating the effectiveness of these innovative models of care, just as there have been no controlled studies in the past 10 years to indicate that inpatient hospitalization or residential treatment for children and adolescents are effective. Recent activities in both the public and private sector are responses to the need for a stronger knowledge base on effective system building and state child mental health policy as well as on individual service strategies.

Research on systems of care indicates

- A reduction in the use of more restrictive and costly services options, such as inpatient hospitalization
- A reduction in out-of-home placement
- A reduction in the per capita cost of children served
- Improved access to an array of services
- Improvement in the functioning of children served
- Improved educational outcomes
- Reduced recidivism rates
- Increased parent satisfaction with services

CASSP Research Demonstration Program

In 1990, the initial request for applications (RFA) for the Child and Adolescent Mental Health Service System research demonstration grants (MH-90-10; NIMH, 1990) was published. In April 1991, this initiative became a standing program announcement (PA-91-40; NIMH, 1991a). The purpose of this announcement was to stimulate investigator-initiated research demonstration projects (R18s) of state- and local-level service systems for children and adolescents with or at risk for serious emotional or mental disorders and their families. This research was expected to contribute to the establishment and maintenance of effective mental health service delivery systems for this population. One of the major factors differentiating this program announcement from earlier demonstrations was that the R18s were expected to use "the most rigorous research design possible as appropriate to the proposed demonstration" (p. 1).

As defined by Sondheimer (1991), research demonstration projects (R18s) are based on the theories and outcomes of prior research, and test particular approaches to providing, organizing, and/or funding services through experimental studies of service interventions applied in actual service settings. They are often used as a mechanism of funding services research. Services research applies clinical disorder efficacy findings to real-world settings and systems of care. The population of children studied in services research is usually broad and heterogeneous, with multiple mental health problems. Two similar types of grants are often used to fund services research: the R01, which is the most flexible mechanism, and the R18 research demonstration project, which funds the service intervention as well as the research component of the grant. Consequently, these latter projects may be relatively more costly. However, in testing the effectiveness of new and innovative services that are not yet widely available, it becomes crucial to keep the services component as constant as possible so as not to jeopardize the validity of the project.

On the basis of the first 21 applications submitted in response to this announcement, Hoagwood of NIMH (K. Hoagwood, personal communication, 1992) identified factors distinguishing successful proposals ($n = 10$), that is, projects receiving funding, from unsuccessful proposals ($n = 11$). Following an examination of the proposals and the initial review group's summary statements, Hoagwood used regression analysis to identify variables with large, moderate, and small effects. The factors most likely to distinguish successful from unsuccessful applications were the feasibility of the project as assessed by the reviewers, the perceived adequacy of the measures to be used in determining outcomes, the quality of the statistical plan, the type of study (i.e., the rigor of the design), and the clarity of the hypotheses. As additional proposals are submitted and funded, it would be instructive to rerun the analysis to determine the stability of these findings.

The Child and Adolescent Mental Health
Service System Research Demonstration Grants

In 1990, two important documents were published. The first was the *National Plan for Research on Child and Adolescent Mental Disorders.* This report, requested by the U.S. Congress and submitted by the National Advisory Mental Health Council (1990), addressed the status of research concerning mental disorders in children and recommended areas requiring support for further study. Broadly categorized, these areas included clinical research focused on the epidemiology, diagnosis, treatment, and prevention of mental disorders; basic neuroscience and behavioral research regarding the causes and effective treatments for these disorders; and clinical services research and service system research to improve the service provided. In April 1991, this document was followed by the publication of *Implementation of the National Plan for Research on Child and Adolescent Mental Disorders* (PA-91-46; NIMH, 1991b). The purpose of this announcement was to expand the spectrum of research related to child and adolescent mental disorders to include a special focus on areas listed in the National Plan and on building the scientific capacity to conduct research. Although clinical services research and service systems research were listed as priority areas, no specific provisions were made for funding R18-type research demonstrations.

The second document published in 1990 was the initial program announcement for the Child and Adolescent Mental Health Service System research demonstration grants released by NIMH (MH-90-10; NIMH, 1990). This announcement, based on recommendations in the National Plan and on the NIMH Public-Academic Liaison Initiative, was intended to stimulate investigator-initiated research demonstration projects (R18s) of state and local service systems for children at risk for serious emotional or mental disorders. Since the release of this program announcement, more than 70 proposals have been reviewed for funding. Of these, 16 have been funded. The research areas and principal investigators are listed in Table 4.1.

Although it is not possible to discuss each of these projects in depth here, several studies, identified by principal investigator, are overviewed. The CASSP emphasis on keeping children in the least restrictive setting appropriate to their needs leads to an examination of the functioning of children in community settings and the establishment of school-based services for children with emotional and behavioral problems. Catron's (1993) evaluation of school-based mental health services, for example, uses a school-wide assessment of the mental health needs of second through fifth graders in each of nine Nashville public schools to identify children with serious behavioral and emotional disturbance. These children are then randomly assigned to a school-based counseling program, academic tutoring, community-based counseling at a local community mental health center, or a no-treatment control condition. Children selected for the study and

Table 4.1 Implementation of the National Plan for Research on Child and Adolescent Mental Disorders Within the Child, Adolescent, and Family Branch, Center for Mental Health Services

Research Areas	Currently Funded	Date Funded
Effectiveness of alternatives to residential treatment/flexible funding	Lubrecht (ID) Wachal (OR)	Fall 1990 Spring 1991
Effectiveness of innovative services	Behar (NC) Lilley (WV)	Fall 1990 Spring 1991
Effects of different reimbursement mechanisms on quality, cost, and appropriateness of care	Wachal (OR)	Fall 1991
Multilevel organization and interrelation of services	Behar (NC)	Spring 1991
Effectiveness of intensive case management models	Evans (NY) Marcenko (PA)	Fall 1990 Fall 1993
Service intervention for children/adolescents in foster care	Hardy (FL)	Fall 1990
Effects of approaches to family involvement	Evans (NY)	Spring 1993
School/mental health interface and effectiveness of mental health services in educational settings	Catron (TN)	Fall 1992
Effectiveness of crisis stabilization interventions	Evans (NY)	Fall 1992
Intensive case management/homeless adolescents	Cauce (WA)	Fall 1990
Children of mentally ill parents	Tebes (CT)	Summer 1993
Serious juvenile offenders/family preservation	Henggeler (SC) Jerrell (CA)	Fall 1991 Fall 1993

their classroom peers receive five assessments of their behavioral, emotional, and social functioning over 3 years. These data will be analyzed to determine whether the school-based program increases accessibility to mental health services and whether it is as effective as or more effective than a community-based program.

Meeting the mental health needs of children served in the child welfare system is of increasing importance given the number of children being served in that system nationwide. This is the focus of a project in Florida that is designing and evaluating a wraparound system of care for foster children (Clark & Boyd, 1993). This study is a community-based, controlled experiment that examines the effects of two levels of service provision on the progress of two groups of high-risk foster children. It establishes an integrated, systemic approach to individualized, wraparound services and supports through the use of an intensive case management team for children 7 to 15 years old who are in foster care and who have severe emotional disturbance or are at risk. Children meeting criteria are randomly assigned to the Individualized Support Team or to standard foster care practice, and are followed over time to determine outcomes such as restrictive placements, emotional/behavioral adjustment, and academic performance.

Providing comprehensive, effective services to children with emotional and behavioral problems who are in crisis and their families is an area in need of further study. A research demonstration being conducted in the Bronx, New York (Evans, 1993b), compares the child, family, system, and provider outcomes associated with three intensive, in-family crisis intervention programs. Children 5 to 18 years old presenting at three psychiatric emergency settings, who are at immediate risk of hospitalization, are randomly assigned to one of the three interventions. The interventions comprise home-based crisis intervention, modeled on Homebuilders; an enhanced, culturally competent home-based crisis intervention program; and crisis case management. The research uses a positive controlled randomized study design: That is, there is no classic no-treatment control group; instead, three treatment conditions are compared with each other, with repeated measures. The outcomes being examined include child placements and functioning; family outcomes such as adaptability, cohesion, and parenting self-efficacy; system outcomes, primarily costs; and provider outcomes such as job tenure and satisfaction.

There is a dearth of knowledge about the mental health status of homeless adolescents. Cauce (1993) is conducting a research demonstration on the effectiveness of intensive case management for homeless adolescents in the state of Washington. The project examines the prevalence of mental disturbance among homeless adolescents, develops an adolescent-centered intensive case management program, and compares the relative effectiveness of this case management program with services as usual in Seattle and with minimal services in Everett, Washington. Outcomes of interest include residential stability, mental health, independent living skills, substance abuse, social functioning, school/employment history and attitude, quality of life, and consumer satisfaction.

Although CASSP principles are highly regarded by professionals and families, problems continue to exist regarding the involvement of parents as partners in caring for their child with an emotional/behavioral disorder. A study being conducted in upstate New York (Evans, 1993a) takes advantage of a natural experiment in which the principle of parent involvement has been taken to its logical limit by a group of parents in one rural county. This parent group has been playing a major role in planning and implementing a system of care for children with emotional/behavioral disturbances. The child, family, and system outcomes of the parent-designed system of care will be compared with the outcomes of a provider-designed system of care in a similar rural county that has been enhanced with the same level of financial resources as the county study. The research design comprises two related outcomes studies—a study of service system outcomes, such as availability and accessibility of services, and a treatment outcome study focused on child functioning and family satisfaction with services.

This section has briefly reviewed the Child and Adolescent Service System research demonstration grants that have been funded to date. A more complete account of these projects can be found in the *Journal of Emotional and Behavioral Disorders*, Vol. 2(1). The two sections that follow identify areas for future research. The first of these sections examines those areas for future research identified in the National Plan (National Advisory Mental Health Council, 1990). The second section discusses the future directions for research in regard to services provided to or needed by children with mental and behavioral disorders and their families and the system of care in which such services are embedded.

Areas for Future Research
Identified in the National Plan

NIMH (1991b) briefly overviewed the major areas in child and adolescent mental disorders needing research and suggested some specific subareas for study under each of these major topic areas. The major topic areas are listed below with illustrative examples of needed research. Not all of the areas lend themselves to services research. All are presented, however, to show how services research fits into the context of the universe of research that is needed. Services research is discussed in greater detail than other major topic areas, however, because it lends itself so well to research demonstrations.

The first of four nonservices areas for research is Developmental Considerations. An understanding of developmental factors is necessary for understanding the evolution of behavior, cognition, mental health, and mental and emotional disorders in children. Suggested study areas include developmental approaches to structural and functional changes in memory, attention, perception, and reasoning; interactions between family dynamics and genetic factors in shaping development and behavior; and developmental psychopharmacological studies.

The second major nonservices area for research is Dimensions of Disorder. This involves an accurate determination of the nature and extent of the problem of mental disorders. Suggested study areas include epidemiologic studies for specific disorders and epidemiologic studies of the mental health of children and adolescents living in abusive situations. Studies are also suggested in the area of assessment and diagnosis to focus on understanding the factors that influence judgments regarding emotional and behavior problems and the methods that would allow accurate and valid measurement of children 10 years of age and younger.

A third nonservices area for research is the Causes and Determinants of Mental Disorders. Specific foci here include the study of biologic factors and brain mechanisms, genetic studies, and animal studies to enable the modeling of the development of mental disorders.

Another major nonservices topic area is Child Development and Psychosocial Risk Factors. Studies in this area would improve our understanding of risk and protective factors for mental disorders. Specific study areas include examination of whether intra- and interpersonal protective factors can be learned and the effects of homelessness on children's development.

The services area identified as needing research is Interventions for Child and Adolescent Mental Disorders. This area includes research on treatment and prevention. Researchable questions include the effects of treatments commonly used in clinical practice, the effects of medication on response to psychological interventions, and how to incorporate developmental processes into prevention research. One area particularly in need of research is emergency mental health services. In April 1993, NIMH released program announcement PA 93-075, "Research on Emergency Mental Health Services for Children and Adolescents," whose purpose is to encourage grant applications on emergency mental health services to children and adolescents in need of acute psychiatric and/or psychosocial intervention for one of a number of reasons, including having a physical condition, such as AIDS, that places them at risk for mental health problems or being a victim of or witness to violence.

NIMH (1991b) also noted the importance of studying special populations such as minorities, rural populations, children with AIDS, and homeless children and adolescents. Building research capacity was seen as important, and the importance of research centers, training, and career development was stressed. Currently, there are two Research and Training Centers for Children's Mental Health, one at the Florida Mental Health Institute at the University of South Florida and one at Portland State University. There are also two Centers for Research on Mental Health Services for Children and Adolescents funded under PA-92-20, one at Johns Hopkins University and the other at Children's Hospital in San Diego.

Future Directions
for Research Demonstrations

One of the areas for research noted in the National Plan is mental health services (National Advisory Mental Health Council, 1990). This area is considered in greater detail here because it is the most common focus of research demonstrations. Services research may be divided into two major types: clinical services research and service system research. According to the National Plan, clinical services research is concerned with the application of clinical knowledge gained in controlled research environments to relatively uncontrolled environments in which children and their families actually function. Its goal is to improve the quality of care of everyday clinical practice. Service system research focuses on studying the organization, delivery, and financing of systems of care, including developing and evaluating strategies for improving systems of care. Service system research is particularly germane to the CASSP program, which was designed to develop systems of care for children with emotional and behavioral disorders and their families. The boundaries between these two types of services research are permeable, and many services research projects, particularly research demonstration projects, contain elements of both.

Another way of thinking about services research is to identify the primary focus of the research—the individual, the family, the treatment program or intervention, or the system of care. Research is needed at all of these levels to further our understanding of who is receiving what services from whom, where, with what effect, and at what cost.

Another review of the research base for child mental health services and policy is that of Burns and Friedman (1990). Their article stresses the importance of maintaining a systems perspective while conducting research on system components. They also identify the need for controlled studies that assess both clinical and cost outcomes, and for studies examining the larger picture of the organization and financing of systems of care. Saxe, Cross, and Silverman's (1988) article on the gap between what we know and what we do provides a useful review of the work that has been done and indicates areas needing further systematic study. A family-centered focus for services is more recent than the child-centered focus, and research in this area is less well developed. Friesen and Koroloff (1990) identified research implications for this approach to services. These include reconceptualizing program effectiveness to include family outcome variables; better specifying program processes and components; designing research that links program characteristics, family characteristics, and outcomes; and developing new research methods to address family and program questions.

At the level of the individual, much descriptive work remains to be done to enhance our understanding of who is receiving services where and with what outcomes, such as level of functioning and quality of life. In particular, we lack longitudinal research that tracks children over a number of years to assess their contact with various categorical agencies and their mental health and functioning as they approach adulthood. Such work is funded by NIMH as part of the UNOCAP research program. In this program, one national and four local surveys will be conducted to study mental health and service use. Additional work needs to be done in the area of risk factors such as homelessness and physical, psychological, and/or sexual abuse, and the impact of various environmental contexts, such as family chemical abuse, on children's mental health. There is a paucity of research using children's perceptions about their life situation, needs, and satisfaction with services. Additional work remains to be done in the area of assessing and responding to the needs of parents/ caregivers of children with serious emotional disturbance and their experiences as they are engaged in self-help and mutual support groups.

With the shift toward community-based services for children with serious emotional disturbance has come recognition of the need for supportive services for families. Research focused on the family with a child with emotional or behavioral disorder as the unit of analysis is in its infancy. Research in this area will need to focus on family-level outcomes and examine the links among family characteristics, interventions, and outcomes. Opportunities exist for the development of assessment instruments, including those to measure family functioning, and the benefits, such as feelings of self-efficacy, not just the burdens, associated with successfully raising a child who has a mental disorder. Because of the complexity of family systems, as Friesen and Koroloff (1990) pointed out, there is a need to expand the repertoire of methods used to study family interventions and outcomes. A services research agenda might include studies to examine the family outcomes of participation in family support groups, in family preservation programs, and in multisystemic interventions.

In regard to the study of treatments or interventions at the program level, many areas have not been adequately explored. In part due to CASSP, a number of studies of community-based programs have been undertaken, but many opportunities remain to be explored as new program models are developed and implemented: for example, family preservation programs, which are intensive in-home services designed to keep families together, and teaching group homes, in which a treatment foster care model is offered to four children per placement home. An area in need of immediate study is the development, implementation, and outcomes of culturally competent programs. Examples of the need for research in the cultural competence of programs would include studies on the effectiveness of services used by minority children, adolescents, and their families, and studies of the barriers that deter service use by children and families of various ethnic/racial minorities. Relatedly, the field of services research is in need of additional instruments to assess the cultural competence of interventions. Finally, with the stress on the development of community-based programs, there has been less recent research on hospitalization of children and adolescents. In particular, we have little understanding of exactly what is done to children in hospitals, the process of linking children to services at discharge, and how these aspects of treatment are related to outcomes such as school, home, and community functioning. To facilitate research in this area, NIMH (1991c) has released a program announcement (PA-91-58) for research on hospitalization of adolescents for mental disorders. We also need to understand in greater depth the hospitalization experiences of and outcomes for younger children.

At the systems level, there is a need for studies of system integration projects designed to remove many of the barriers that exist in systems in which services are provided by categorical child-serving agencies. There is also a need for projects designed to study the process and outcomes of involving parents as partners in developing and implementing service systems. A host of projects could be developed to examine the funding of children's mental health services, including studies of the consequences of managed care, capitated systems of care, providing vouchers for parents to purchase services needed by their child, and incentives to providers for accepting hard-to-serve children. Many currently funded projects focusing on the individual, family, or program level could benefit from the addition of a cost-effectiveness component designed and directed by an economist specializing in children's services. Finally, there are opportunities to develop instruments and methods in the areas of assessing systems change. Such instruments and methods would be helpful in stimulating additional research at the systems level.

One of the major features of services research in the area of children and adolescents is that there are so many interesting areas to explore with the potential to affect policy development. In addition to the types of single-level projects noted above, there is need for more multilevel projects, such as the Ventura County study (see Attkisson et al., Chapter 11 of this book), and multisite projects. Multisite studies should be facilitated by the adoption of the Mental Health Statistics Improvement Program minimum data set for children, expected to be released in the near future, and the availability through NIMH of R10 funding for multisite research that may involve the implementation of a consensus research protocol at several sites, perhaps in different states. The support for multisite work may be particularly important in facilitating studies of rural services projects in which small numbers of children may be enrolled in the interventions at any one site.

Finally, there is a need for replication studies. Clinical and psychosocial interventions are implemented and evaluated in service systems with unique characteristics. It cannot be assumed that transplanting a successful program from one venue—for example, city, county, or state—or one type of child-serving agency to another—for example, child welfare to mental health—will result in a successful program in the second site. Research demonstration projects need to specify clearly the nature of the intervention(s), the characteristics of the clients served, and the techniques used for program implementation, monitoring program fidelity, and evaluating programs to maximize the chance for program success when services and/or programs are disseminated. Researchers need to be actively involved in testing the most effective dose of a treatment or intervention and determining for whom the intervention works most effectively and under what conditions the intervention is most effective.

Discussion

Continuing support for additional controlled studies of the effectiveness of multiple services for children and adolescents is a high priority for the Center for Mental Health Services and NIMH. The next several years will bring the results from the first generation of research demonstration grants and the outcomes from studies on emergency services and hospitalization of adolescents. The funding of additional Centers for Research on Mental Health Services for Children and Adolescents will probably result in the generation of additional grant applications requesting funding for studies regarding the organization, financing, delivery, effectiveness, and outcomes of mental health services for children and adolescents and their families.

Prior research on children's mental health has provided useful information regarding effective intervention strategies. It remains for the current generation of services researchers to employ rigorous research designs and sophisticated analytic strategies to answer questions regarding what works for whom under what conditions and at what cost. The challenges are many, including assessing the relationships between developmental level, interventions, and outcomes; developing, implementing, and evaluating culturally competent services, programs, and systems of care; assessing differential outcomes associated with varying degrees of family engagement as partners in treatment; determining the cost-effectiveness of primary, secondary, and tertiary prevention programs; and assessing the outcomes associated with systems-level interventions involving multiple child-serving agencies.

Research on effectiveness of services for children with serious emotional and behavioral problems and their families, particularly R18 services demonstration research, should continue to be a priority for funding agencies at the federal level because of the immediate policy relevance of these projects. Beyond fostering the development of such research, it is important to develop effective strategies for disseminating the outcomes of this research to policy makers, practitioners, and consumers/advocates, as well as to other investigators.

References

Bickman, L. (1993, March). *Evaluation and research issues in system of care research at Fort Bragg*. Paper presented at the Sixth Annual Research Conference of the Florida Research and Training Center on Children's Mental Health, Tampa, FL.

Brandenburg, N., Friedman, R., & Silver, S. (1990). The epidemiology of childhood psychiatric disorders: Prevalence findings from recent studies. *Journal of the American Academy of Child and Adolescent Psychiatry, 29*, 76-83.

Burns, B. J. (1989). Critical research directions for child mental health services. In A. Algarin, R. M. Friedman, A. J. Duchnowski, K. M. Kutash, S. E. Silver, & M. K. Johnson (Eds.), *Children's mental health services and policy: Building a research base. Second annual conference proceedings* (pp. 8-13). Tampa: Florida Mental Health Institute.

Burns, B. J. (1991). Mental health services use by adolescents in the 1970s and 1980s. *Journal of the American Academy of Child and Adolescent Psychiatry, 30*(1), 144-150.

Burns, B. J., & Friedman, R. M. (1990). Examining the research base for child mental health services and policy. *Journal of Mental Health Administration, 17*, 87-98.

Catron, T. (1993). *Evaluation of school-based mental health services*. Abstract submitted to the Center for Mental Health Services, Rockville, MD.

Cauce, A. M. (1993). *Effectiveness of intensive case management for homeless adolescents*. Abstract submitted to the Center for Mental Health Services, Rockville, MD.

Clark, H. B., & Boyd, L. A. (1993). *Fostering individualized mental health care: A study of a wraparound system of care for foster children with emotional/behavioral disturbances*. Abstract submitted to the Center for Mental Health Services, Rockville, MD.

Costello, E. J., Burns, B. J., Angold, A., & Leaf, P. J. (1993). How can epidemiology improve mental health services for children and adolescents? *Journal of the American Academy of Child and Adolescent Psychiatry, 32*, 1106-1114.

Dugger, C. W. (1993, August 6). Program to preserve families draws child-welfare debate. *New York Times*, pp. B1, B2.

Evans, M. E. (1993a). *Outcomes of parent and provider designed systems of care*. Abstract submitted to the Center for Mental Health Services, Rockville, MD.

Evans, M. E. (1993b). *Outcomes of three children's psychiatric emergency programs*. Abstract submitted to the Center for Mental Health Services, Rockville, MD.

Fisher, P. W., Shaffer, D., Piacentini, J. C., et al. (1993). Sensitivity of the Diagnostic Interview Schedule for Children, 2nd edition (DISC 2.1) for specific diagnoses of children and adolescents. *Journal of the American Academy of Child and Adolescent Psychiatry, 32*, 666-673.

Fraser, M. W., Pecora, P. J., & Haapala, D. A. (1991). *Families in crisis: The impact of intensive family preservation services*. New York: Aldine.

Friedman, R. M., & Kutash, K. (1992). Challenges for child and adolescent mental health. *Health Affairs, 11,* 125-136.

Friedman, R. M., & Street, S. (1985). Admission criteria for children's mental health services: A review of the issues and options. *Journal of Clinical Child Psychology, 14,* 229-235.

Friesen, B. J., & Koroloff, N. M. (1990). Family-centered services: Implications for mental health administration and research. *Journal of Mental Health Administration, 17,* 13-25.

Goldfine, P. E., Heath, G. A., Hardesty, V. A., Berman, H. G., Gordon, B. J., & Lind, N. W. (1985). Alternatives to psychiatric hospitalization for children. *Psychiatric Clinics of North America, 8,* 527-535.

Henggeler, S. W., Melton, G. B., & Smith, L. A. (1992). Family preservation using multisystemic therapy: An effective alternative to incarcerating serious juvenile offenders. *Journal of Consulting and Clinical Psychology, 60,* 953-961.

Johnson, K. (1987). *Report on SRS substitute care and intensive family-based services in Vermont.* Montpelier, VT: Vermont Coalition of Runaway Youth Services Intensive Family-Based Services Project.

Kiesler, C. A., & Simpkins, C. G. (1991). Changes in psychiatric inpatient treatment of children and youth in general hospitals, 1980-85. *Hospital and Community Psychiatry, 42,* 601-604.

Knitzer, J. (1982). Mental health services to children and adolescents. *American Psychologist, 39,* 905-911.

National Advisory Mental Health Council. (1990). *National plan for research on child and adolescent mental disorders* (NIMH ADM 90-1683). Rockville, MD: Author.

National Institute of Mental Health (NIMH). (1990). *Child and mental health research demonstration grants* (MH-90-10). Rockville, MD: Author.

National Institute of Mental Health (NIMH). (1991a, April). *Child and Adolescent Mental Health Service System Research Demonstration Grants* (PA-91-40). Rockville, MD: Author.

National Institute of Mental Health (NIMH). (1991b, April). *Implementation of the national plan for research on child and adolescent mental disorders* (PA-91-46). Rockville, MD: Author.

National Institute of Mental Health (NIMH). (1991c, April). *Research on hospitalization of adolescents for mental disorders* (PA-91-58). Rockville, MD: Author.

National Mental Health Association. (1988). *America's invisible children need visible services.* Alexandria, VA: Author.

Roghmann, K. J., Zastowney, T. R., & Babigan, H. M. (1985). Mental health problems of children: Analysis of a cumulative psychiatric case register. *Annual Progress in Child Psychiatry and Child Development,* 475-495.

Saxe, L., Cross, T., & Silverman, N. (1988). Children's mental health: The gap between what we know and what we do. *American Psychologist, 43,* 800-807.

Sondheimer, D. (1991, March). *Developing an NIMH research demonstration project for children and adolescents with or at risk for severe mental and emotional disorders.* Bethesda, MD: National Institute of Mental Health.

Stroul, B. A., & Friedman, R. M. (1986). *A system of care for severely emotionally disturbed children and youth.* Washington, DC: Georgetown University Child Development Center.

Tuma, J. M. (1989). Mental health services for children: The state of the art. *American Psychologist, 44,* 188-199.

U.S. Department of Education, Office of Special Education and Rehabilitative Services, Division of Educational Services, Special Education Programs. (1984). *Sixth annual report to Congress on the implementation of the Education of the Handicapped Act.* Washington, DC: Government Printing Office.

PART III

Selected Components of a
System of Care

Stroul and Friedman (1986) developed a model system of care to guide the initial efforts of states and communities in developing service delivery systems. In addition to providing a full array of needed services, a system of care ideally bridges the multiple settings in which children with mental health needs are found, including health, mental health, education, and juvenile justice settings. This section describes four of these settings that should be linked within an ideal system of care and highlights the role each can play in serving children with mental health needs. The settings described are the primary care setting, the school, juvenile court, and the psychiatric hospital.

Primary health clinics and doctors' offices, as well as schools, are two settings that offer great potential for mental health intervention with children. Both settings offer the potential to identify children who otherwise might not come to the attention of mental health professionals. Both settings also offer "natural," regular environments for most children, where prevention, diagnosis, and treatment can occur. However, as Mark L. Wolraich and Sarah Ring-Kurtz, Susan Sonnichsen, and Kathleen V. Hoover-Dempsey indicate, both the primary care and education settings have rarely had a role in the delivery of mental health services.

Wolraich (Chapter 5) highlights the role that primary care professionals *can* play in treating children with mental disorders. Although the primary care setting is often the first potential area of identification for mental disorders, the research to date indicates that primary care physicians underidentify mental disorders in children. Wolraich discusses the multiple reasons that primary care professionals underdiagnose mental disorders in children and offers strategies for these professionals to use in facilitating the identification of mental health problems. Wolraich also describes primary care professionals' role in treating children as well as the role they can play in primary and secondary prevention. In particular, providing well-child-care education and detecting detrimental situations for children, such as abuse and neglect, divorce, and illness, are activities that can be easily incorporated within the role of the primary care physician. Finally, Wolraich outlines the research needs in further understanding the factors that contribute to underdiagnosis, appropriate and effective psychosocial interventions, and new models for delivery of services.

Ring-Kurtz, Sonnichsen, and Hoover-Dempsey (Chapter 7) describe the role of school-based services in the system of care for children. Like the primary care settings, schools offer a natural point of assessment, prevention, and intervention in a child's life. School is the most universal environment for children and can provide a relatively nonstigmatizing base for service delivery. Moreover, several features of the educational setting offer advantages for mental health service delivery to children, including the commitment to parent involvement and educational processes that support a focus on preventive services. In addition to the positive aspects of the school setting for mental health services, Ring-Kurtz and her colleagues describe some of the problems inherent in working in a school environment and strategies for dealing with these constraints. In particular, the authors close their chapter with a discussion of the major challenges engendered by current policy that hinder the development and implementation of school-based mental health services.

Another setting discussed in this section is the juvenile justice setting, long recognized as serving children with mental health problems. As Kathleen A. Maloy describes in Chapter 8, the overall structure of the system, with a focus on treatment and rehabilitation, acknowledges the mental health needs of the children and the fact that juvenile justice is one of the major points of entry for children who come to the attention of the state. In her chapter, Maloy reviews the historical roots of the juvenile justice system and the intersection of the juvenile justice and mental health systems. Because the juvenile justice system often is the gatekeeper for troubled families and youth, it can offer a key area of mental health intervention. Moreover, as Maloy suggests, this gatekeeping role, together with the juvenile court's authority to mandate other agencies to provide services to a child and his or her family, positions the juvenile justice system as a key and integral player in implementing an integrated mental health system for children.

The final setting within the mental health system highlighted in this section is the psychiatric hospital. In Chapter 6, Barry Nurcombe discusses the criticisms of long-term hospitalization for children that have been common in the field and reviews the inadequacy of the research basis for either supporting or refuting these criticisms. However, funding realities and pressures have curbed lengths of hospital stays with little evidence of quality and efficacy of the care provided. Thus, given the current economic environment, Nurcombe posits a model for short-term hospitalization that could fit within an integrated system of care for children with mental health service needs. As hospitals converted from what Nurcombe has termed a reconstructive model to a stabilization model of care when they moved from long-term to brief hospitalization, so must they now adapt to an ultrabrief model of care. Nurcombe suggests that ultrabrief hospitalization, in contrast to brief hospitalization, should have crisis alleviation as its primary purpose. Therefore, to provide for stabilization, reintegration, and aftercare, hospitalization should be one of the many components within a comprehensive, intertwined system of care. As Nurcombe indicates, the current state of mental health care financing is based on an episodic model of care and thus requires an integrated array of services if appropriate care is to be provided.

Reference

Stroul, B. A., & Friedman, R. M. (1986). *A system of care for severely emotionally disturbed children and youth*. Washington, DC: Georgetown University Child Development Center.

5

Services in the Primary Care Context

MARK L. WOLRAICH

As has been covered by others in this volume, mental disorders are a frequent problem in children and require help from more mental health clinicians than are currently available. Because it is impossible for all the children with diagnosable mental disorders, let alone those with mental problems, to be treated by mental health professionals, many families have to depend on other sources for help or get no help at all. Primary care professionals are an important alternative source. In fact, recent research has found that the majority of children with mental disorders receive their treatment in primary care or outpatient medical settings (Offord et al., 1987). Therefore, it is important to include a discussion of the primary care context when trying to characterize mental health services for children.

This chapter first discusses some of the issues relating to diagnosis. How well primary care clinicians are able to recognize mental disorders in children is key to their ability to identify which children are in need, who can benefit from their services, and who must be referred for more specialized mental health services. The chapter then discusses the range of mental health services provided in primary care contexts, including preventive services such as anticipatory guidance. Such services are believed to contribute to the prevention or diminution of mental problems by addressing them early. The chapter concludes with a discussion of existing needs and implications for future research.

Diagnosis

A concern raised in some of the current research is that primary care physicians underdiagnose mental disorders in children. Although the prevalence of mental disorders based on epidemiological surveys of children ranges from 10% to 20% (Offord et al., 1987), the prevalence of those diagnosed by the primary care clinicians has been in the range of 2% to 5% (Costello, Costello, et al., 1988). The epidemiologic studies are based on structured psychiatric interviews with parents and/or patients using the criteria of the *Diagnostic and Statistical Manual of Mental Disorders* (3rd ed., Rev.; *DSM-III-R*; American Psychiatric Association, 1987). Using such rigorous identification methods, Costello, Edelbrock, et al. (1988) found that primary care physicians were reasonably specific (84%) but not very sensitive (17%) to mental disorders in children. By *specific*, it is meant that they accurately identify children who do not have mental illness, and by *sensitive*, it is meant that they accurately identify children with mental disorders. Results were better in a study examining the diagnosis of attention deficit hyperactivity disorder only, with a specificity of 97% and a sensitivity of 44% (Lindgren et al., 1989). However, both studies suggest that primary care physicians tend to underdiagnose mental disorders in children.

A number of factors contribute to these findings. Primary care physicians receive relatively little training about mental disorders in children. A review of the pediatric curriculum in 1979 (American Academy of Pediatrics, 1978) reported that many residency training programs offered minimal or no training in the psychosocial aspects of pediatrics. Even with programs that have increased behavioral pediatrics in their curricula, most limit that training to 1 month unless the residents themselves elect to pursue the area further during their elective time. In addition, because the major emphasis of behavioral pediatric rotations in many of the programs is on milder problems and preventive issues, it is likely that little or no time is spent devoted to diagnostic criteria for mental disorders or particularly about the *DSM* system.

This lack of exposure to mental health diagnostic criteria is reflected in the practice of primary care physicians. In a national survey of pediatricians and family practitioners related to attention deficit hyperactivity disorder (Wolraich et al., 1990), only 24% reported using *DSM* criteria to make the diagnosis. Most primary care physicians do not use *DSM* criteria and are therefore not likely to identify many of the children diagnosed on the basis of interviews specifically employing those criteria.

In addition to the lack of information about diagnostic criteria, primary care physicians rarely have sufficient practice time to address psychosocial problems. The average primary care visit is 15 to 20 minutes. In that time, it is difficult, if not impossible, to adequately explore the issues pertinent to making mental illness diagnoses. Consequently, primary care physicians must deal with issues with which they have relatively little training in too short a time. Thus, it is not surprising to find that primary care physicians are reluctant to address these issues. Several suggestions to help alleviate these problems are presented in this chapter.

The trend of underdiagnosis of mental disorders is further compounded because mothers do not perceive the primary care visit as an appropriate time to raise such issues. In a study by Hickson, Altemeier, and O'Connor (1983), 70% of the mothers had psychosocial concerns about their children, but only 28% of those mothers raised them with their physician. The major reason for not doing so was that the mothers were unaware that their pediatricians could help them with these concerns.

It does appear, however, that parents' concerns may be a useful screener for mental health problems. In a study that examined both physician and parent identification of child mental health disorders, parents' concerns were found to be a useful source of identification, with a sensitivity of 85%, but were found to overidentify disorders, with a specificity of 55% (Costello, Edelbrock, et al., 1988). However, the children overidentified may be those who do not quite meet the criteria for diagnosis but have significant problems that warrant attention. Utilizing parental concerns as a screening method provides the practical benefit of time and cost and has the advantage of specifically addressing parental concerns. Primary care physicians therefore need to make parents aware that they can discuss these issues as part of their physician visits.

Another method used to screen children more efficiently has been the use of parent rating scales (Jellinek, Murphy, & Burns, 1986). These are not yet used extensively by physicians, but do show some promise in helping to identify children in need. They provide the benefit of collecting information from the parent and/or teacher without taking up much physician time, and because the scales have normative data, it is possible to compare the responses to ratings of normal children.

A practice being instituted as part of family practitioner training may also contribute to the identification of mental health problems in children. Family practitioner training programs have increased their interest in family systems (Doherty & Baird, 1984). This has led more recently trained family practitioners to address psychosocial and mental health issues in their explorations of family dynamics. Use of such procedures as the genogram may help family practitioners to explore family psychosocial issues and to improve their identification of problems in the family that have potentially adverse effects on the children. However, identifying these issues does not necessarily increase the abilities of family practitioners to identify and diagnose mental disorders in children.

A further factor contributing to the low level of identification of mental disorders by primary care physicians is their reluctance to place a mental disorder label on a child. This is suggested in a study by Starfield and Barkowf (1989). Psychiatric diagnoses still carry social stigma. The negative perceptions are further reinforced by a commonly held belief that many mental disorders imply inadequate child rearing. There is also a belief that for many disorders treatment has limited benefit. All of these beliefs make mental disorder diagnoses upsetting to parents and are likely to make primary care physicians reluctant to place this added burden on the families.

In addition, mental disorder labels can have adverse effects on health insurance. There have been instances in which insurance policies have been denied or restricted in their mental services coverage because of the diagnosis carried by a family member. Further, some insurance companies limit reimbursement for mental disorders to care received by psychiatrists, so that the label, in a primary care context, does not help the physician receive adequate compensation.

The diagnoses are made more difficult because primary care physicians are faced with a broad spectrum of psychosocial problems, including normal variations in behaviors, developmental variations dependent on the child's age, subthreshold conditions, and actual disorders. The criteria for disorder diagnoses are not always clear enough for the physician to decide if the presenting behaviors are severe enough to meet the criteria required in making a specific mental disorder diagnosis. Given the belief that a mental disorder diagnosis is likely to be stigmatizing, the physician is likely to err on the side of underdiagnosing if he or she is unsure of the diagnosis.

The *DSM* system was developed for psychiatric use, and its emphasis has been on psychiatrists defining those disorders so that psychiatric clinicians can become more precise in their terminology and so that empirical studies of these disorders can be pursued. This has very effectively increased the empirical knowledge of mental disorders. However, the range of mental problems seen in primary care is much broader than that seen by psychiatrists. Horwitz, Leaf, Leventhal, Forsyth, and Speechly (1992) found that when a system designed for primary care is used, primary care physicians are better able to identify psychosocial problems. Therefore, efforts are currently underway to develop a classification system of psychosocial and mental problems focusing on the primary care context. This is a joint effort of the American Psychiatric Association and the American Academy of Pediatrics. The process will include joint activities of pediatricians, child psychiatrists, and child psychologists.

An additional important diagnostic role played by primary care physicians has been to identify children who are developmentally delayed. This has been emphasized recently with the government's effort (Individuals With Disabilities Education Act of 1991, Part H) to identify and provide early intervention services for children under the age of 3 years. Through a combination of developmental screening and surveillance and the identification of medical conditions likely to cause developmental disabilities during frequent contacts provided as part of well-baby care, primary care physicians are one of the major identifiers of developmentally delayed infants.

Treatment

Most primary care physicians limit their treatments to those interventions that require little time and are not complex. Therefore, most primary care physicians limit the number of mental disorders that they treat directly. The two mental disorders they most frequently treat among children are enuresis and attention deficit hyperactivity disorder (ADHD). Both are high-frequency, low-severity conditions, and both can be treated with relatively safe and effective pharmacologic agents: enuresis with DDAVP or imipramine, and ADHD with stimulant medications such as methylphenidate, dextroamphetamine, or pemoline. Whereas a pharmacologic agent for enuresis can frequently be effective as a single form of treatment, ADHD frequently requires a multimodal approach (i.e., pharmacotherapy and behavior modification) for long-term efficacy (Hechtman, 1985).

Other disorders, mostly in Axis II (i.e., mental retardation) of the *DSM-III-R* and *DSM-IV* (*Diagnostic and Statistical Manual of Mental Disorders*, 4th ed.; American Psychiatric Association, 1994), are also frequently evaluated and treated in primary care settings. These include learning disabilities and mental retardation. Treatment of learning disabilities has mostly entailed ruling out other contributing causes such as hearing loss due to otitis media or visual acuity problems and helping parents as a third party when the parents are in conflict with the educational system. With mental retardation, physicians are usually involved in establishing the underlying cause, such as fragile X or Williams syndrome, and providing treatment for that cause where appropriate, as in the case of phenylketonuria or hypothyroidism. Many causes of mental retardation also have other physical conditions as part of the diagnosis. For example, children with Down's syndrome may have congenital heart disease, middle ear disease, and a greater risk for leukemia. For children with mental disorders, seizures are a frequently associated condition. Their treatment must balance the benefits of the seizure control with the significant side effects of the anticonvulsive therapy. Counseling parents about their child's condition is also an important role played by primary care physicians. Physicians can help parents to understand and deal with their child's condition and also to understand the impact of their child's condition on siblings.

Prevention

Primary care physicians also focus a great deal of attention on preventive issues. The preventive efforts take two forms. One is primary prevention, which seeks to prevent the condition, and the other is secondary prevention, which seeks to diminish the impact of a condition once it has occurred. An example of primary prevention is using neonatal screening to identify phenylketonuria or hypothyroidism in the newborn period and allow the initiation of treatment to prevent mental retardation. An example of secondary prevention is obtaining educational services for children with learning disabilities to maximize their functioning in school and to minimize their failure experiences.

Primary prevention constitutes the major psychosocial activity of primary care physicians. Much of this is provided as well-child care when physicians give parents information and advice about normal cognitive and behavioral development. They try to help parents understand expected normal patterns. They help parents by anticipating minor problems that are likely to occur at different stages of a child's development, such as colic, sleep difficulties, toilet training, and adolescent rebellion. By helping parents to understand and anticipate normal variations in child development, they provide what is referred to as anticipatory guidance. This helps parents plan for these possibilities and realize that the problems are common and do not necessarily reflect significant pathology.

Another primary prevention role played by primary care physicians is that of detecting environments that are likely to be detrimental to a child's development. One such role is identifying physical or sexual abuse. Because abuse frequently includes some physical manifestations or somatic symptoms, primary care physicians need to be sensitized to signs that suggest it. Often the signs are not obvious, as in the "shaken baby syndrome." Almost all state laws currently require health care professionals to report all suspicions of abuse, such as inadequately explained injuries. However, the physician does not have to make a definitive decision. The decision is the responsibility of the state's child protective agency and, if needed, the court. The physician can be helpful in identifying stress factors and appropriate resources.

More frequently than actual abuse, primary care physicians see neglect, which is frequently manifested in infants by a failure to thrive. The physician must identify the extent that each of potentially multiple factors contributes to the child's failure to thrive. These include an underlying organic cause in the child, such as an inborn error of metabolism or gastrointestinal reflux; serious emotional problems in the caregiver; and difficulties in the parent-child interaction.

Some family events also have adverse effects on children. The most prominent are marital discord and divorce. If primary care physicians develop good relationships with parents and are careful observers, they can detect problems early and help influence the parents to seek help. Primary care physicians are also in a good position to help parents understand the impact of their actions on their children and to provide them with advice about dealing with their children when there are family problems.

Another common problem is death or serious illness of a family member. Family practitioners frequently are the physician for all family members, and, in the case of pediatricians, they are frequently the physician for all the children in a family. This allows the primary care physician to address not only the needs of the patient with a chronic illness but also those of the patient's siblings, who are at risk for developing psychological problems (Tritt & Estes, 1988). Through anticipatory guidance, the primary care physician can help parents to be aware of the needs of those siblings and to seek counseling, if appropriate, before the problems become more serious.

Research

The research needed for mental services in primary care settings falls into the three categories already discussed: diagnosis, treatment, and efficacy of interventions. As was stated earlier in the chapter, most of the previous research on diagnosis has examined the role that primary care physicians play in diagnosing mental disorders. Most of these studies have examined the inaccuracy and particularly the underdiagnosing of disorders (Costello, Edelbrock, et al., 1988). However, much more information is required if we are to address the problem. We need to know to what extent each of the contributing factors outlined here (i.e., time, physician knowledge, and classification system) plays a role. For example, additional training will be of limited benefit if what is taught is not practical to the primary care setting or does not address the types of problems seen in primary care settings.

Because most of the current classification efforts have dealt with mental disorders in psychiatric settings, the type of problems and range of severity need to be better defined. The suspicion is that the spectrum of mental problems is broader than that usually seen in psychiatric settings, and it may be more difficult to differentiate problems from disorders in primary care settings. Few specific data to support or refute this hypothesis are available at this time. Such information will be important in the process of developing the classification system for primary care *(DSM-PC)*.

Because preventive activities have been a major focus of the psychosocial activities of primary care physicians, it is important to improve the definition and identification of the important issues. We need to be able to identify specific potential problems to determine how they affect future mental health and whether specific interventions can ameliorate the problems and prevent more serious mental illness. For instance, some recent research has examined the impact of parent mental illness on children (Radke-Yarrow, Nottelmann, Martinez, Fox, & Belmont, 1992). The various adverse factors need to be defined and studied individually for progress to be made in determining what interventions are likely to help prevent subsequent problems.

The other important need is for research to show what are appropriate psychosocial interventions by primary care physicians. The provision of anticipatory guidance is strongly recommended (Casey, Sharp, & Loda, 1979). However, much more needs to be known about what is appropriate content for that guidance and whether providing that guidance makes any difference in the behavior of parents or children. Another broad area of preventive activities pertains to child neglect and abuse. What are effective activities for primary care physicians apart from reporting abuse and neglect? This area requires a good deal of further investigation.

The third important area of research deals with efficacy of treatment. Based on naturalistic studies such as those suggested for research into diagnosis and treatment, hypotheses will be generated about how to improve primary care services on psychosocial issues. It will be important to rigorously examine planned changes. For example, improving the abilities of primary care physicians to better detect mental disorders may require providing them with more knowledge about the condition, but it also may require better training in physician-patient communication or a change in the diagnostic procedures to enable physicians to screen patients in a short period of time. All of these issues need to be examined in an objective fashion and are part of the broad area of research in mental health services.

It will also be necessary to try new models for the delivery of services. For example, Schroeder, Gordon, Kanoy, and Routh (1983) proposed a model of collaborative service between pediatricians and psychologists. They described the experience of a child psychologist working with a pediatric group to provide diagnostic and counseling services to the group's families. Such models must be studied to determine their clinical impact as well as their cost. On a systems level, reimbursement structures and the impact of changes in that system on the delivery of mental health services in primary care must be examined.

In addition to research on new models, a larger systems-level approach also requires further research. For example, it will be important to determine how changes in reimbursements to primary care physicians can be used to improve their ability to address mental issues while not adding an undue burden on an already overly expensive health care system.

Summary

Primary care physicians play an important role in providing mental health services to children, especially because the number of children with mental health problems far exceeds the number of mental health professionals available. However, current information would suggest that primary care physicians significantly underidentify mental disorders in children. Less is known about their greater scope of activities in preventing mental problems as part of well-child care.

Much research is needed to better identify the issues, develop solutions, and assess the efficacy of the proposed solutions.

References

American Academy of Pediatrics, Task Force on Pediatric Education. (1978). *The future of pediatrics*. Evanston, IL: Author.

American Psychiatric Association. (1987). *Diagnostic and statistical manual of mental disorders* (3rd ed., Rev.). Washington, DC: Author.

American Psychiatric Association. (1994). *Diagnostic and statistical manual of mental disorders* (4th ed.). Washington, DC: Author.

Casey, P., Sharp, M., & Loda, F. (1979). Child-health supervision for children under 2 years of age: A review of the content and effectiveness. *Journal of Pediatrics, 95*, 1-9.

Costello, E., Costello, A., Edelbrock, C., Byrns, B. J., Dulcan, M. K., Brent, D., & Janisz-Ewski, S. (1988). Psychiatric disorders in pediatric primary care: Prevalence and risk factors. *Archives in General Psychiatry, 45*, 1107-1116.

Costello, E. J., Edelbrock, C., Costello, A. J., Dulcan, M. K., Burns, B. J., & Brent, D. (1988). Psychopathology in pediatric primary care: The new hidden morbidity. *Pediatrics, 82*, 415-424.

Doherty, W., & Baird, M. (1984). A protocol for family compliance counseling. *Family and Systemic Medicine, 2*, 333-336.

Hechtman, L. (1985). Adolescent outcome of hyperactive children treated with stimulants in childhood: A review. *Psychopharmacology Bulletin, 21*, 178.

Hickson, B., Altemeier, A., & O'Connor, S. (1983). Concerns of mothers seeking care in private pediatric offices: Opportunities for expanding services. *Pediatrics, 72*, 619-624.

Horwitz, S. M., Leaf, P. J., Leventhal, J. M., Forsyth, B., & Speechly, K. N. (1992). Identification and management of psychosocial and developmental problems in community-based primary care pediatric practices. *Pediatrics, 89*, 480-485.

Jellinek, A., Murphy, M., & Burns, J. (1986). Brief psychosocial screening in outpatient pediatric practice. *Journal of Pediatrics, 109*, 371-378.

Lindgren, S., Wolraich, L., Stromquist, A., Davis, C., Milich, R., & Watson, D. (1989, September). *Diagnosis of attention deficit hyperactivity disorder by primary care physicians.* Paper presented at Mental Health Services for Children and Adolescents in Primary Care Settings: A Research Conference, New Haven, CT.

Offord, R., Boyle, H., Szatmari, P., Rae-Grant, I., Links, S., Cadman, T., Byles, J., Crawford, W., Blum, M., Byrne, C., Thomas, H., & Woodward, A. (1987). Ontario Child Health Study. II. Six-month prevalence of disorder and rates of service utilization. *Archives in General Psychiatry, 44*, 832-836.

Radke-Yarrow, M., Nottelmann, E., Martinez, P., Fox, B., & Belmont, B. (1992). Young children of affectively ill parents: A longitudinal study of psychosocial development. *Journal of the American Academy of Child and Adolescent Psychiatry, 1*, 68-77.

Schroeder, C., Gordon, B., Kanoy, K., & Routh, K. (1983). Managing children's behavior problems in pediatric practice. In M. L. Wolraich & K. Routh (Eds.), *Advances in developmental and behavioral pediatrics* (Vol. 4, pp. 25-86). London: JAI.

Starfield, B., & Barkowf, S. (1989). Physicians' recognition of complaints made by parents about their children's health. *Pediatrics, 43,* 168-172.

Tritt, G., & Estes, L. (1988). Psychosocial adaptation of siblings of children with chronic medical illnesses. *American Journal of Orthopedic Psychiatry, 58,* 211-220.

Wolraich, M., Lindgren, S., Stromquist, A., Milich, R., Davis, C., & Watson, D. (1990). Stimulant medication use by primary care physicians in the treatment of attention deficit hyperactivity disorder. *Pediatrics, 86,* 95-101.

6

The Future of Psychiatric Hospitalization for Children and Adolescents

BARRY NURCOMBE

Until the mid-1970s, it was difficult for a clinician to locate a psychiatric hospital bed for a severely disturbed child or adolescent. The few patients who were able to access inpatient care had three options: state hospitals, general hospital units, or, rarely, specialized psychiatric units.

State hospitals, as a rule, provided substandard medical care for patients housed in chronic wards. The inmates of these mental hospital units were typically abandoned children with intractable psychosis, conduct disorder, or pervasive developmental dysfunction. General hospitals mixed adolescents (and sometimes children) with adults, without benefit of the educational or recreational services suitable for a younger population. As a result, children and adolescents absorbed a disproportionate amount of staff time and were often regarded as a nuisance to older patients. Sporadic attempts were made to open units designed specially for children or adolescents. Some of these programs took their philosophy from Aichorn (1935) and espoused policies opposed to the application of structure. Either they changed or they foundered (Holmes, 1964). Aware of the expense and liability risks such programs created, hospital administrators resisted their proliferation. Here and there, a few highly specialized units prospered. These programs were often based upon the original views of their persuasive psychoanalytic founders (e.g., Bettelheim, 1955; Szurek, Berlin, & Boatman, 1971). Other programs such as Close-Holton (Jessness, 1975), KYC (Levinson & Gerard, 1973), Achievement Place (Braukmann, Kirigin, & Wolk, 1976), and Project ReEd (Kirby, Wilson, & Short, 1977) employed or contrasted different combinations of behavior therapy, counseling, and transactional analysis. Because they involved long-term care in an open, nonmedical environment, they are appropriately regarded as residential treatment centers and will not be considered further in this chapter.

Though seldom described in this manner, the aim of long-stay hospital treatment was essentially reconstructive (or, in the worst instances, merely custodial). Highly selective in their admission policies and leisurely in their diagnostic evaluation, hospitals usually relied upon a particular therapeutic technique, such as intensive psychotherapy, supplemented with group therapy and parental counseling. Their purpose was nothing less than a radical alteration of personality, behavior, and family functioning. They generally regarded advances and innovations in pharmacotherapy, family therapy, and behavior therapy as charlatanic or irrelevant, and were often resistant to research. Thus, they were left with little more than rhetoric with which to answer their critics.

The chief criticisms of long-term hospitalization were as follows: Psychiatric patients could be stigmatized; patients might become so dependent on hospital staff that they would be unable to cope with the world outside; patients might get the idea they had mental diseases rather than coping problems; hospitals are overrestrictive; families are disrupted by hospitalization of a family member; and patients might become estranged from their parents. There has been little research into the validity of these criticisms. But there also is inadequate scientific evidence for the efficacy of long-term hospitalization. Moreover, concern was expressed that the expenditure of a disproportionate amount of public funds on a small number of very disturbed patients detracts from others who need treatment and retards the development of alternative services (American Psychiatric Association, 1989; Friedman, Ichinose, & Greer, 1990; Knitzer, 1982).

This chapter reviews existing research on the efficacy of hospitalization. It goes on to propose a model for short-term hospitalization that both recognizes contemporary economic constraints and has the potential to complement and enhance a comprehensive array of mental health services for children and adolescents.

Research Into the
Efficacy of Inpatient Treatment

Most research into the outcome of hospitalization was conducted at a time when lengths of stay were measured in months rather than weeks. Few studies were controlled in terms of random assignment to hospital or a comparison treatment, and only some used standardized measures in order to evaluate outcome at the time of discharge or at follow-up. Reviews of this research have been provided by Blotcky, Dimperio, and Gossett (1984), Gossett, Lewis, and Barnhart (1983), and Pfeiffer and Strzelecki (1990).

Blotcky et al. (1984) surveyed 24 outcome studies involving children under 12 years of age. Only 5 of these reports were prospective. No study was controlled, and methods of data collection varied considerably in rigor. Nevertheless, the reviewers felt able to conclude that the following factors were associated with less favorable outcome: (a) lower intelligence, (b) organicity, (c) diagnosis (especially pervasive developmental disorder, psychosis, and conduct disorder), (d) symptomatology (especially autism, bizarre symptoms, antisocial behavior, and severely impaired peer relationships), and (e) severe parental psychopathology (especially psychosis or criminality). Longer hospitalization, completion of treatment, and the provision of aftercare were found by several investigators to be associated with favorable outcome. Neither age nor sex was consistently related to outcome.

Gossett et al. (1983) reviewed 22 studies published between 1942 and 1980 concerning the outcome of hospitalization in adolescents aged 13 to 19 years. They found several factors to be related to outcomes:

1. Eighty percent to 90% of neurotic patients were functioning well at follow-up compared to 50% to 60% of those with personality disorder and 30% of those with psychosis.

2. An unfavorable outcome was associated with early childhood trauma, early neuropathic traits, academic failure, isolation from peers, marked passivity, early and gradual onset, and an absence of clear precipitation. (In contrast, psychotic adolescents with normal childhood, good academic performance, later onset, clear precipitation, stormy symptomatology, and rapid symptomatic improvement had a better long-term outcome.)

3. Below-average intelligence was associated with poorer long-term functioning.

4. Poorer outcome was related to having several relatives who suffered from severe psychopathology (e.g., psychosis, substance abuse, or criminality).

5. Better outcome was associated with the provision of a program especially designed for adolescents (particularly in the case of schizophrenia and personality disorder), the completion of the treatment program, and the continuation of therapy following discharge.

In summary, seven factors correlated with outcome: severity of symptomatology, process-reactive psychopathology, intelligence, family dysfunction, specialized adolescent programming, completion of treatment, and aftercare. Gossett et al. (1983) compared these findings to the more extensive research that had been conducted on adult inpatient treatment (e.g., Erickson, 1975). The adult studies are consistent with those concerning adolescents: Better outcome was associated with the provision of specialized, semiautonomous programs with high staff-patient ratios, adequate length of stay, and appropriate aftercare.

Pfeiffer and Strzelecki (1990) surveyed 34 studies published since 1975 regarding inpatient treatment for children and adolescents. Six concerned children, 17 dealt with adolescents, and 11 involved both children and adolescents. Because only two studies presented the means and standard deviations of their outcome measures, conventional meta-analysis was not possible. Instead, the authors employed an innovative statistic, weighted predictive value (WPV), which favored outcome studies with greater sample size. Using the WPV, they evaluated the hypothetical association between treatment outcome and 10 variables—intelligence, organicity, diagnosis, symptom pattern, age, sex, family functioning, treatment, length of stay, and aftercare.

To summarize, Pfeiffer and Strzelecki's (1990) findings were consistent with those of Blotcky et al. (1984). The following four factors had the highest association with outcome: treatment variables, aftercare, organicity, and symptom pattern. Four factors had a moderate association with outcome: family variables, diagnosis, length of stay, and intelligence. Two factors had little or no association: age and sex. The treatment variables most strongly associated with favorable outcome were positive therapeutic alliance between patient, family, and therapist; planned discharge; completion of treatment; and (in one study) the provision of a specialized mode of therapy (cognitively based problem solving). The aftercare variables cited were outpatient therapy, foster home placement, and level of stress following discharge. Central nervous dysfunction was strongly associated with negative outcome, as were bizarre, primitive, or antisocial symptomatology; alienation; psychosexual problems; acting out; psychotic symptoms; and anergia. The diagnosis of psychosis or conduct disorder was associated with poor outcome in some studies but not others. The family variables moderately associated with outcome were level of family functioning, marital conflict, frequency of early separations or disruptions, parental involvement in treatment, and parental denial. Length of stay emerged as an inconsistent predictor: Three studies found a positive association and four failed to do so. Intelligence was not consistently related to outcome. Neither age nor sex predicted outcome.

All three reviews noted deficiencies in the research available. Ethical constraints impeded the introduction of controls or comparisons: The random assignment of dangerously suicidal or violent patients between hospital and control settings is impracticable. Few studies were prospective. The measures of outcome employed varied in objectivity and reliability, and data were rarely reported in a sophisticated manner (many lacked even means and standard deviations). Future research will need to delineate the critical dimensions and quality of inpatient treatment (e.g., ward environment, organization, hierarchy, staff attitudes, and modes of therapy provided), define quality of outcome in a multidimensional manner, and expand the number of predictor variables. More powerful analytic methodologies such as multivariate statistical techniques are required. If random assignment is ethically precluded, strong quasi-experimental designs should be implemented. For example, the effect of different lengths of stay or contrasted treatments could be evaluated across hospitals with regard to comparable types of patient.

Whatever the merits and deficiencies of these studies, they have been rendered irrelevant by the recent history of American health care funding. Starting in the mid-1970s, hospital practices began to change, at first slowly and then with a rush. Aware of shrinking occupancy as clinical advances and utilization review cut lengths of stay in medicine and surgery, hospitals sought new markets. The formerly shunned adolescent psychiatric population lay virtually untapped. Between 1980 and 1984, the number of patients under 18 years of age admitted to private psychiatric hospitals increased by 350% (Miller, 1985). Apparently unaware that this expansion was from a very low base, a number of writers expressed alarm that private hospitals were being used in lieu of adequate ambulatory care and that many admissions were inappropriate (Schwartz, 1989; Schwartz, Beeck, & Anderson, 1984; Weithorn, 1988). In fact, aside from a true increase in admissions to private hospitals as Medicaid funding became available, there was a noticeable movement away from state hospitals and correctional institutions toward private and general hospitals (Burns, 1991).

Since 1985, however, hospitals have been scoured by managed care. Lengths of stay have plummeted from 2 months to as little as 2 weeks. The drastic reduction of length of stay has been imposed without consideration of quality of care, and so abruptly that nothing is known of its impact. Future research must focus on the outcome of ultrabrief hospitalization. In the meantime, hospitals should redefine their purposes and deploy their resources accordingly. This chapter discusses how the principles of *stabilization* and *crisis alleviation* might be used to this end in a time of constraint and transition.

Brief Hospitalization

Definition

Brief hospitalization can be defined as lasting 3 to 5 weeks. Hospitalization of 3 weeks' to 3 months' duration can be regarded as *inter-*

mediate in length. Anything more protracted is *long-term. Ultrabrief* hospitalization lasts 1 to 21 days. Intermediate-term and long-term care have all but disappeared today, and brief hospitalization is being slowly throttled by draconian managed care. Most hospital populations today mix brief and ultrabrief lengths of stay.

Criteria for Admission

Hospitalization is expensive, restrictive, and disruptive. It should be reserved for those who truly need it. The following criteria (Nurcombe, 1991) exemplify those that typically operate today.

1. *General Criteria.* All of the following four criteria should apply:
    a. The patient is of an age appropriate to a hospital program (typically 4 to 18 years). Young adults may be occasionally admitted if they are developmentally immature or if they have previously been inpatients and would benefit from a further exposure to a specialized program.
    b. The patient suffers from a psychiatric disorder for which inpatient treatment is potentially effective (e.g., an uncomplicated conduct disorder).
    c. The patient has had an adequate trial of outpatient treatment, or outpatient treatment would be clearly inappropriate in view of the acuity of the problem (see below).
    d. The patient is physiologically stable. Patients affected by coma, delirium, or stupor (caused, for example, by intoxicants, hypnotic or sedative overdose, infection, or biochemical or electrolytic disequilibrium) should not be admitted until they have been medically stabilized in a pediatric hospital.
2. *Special Criteria.* One or more of the following must apply:
    a. The patient is dangerous to him- or herself or others by virtue of suicidal, self-injurious, reckless, interpersonally provocative, assaultive, destructive, or homicidal behavior.
    b. The patient is unable to protect him- or herself from common dangers or attend to his or her basic needs unless under close observation. This condition is most likely to occur in psychosis or organic brain dysfunction.
    c. The patient refuses, or is afraid of taking, adequate fluids or nourishment. This condition usually applies to patients with eating disorder, somatoform disorder, dissociative disorder, or paranoid schizophrenia.

d. The patient refuses to comply with medical treatment for a potentially lethal or deleterious medical condition: for example, brittle diabetes mellitus, sickle-cell anemia, hemophilia, epilepsy, paraplegia, or cerebral palsy. Some patients refuse prescribed diet, drugs, or catheterization. Others produce factitious symptoms by excessive or irregular self-medication.

e. The patient would deteriorate unless he or she were receiving close observation and intensive medical and nursing care. This criterion generally applies to psychotic patients who do not fit Criterion 2a or 2b.

Purpose

Brief inpatient treatment serves the following purposes:

1. Protection
2. Diagnosis and treatment planning
3. Stabilization
4. Preparation for discharge
5. Reintegration to home, school, and community

These aims can be achieved in many cases with a length of stay of about 1 month.

Protection refers to the prevention of patients' harming themselves or others by virtue of suicidal, self-injurious, reckless, assaultive, provocative, or homicidal behavior, or as a result of noncompliance with medical care for a potentially dangerous physical disorder (e.g., diabetes mellitus or sickle-cell anemia). It also refers to the nursing of patients so ill that they cannot avoid common dangers or take care of their basic needs.

During the diagnostic phase, patients receive a rapid, comprehensive, multidisciplinary, biopsychosocial diagnostic evaluation. In all cases, laboratory, pediatric, psychiatric, psychological, psychosocial, psychoeducational, and nursing assessments are undertaken. Particular cases may require special nutritional, vocational, speech and language, radiological, neuroimaging, neurological, electroencephalographic, chemical dependency investigations, or specialized medical consultation.

Thus, the patterns of symptomatology required for categorical diagnosis and biopsychosocial formulation are expanded by information concerning the patient's biopsychosocial *predisposition, precipitation, perpetuation,* reason for *presentation,* and *prognosis,* together with an inventory of the patient's strengths and *potentials* (Nurcombe & Gallagher, 1986). It is from the biopsychosocial formulation that a goal-directed *focal treatment plan* is derived (Nurcombe, 1989). The technique of focal treatment planning for the purpose of stabilization will be summarized below.

Specialization

There is evidence that specialized programs are more effective than those that mix disparate patients in a generic milieu (e.g., Beavers & Blumberg, 1968; Becket, Pearson, & Rubin, 1962; Garber, 1972; Gossett, Barnhart, Lewis, & Phillips, 1977; Kazdin, Esveldt-Dawson, French, & Unis, 1987; King & Pittman, 1969). A specialized staff builds teamwork through a shared philosophy and clarity about their strengths and limitations. On the other hand, a treatment approach helpful for one type of patient is likely to be ineffective or deleterious for others. For example, the relatively intrusive group-oriented style of treatment that suits posttraumatic stress disorder can be disruptive to adolescent schizophrenics.

Programs may be designed according to age groups (children, preadolescents, adolescents), diagnostic groups (e.g., psychosomatic problems, eating disorders, trauma spectrum disorders, affective disorders, neuropsychiatric disorders, disruptive behavior disorders, psychosexual disorders), or functions (e.g., crisis intervention, forensic evaluation, long-term psychotherapy).

Stabilization

Brief hospitalization is based on the principle of *stabilization* (Nurcombe, 1989). In essence, the treatment team asks the following question: In what way must the patient change in order to enable early discharge and treatment at a less intensive level of care? In contrast to the reconstructive plans of long-term hospitalization, stabilization plans are unambitious. They are, on the other hand, precise, focused, and designed to be closely monitored.

Focal Treatment Planning

The natural, intuitive approach to planning is therapy oriented. Given a particular diagnostic configuration, clinicians tend to match to it a set of therapies. Unfortunately, therapy-oriented planning lacks target dates or criteria for termination and is a hindrance when, as today, the team is pressed for time. The problem-oriented approach (Weed, 1969), which was introduced in order to improve the organization of medical-surgical diagnosis and treatment planning, failed in psychiatry because problem-oriented plans typically collapsed into fragmented, unintegrated, behavioral laundry lists. In order to provide a systematic approach to stabilization, Nurcombe (1989) introduced focal or goal-directed treatment planning. The goal-directed treatment team extracts from the biopsychosocial formulation those focal areas that must change in order to allow early discharge. Foci usually refer to symptoms in the pattern of psychopathology, unresolved psychological conflicts, physical problems that aggravate psychopathology, social skill impairments, perpetuating factors in the family environment, or educational deficits that affect adaptation.

For each focus, an objective is written. Whereas foci are general and abstract (e.g., *depressive mood/suicidal ideation*), objectives are observable, behavioral, and (if possible, without distorting reality) measurable (e.g., *no evidence of depression or suicidality on daily mental status examination or in milieu for a period of 1 week*). In general, four to six foci are sufficient. Each focus requires a target date (because some foci may be alterable before others). Progress notes are recorded in the focal format. For each focus, a mode or modes of therapy must be designed in accordance with the patient's formulation and the resources of the treatment team. One form of treatment (e.g., psychotherapy) may be appropriate for more than one focus. Each form of therapy should have a strategic plan (see below). Many foci (e.g., family dysfunction) are too complex to be resolved by the end of a brief hospitalization. However, objectives can be written in such a manner as to reflect the aim of the team to orient the patient and family to the problem and to prepare them to address it following discharge.

The treatment team meets regularly and monitors treatment according to the stated objectives. Focal objectives are very practical. They represent the amount of change required to allow discharge. When all objectives are attained, the patient is discharged from the hospital. Continued hospitalization is justified by active treatment and discharge planning, continued danger to self or others, serious risk of harm to self or others if prematurely discharged, complications that have arisen in the course of treatment, and incomplete stabilization (gauged according to the stipulated objectives).

Inpatient Therapies

The clinical team should be eclectic and integrative. According to their training, different team members provide individual psychotherapy, group psychotherapy tailored to fit special populations (e.g., different therapeutic groups emphasizing goal setting, family problems, sexual abuse, eating problems, chemical dependency, the problems of children of alcoholics, or the development of social skills), family therapy, cognitive behavioral therapy, or pharmacotherapy. Speech therapy, nutritional therapy, and remedial education are also available as needed. For each mode of therapy, an individualized strategic statement is required (e.g., individual psychotherapy may be supportive, reality oriented, exploratory, or interpretive).

Discharge Planning

Discharge planning should commence on admission and be clarified during master treatment planning. The team identifies the person or agency into whose custody the child will be discharged and the mental health clinician who will assume responsibility for the case following discharge. The team also identifies the obstacles to discharge (other than the failure to reach stabilization objectives), what needs to be done to remove the obstacles, and the clinician who is responsible for doing so. For example, the teacher may be required to contact the local school or psychologist, or the psychiatrist may need to alert a referring pediatrician that a patient is about to be discharged.

Ultrabrief Hospitalization

Five years ago, hospitals struggled to convert from a reconstructive to a stabilization model. What now? What is the point of inpatient care that lasts 2 weeks? No conceptual model has been defined for ultrabrief care. We are left, today, with amputated stabilization programs in which patients are discharged before treatment gains have been consolidated. Worse still, hospitals that have been slow to adapt are left with the remnants of an obsolete reconstructive doctrine.

Arguably, ultrabrief hospitalization has the same initial aims as brief hospitalization: *projection, diagnosis,* and *treatment planning.* Beyond the three fundamental aims, the primary therapeutic purpose is *crisis alleviation.* The treatment team puts its effort into intensive care, rapid diagnostic evaluation, and discharge disposition, aware that unstable patients must often be transferred to community care and to parents unprepared for their homecoming.

If unstable discharge is to be the norm, reintegration services will be required, and the neglected area of aftercare must receive more attention. Although the daily cost of inpatient treatment will increase due to the intensity of care required for greater proportions of acutely disturbed patients, some of the money saved by shortening length of stay should be expended on providing home-based services in order to facilitate the reintegration of patients into home, school, and community, and the empowerment of parents to find the care their children require. These services will need to commence well before discharge and to continue for several months thereafter.

Treatment foci and objectives will be required for ultrabrief hospitalization; however, in contrast to the treatment plans of briefly hospitalized patients, the number of foci will be reduced, and the objectives will be even less ambitious than in the stabilization model. No attempt will be made to address dynamic issues, alter family dysfunction, or remediate social or educational deficits. The key foci will relate to suicidality, assaultiveness, and acute dysphoria. The inevitable sense of clinical urgency will introduce the serious risk of an overreliance on drug treatment. Other issues relate to the mixing of ultrabrief and brief patients, the means of preparing families for discharge, and the need for a step-down service (Gold, Heller, & Ritorto, 1992). The function of the hospital school will also require revision. Hospital schools were typically designed to fit the reconstructive model of long-term inpatient care. Will they become no more than custodial? Should they be oriented more toward diagnosis than toward remedial education?

An Integrated
Array of Graduated Services

Though mental illness is usually protracted, hospital care is but an episode. Therein lies the nub of a problem. It is not sensible to design or evaluate hospitalization alone, for continuity of care must be considered. Inpatient treatment is the most intensive, specialized, and restrictive service in the panoply of mental health services. It should be imbedded in a comprehensive continuum of care devoted to linkage and graduation. Unfortunately, the current state of affairs falls far short of this ideal.

In large cities, private hospitals, public hospitals, state mental hospitals, community mental health centers, private practitioners, child welfare agencies, juvenile correctional agencies, the courts, and the educational system act independently, guarding their territories against those they perceive as rivals. The public system is in decline. General hospitals compete with specialized psychiatric hospitals by offering generic (and less expensive) ultrabrief care. Private hospitals compete with each other on the basis of cost, efficiency, perceived quality, and publicity. Residential treatment centers and alternatives to hospital such as home-based intensive care compete with hospitals rather than complementing them. The linkage between hospitals, private outpatient practice, and community mental health depends on personal contact between clinicians rather than systematic design.

The contemporary mode of mental health care financing promotes fragmentation, competition, and waste, and has recently introduced an adversarial form of managed care that attempts to curb the growing expense of the disjunctive system. Well-established modalities such as day hospitalization and intensive outpatient treatment are difficult to fund because health insurance is based upon an episodic model of medical care.

The American system resists central planning, largely out of a fear of stagnant bureaucracies. The future may lie in the development of comprehensive local systems allied to informal networks of care. Hospitals, for example, could take the lead by evolving into graduated mental health complexes providing inpatient, residential, day hospital, and outpatient care together with external consultation to hospitals, schools, community mental health centers, courts, and the correctional system. Given the vagaries of mental health funding, an evolution of this sort is bound to be cautious. It is long overdue.

References

Aichorn, A. (1935). *Wayward youth*. New York: Viking.

American Psychiatric Association. (1989). *Statement on psychiatric hospitalization of children and adolescents*. Washington, DC: Author.

Beavers, W., & Blumberg, S. A. (1968). A follow-up study of adolescents treated in an inpatient setting. *Diseases of the Nervous System, 29*, 606-612.

Becket, P., Pearson, C., & Rubin, E. A. (1962). A follow-up study comparing two approaches to the inpatient treatment of adolescent boys. *Journal of Nervous and Mental Disease, 134*, 330-338.

Bettelheim, B. (1955). *Love is not enough: The treatment of emotionally disturbed children*. New York: Free Press.

Blotcky, M. J., Dimperio, T. L., & Gossett, J. T. (1984). Follow-up of children treated in psychiatric hospitals. *American Journal of Psychiatry, 141*, 1499-1507.

Braukmann, C. J., Kirigin, K. A., & Wolf, M. W. (1976). *Achievement place: The researcher's prospective*. Paper presented at the annual meeting of the American Psychological Association, Washington, DC.

Burns, B. J. (1991). Mental health service use by adolescents in the 1970s and 1980s. *Journal of the American Academy of Child and Adolescent Psychiatry, 30*, 144-150.

Erickson, R. (1975). Outcome studies in mental hospitals: A review. *Psychological Bulletin, 82*, 519-540.

Friedman, R. M., Ichinose, C. K., & Greer, S. (1990). *Psychiatric hospitalization of children and adolescents: Testimony to the HRS Committee, Florida Senate*. Tampa: University of South Florida, Florida Mental Health Institute.

Garber, B. (1972). *Follow-up study of hospitalized adolescents.* New York: Brunner/Mazel.

Gold, I., Heller, C., & Ritorto, B. (1992). A short-term psychiatric inpatient program for adolescents. *Hospital and Community Psychiatry, 43,* 58-61.

Gossett, J. T., Barnhart, F. D., Lewis, J. M., & Phillips, V. A. (1977). Follow-up of adolescents treated in a psychiatric hospital. *Archives of General Psychiatry, 34,* 1037-1042.

Gossett, J. T., Lewis, J. M., & Barnhart, F. D. (1983). *To find a way: The outcome of hospital treatment of disturbed adolescents.* New York: Brunner/Mazel.

Holmes, D. J. (1964). *The adolescent in psychotherapy.* Boston: Little, Brown.

Holmes, D. J. (1984). *Psychotherapy with the disturbed adolescent.* Boston: Little, Brown.

Jessness, C. F. (1975). Comparative effectiveness of behavior modification and transactional analysis programs for delinquents. *Journal of Consulting and Clinical Psychology, 43,* 758-779.

Kazdin, A. E., Esveldt-Dawson, K., French, N. H., & Unis, A. S. (1987). Problem-solving skills and relationship therapy in the treatment of antisocial child behavior. *Journal of Consulting and Clinical Psychology, 55,* 76-85.

King, L., & Pittman, G. (1969). A six-year follow-up study of 605 adolescent patients: The predictive value of the presenting clinical picture. *British Journal of Psychiatry, 115,* 1437-1441.

Kirby, T. F., Wilson, C. T., & Short, M. J. (1977). A follow-up study of disturbed children treated in a Re-ed program. *Hospital and Community Psychiatry, 28,* 694-697.

Knitzer, J. (1982). *Unclaimed children: The failure of public responsibility to children and adolescents in need of mental health services.* Washington, DC: Children's Defense Fund.

Levinson, R. B., & Gerard, R. E. (1973). Functional units: A different correctional approach. *Federal Probation, 39,* 8-16.

Miller, G. (1985). Opening statement: Emerging trends in mental health care for adolescents. In *Hearings in the U.S. House of Representatives—Select Committee on Children, Youth and Families,* Washington, DC.

Nurcombe, B. (1989). Goal-directed treatment planning and the principles of brief hospitalization. *Journal of the American Academy of Child and Adolescent Psychiatry, 28,* 26-30.

Nurcombe, B. (1991). *Criteria for admission to Vanderbilt Child and Adolescent Psychiatric Hospital.* Nashville, TN: Vanderbilt Child and Adolescent Psychiatric Hospital.

Nurcombe, B., & Gallagher, R. M. (1986). *The clinical process in psychiatry: Diagnosis and treatment planning.* New York: Cambridge University Press.

Pfeiffer, S., & Strzelecki, S. C. (1990). Inpatient psychiatric treatment of children and adolescents: A review of outcome studies. *Journal of the American Academy of Child and Adolescent Psychiatry, 29,* 847-853.

Pollack, M., Levenstein, S., & Klein, D. (1968). A three-year post-hospital follow-up of adolescent and adult schizophrenics. *American Journal of Orthopsychiatry, 38,* 94-109.

Schwartz, I. M. (1989). Hospitalization of adolescents for psychiatric and substance abuse treatment. *Journal of Adolescent Health Care, 10,* 473-478.

Schwartz, I. M., Beeck, M. J., & Anderson, R. (1984). The "hidden" system of juvenile control. *Crime and Delinquency, 30,* 371-385.

Szurek, S. A., Berlin, I. N., & Boatman, M. J. (1971). *Inpatient care for the psychotic child.* Palo Alto, CA: Science and Behavior Books.

Weed, L. L. (1969). *Medical records, medical evaluation and patient care.* Cleveland: Case Western Reserve University Press.

Weithorn, L. A. (1988). Mental hospitalization of troublesome youth: An analysis of skyrocketing admission rates. *Stanford Law Review, 40,* 773-838.

School-Based Mental
Health Services for Children

SARAH E. RING-KURTZ
SUSAN SONNICHSEN
KATHLEEN V. HOOVER-DEMPSEY

A theme of all of the chapters in this volume is the persistent, unmet need for appropriate mental health services for children in the United States. The disparity between the number of children in need of mental health services and those who receive any service at all reflects a need that has persisted for decades and is documented in the literature (e.g., Institute of Medicine, 1989; Knitzer, 1982; Knitzer, Steinberg, & Fleisch, 1990; Rog, 1990; Tuma, 1989). Federal efforts to address this problem have emphasized community-based services in keeping with the principle of the "least restrictive environment" (Stroul & Friedman, 1986). Although interagency coordination has been strongly encouraged, schools traditionally have not been central to this movement (Knitzer et al., 1991; Knoff & Batsche, 1990). The important role played by schools in children's lives has long been recognized, and the concept of the school as a center for service delivery is not a recent development (Cowen et al., 1975; Hobbs, 1975).

School-based mental health services, however, have not been widely implemented (Knoff & Batsche, 1990; Tuma, 1989), often due to insufficient funding and lack of multiagency coordination (Saxe, Cross, & Silverman, 1988). The growing voice of advocacy organizations over the past two decades has brought the possibility of school-based services to the attention of policy makers and legislators (Craig, 1990; Melaville & Blank, 1991), and the feasibility of providing mental health services through the school system is being reconsidered (Knitzer et al., 1990; Knoff & Batsche, 1990; Linney & Seidman, 1989; Will, 1990).

One of the major reasons for considering school-based mental health services is that teachers, beyond their role as educators, represent potentially critical agents of social and psychological interventions (Entwisle & Stevenson, 1987; Knitzer et al., 1990). While in school, children and adolescents learn socialization skills; develop self-control, responsibility, independence, and self-esteem; and formulate their concepts of themselves and others (Good & Weinstein, 1986). They are educated, receive health care, develop friendships, choose vocations, and often plan families in the course of their school lives. Thus, although schools are clearly not without obstacles to mental health service delivery, they offer an environment that may be critical to families, professionals, and policy makers seeking to increase the availability and accessibility of effective mental health services to children and adolescents in need.

In this chapter we review the rationale for school-based mental health services, principles essential for successful school-based programs, examples of the types of mental health services currently being provided through school systems, and critical policy issues that administrators, legislators, and service providers face in developing coordinated, comprehensive school-based systems of mental health care for children. We conclude with recommendations for researchers and policy makers.

Rationale for
School-Based Treatment

Schools represent a natural and significant locus for the delivery of mental health services to children and adolescents. The most compelling rationale for school-based services is found in the statistics chronicling the long-term failure of a variety of mental health efforts to reach even a fraction of the children in need of such services (Dougherty, 1988; Saxe et al., 1988; Shore & Mannino, 1976; Tuma, 1989). Many have called for a standard of universal eligibility (i.e., all children and families who need services may have access to them, regardless of income or other variables sometimes used as eligibility criteria) for a variety of child and family services designed to enhance the mental health and well-being of children (e.g., Dokecki & Moroney, 1983; Hobbs et al., 1984; Powell, 1991; Shore & Mannino, 1976; Weissbourd, 1987). Schools meet this criterion very well. They are "regular" socializing agencies; they are seen as having normal functions in the everyday life of communities and families (Hobbs et al., 1984; Tarico, Low, Trupin, & Forsyth-Stephens, 1989). There are minimal negative characteristics associated with school involvement. For example, there are no stigmatizing eligibility criteria for entry into the school system (e.g., means testing for income levels) or for the use of most services in the school. Thus, the use of schools as a primary locus for the delivery of mental health services to children and adolescents offers the immediate advantages of allowing service delivery on a universal basis with lower probabilities of the stigmatization so often associated with utilization of services within identifiable and special-purpose service locations (see Hobbs, 1975).

Further, schools offer the possibility, in ways unavailable to almost any other social institution, of responding to both local need and the greater common good (Hobbs et al., 1984). This is of particular importance to those concerned with children's mental health. Although improved mental health among children and adolescents clearly serves the common good, it is often within local communities that evidence of unmet need and underserved populations is strongest. Thus, selection of the schools as a primary delivery system for child and adolescent mental health services offers the possibility of local control over service delivery, permitting a focus on currently underserved populations (e.g., poor and minority populations; see Shore & Mannino, 1976; Tuma, 1989), a need identified repeatedly by professionals in the field (see Dougherty, 1988; Meyers, 1985). Schools, as the primary locus of children's mental health programming services, also offer the possibility of focusing services simultaneously on the child, the family, the school, and the community (Saxe et al., 1988; Tuma, 1989). Finally, they also offer the potential for public-private cooperation (e.g., a private, nonprofit agency offer; child care or child mental health services in the school), an arrangement that may benefit several child and family service options through school-based coordination (Hobbs et al., 1984).

The ongoing and publicly accepted purpose of schools is to enhance the developmental capabilities of children. Schools operate within the clear mandate to educate children in both academic and socialization functions (Hamilton, 1983). In fact, several authors have noted that within a school's educational mandate, noncognitive developmental outcomes—social and emotional—may be as important as the cognitive or academic outcomes (Entwisle & Stevenson, 1987; Rutter, 1983). Schools offer an increasing variety of educationally related services that function to support families' abilities to educate and nurture children. They have become involved in offering pre-school education, recreation, and nutritional services (Linney & Vernberg, 1983), and are expanding their involvement in services that support child and family functioning, for example, through the provision of before- and after-school child care to meet the needs of dual-earner and single-parent families (Hobbs et al., 1984; Zigler, 1989).

The delivery of mental health services fits well within the general mandate followed by schools in offering full educational services to children. Indeed, the success of a small but varied range of primary and secondary prevention programs within schools has been noted by several authors (Cowen et al., 1975; Linney & Seidman, 1989; Price, Cowen, Lorion, & Ramos-McKay, 1988; Saxe et al., 1988; Tuma, 1989), as has the general need for the delivery of services to the more broadly based constituency (Meyers, 1985) usually found in schools. Because schools specialize in education, they seem particularly well suited to respond to the call for an increased focus on preventive services in children's mental health programming (Dougherty, 1988; Shore & Mannino, 1976; Tarico et al., 1989), aimed at helping children, adolescents, and their families deal effectively with developmental crises (Powers, Hauser, & Kilner, 1989).

Schools have a long-standing commitment, albeit in varying degrees across time and communities, to parent involvement (Kagan,

1987; Powell, 1991). Parent involvement is aimed at improving parents' abilities both to support children's educational achievement and to do their parenting jobs well (Hobbs et al., 1984; Hoover-Dempsey, Bassler, & Brissie, 1987; Schlossman, 1983). This tradition of parent involvement is consonant with the mental health area regarding empowering parents and families to take a more active and enabling role in the mental health needs of their children (Tarico et al., 1989). Further, the close involvement of parents in the services holds the possibility of improving the services and their outcomes (Hobbs et al., 1984; Tarico et al., 1989), as demonstrated in programs intended to improve the academic performance of children with special needs (Dougherty, 1988; Hobbs et al., 1984).

At a pragmatic level, schools also offer several advantages to those concerned with increasing the impact and accessibility of mental health services for children. One of the most significant advantages is that the schools contain a "captive" population (Powell, 1991); almost all children and adolescents between specified ages are required by law to be in school. Thus, children who need services are already in a known setting for a given number of hours per day, during which mental health services could be delivered with improved efficiency and coverage. Schools also are staffed by a professional population generally well educated in the demands of observing the well-being and progress of children. Teachers and related professionals constitute a potentially valuable and valid source of information regarding the mental health status and progress of children. Indeed, the use of school personnel to identify children's mental health problems has been ongoing for many years (Shore & Mannino, 1976). Further, the administrative structure of schools, already in place, may be adapted to coordinate the services and funding of mental health programs for children (Dougherty, 1988; Hobbs et al., 1984; Meyers, 1985; Powell, 1991; Zigler, 1989). Such school-based coordination may improve the administrative and funding fragmentation that so often, and with negative impacts, characterizes such services (Hobbs, 1975; Meyers, 1985; Saxe et al., 1988).

The possibility of using schools as a primary locus for the delivery of mental health services to children and adolescents is not without problems. Of major importance to our advocacy of school-based service delivery, however, is our fundamental reading of the evidence that the problems, even when significant, can be solved. Given adoption of effective solutions, the use of schools as a primary locus of service holds the promise of delivering a needed range of programming to children and adolescents without the difficulties of access and stigmatization that now affect so many families' efforts to obtain services for their children.

Perhaps foremost among the problems is the reality that efforts to change and improve school operations often meet with resistance. For example, administrators may not consider the proposed improvements to be a legitimate part of school operations, and teachers may object to anticipated increases in noninstructional responsibilities (Hamilton, 1983; Powell, 1991; Sarason, 1971). Nonetheless, there are numerous precedents for offering school-based mental health services, precedents incorporating models for successful implementation of prerequisite change and service provision (Cowen et al., 1975; Fine & Carlson, 1992). In addition, principles of successful organizational management and change can be applied well to the task of expanding school missions to include education-enhancing mental health services (Cowen et al., 1975; Price et al., 1988).

Related concerns focus on the overburdened status of many school professionals (e.g., multiple instructional responsibilities, disciplinary issues, increases in record keeping). These concerns suggest that although school-based mental health services may be coordinated well with existing school programs, they might most optimally be administered and staffed by a distinct team of mental health professionals (see, e.g., Zigler's 1989 discussion of this issue in relation to child care programs located within school settings and Sondheimer and Evans's discussion of Catron's research described in Chapter 4 of this book). Of further concern at an organizational level is the possibility that funding problems may be very difficult to overcome. Rubin (1983), for example, observed that in periods of financial austerity, joint financial agreements between cooperating service agencies may break down. It is important, therefore, that the financial foundations of service delivery through schools be fully integrated into school funding programs (i.e., not subject to general school budget trimming or reallocation into other school programs) or secured on a freestanding basis within the schools.

Other potential problems center on the possibility of stigmatization of client children. Although schools offer excellent opportunities for delivery of "normal" services, issues related to stigmatization growing from any kind of "sorting" practices may have serious and negative impacts on children selected for special programs (Hamilton, 1983; Hobbs, 1975).

The success of school-based mental health programs will depend, in large part, on their ability to minimize the segregation of special populations in schools and maximize the opportunities for least restrictive and integrated involvement of students receiving mental health services in the full school program (Tarico et al., 1989; Tuma, 1989). Finally, Powell (1991) and Weiss (1989) noted further that when services are offered on a universal basis, more able families may be more effective than others in actually gaining access to the services. School-based mental health programming will have to develop mechanisms for ensuring that services are equitably distributed across the full range of families in need.

Services and Programs

When child behavior problems arise (e.g., poor grades, poor attendance), parents frequently turn to the schools for help with guidance. In fact, it has been reported that families would use the schools with which they were familiar for help with a child's behavior rather than go to an outside agency (Merrill, Clark, Varvil, Van Sickle, & McCall, 1992). With the growing realization that the school and the family have a common goal of educating and socializing the child, many programs have sought to bring these two entities together to see that this goal is met. In one such approach, Everett's (1976) model of family assessment and intervention, the family problems are assessed and a short-term family intervention is implemented to resolve the child's school-related problem. This model has been found to be appropriate for use in many schools, in part because families are often receptive to receiving assistance regarding their child's problem from the school psychological staff. This reception is believed to be due to the staff's knowledge of child development, their established relationship with the family, their understanding of the school system, and their knowledge about the relationship between school performance and family functioning. In a situation in which the child needs treatment more extensive than can be provided in the school, the family is referred to an outside agency. However, the school's involvement and the information it provides often greatly affect the outcome of the child's treatment, making the referral process more effective by motivating families to seek treatment and support for movement between services (Donovan, 1992).

There are three general mental health services that the schools can provide to children and families: assessment, prevention, and intervention. Although the family has significant influence in the development and education of the child, most assessment procedures are traditionally focused on the child rather than the child and the family. Evaluation procedures in general, however, seem to be progressing toward the acknowledgment of the importance of the family role in the development of the child's behavior; thus, family assessment is becoming more and more prevalent (Carlson, 1992).

The purpose of mental health assessment is to enable the provider to select an appropriate form of treatment for the child or the child and family. Carlson (1992) suggested three methods of assessment useful in the evaluation of families, schools, and their interactions: interviews, observations, and self-report methods. The purpose of the interview is to gather information to understand how and why a particular behavior occurs and what is happening within the family and school environment that allows this behavior to continue. The hope is that the interview will clarify how the problem evolved and thus aid in the development of a solution. Observation, which has become the chosen technique by researchers and clinicians for identifying dysfunctional patterns of family and family-school interaction, often provides valuable information related to causal factors regarding the child's problem. Carlson warned, however, that the process of observing the child's behaviors and interactions must be systematic to avoid unnecessary subjectivity and bias. Self-report measures are usually utilized to determine the family's perceptions and feelings about the problems in question. They have been used in the process of diagnosing children within the schools for a long time, and can be adapted to work more extensively in school psychological practices (Carlson, 1992; see also Carlson, 1987, 1991; Grotevant & Carlson, 1989).

Another mental health service that schools can provide to children is prevention. Prevention is recognized as highly valuable in the circumvention of maladaptive and troublesome behaviors. As noted by the American Psychological Association (APA) Task Force on Promotion, Prevention, and Intervention Alternatives, "Prevention efforts reflect the popular wisdom that an ounce of prevention is worth a pound of cure" (Price et al., 1988, p. 2). Children are seen as perfect candidates for prevention programs given their flexibility and adaptability. Furthermore, the common belief that good health from the beginning can circumvent serious and expensive problems for individuals and society in general makes prevention all the more attractive. Given that children spend much of their time in school and that education is a perfect venue for prevention, schools offer an optimal location for the delivery of these services.

According to Price et al. (1988), there are two major approaches to prevention. The first is a system-directed approach that includes social policy development and adjustments of social environments aimed at decreasing stress and improving life opportunities. The second approach is aimed at specific groups of people and includes services such as educational programs providing the opportunity to learn adaptive skills and programs for groups who are at risk (e.g., children transitioning from one school to another or children of divorced parents). In 1982, the APA task force began to identify valuable prevention efforts under the second approach that were in progress, in the hope that this discovery would lead to increased knowledge regarding which services were most effective. The task force identified 52 of the 300 programs worthy of further analysis. Of those 52 programs, 14 were considered to be exemplary and were discussed at length in the task force report (Price et al., 1988). Regrettably, only a few of those included were school based, demonstrating again the need for further development of effective school-based prevention programs.

Among school-based programs described in the literature, several offer useful possibilities for replication and further development. The Carolina Early Intervention Program (Ramey, Bryant, Campbell, Sparling, & Wasik, 1988), for example, focused on high-risk children and was effective in preventing developmental delay through providing children and families with supplementary education and support services. On the basis of program results, the authors concluded:

> The 15-point IQ difference typically reported between Blacks and Whites in the United States can be effectively eliminated during the preschool years, and . . . high-risk, socially disadvantaged children can perform at least at national average on standardized tests of intelligence if they and their families are provided additional education and family support services. (p. 43)

The effectiveness of this program is heartening and raises the hope that well-designed prevention efforts can help children of disadvantaged families avoid educationally damaging developmental delays.

In another school-based approach to prevention, the Houston Parent-Child Developmental Center developed a program for the primary prevention of behavior problems in young children. Research on the program found that even 5 to 8 years after the completion of the program, effects remained (Johnson, 1988). Johnson reported that probable reasons for the program's success are such qualities as extensive parent education and involvement, which encourage parents' sense of efficacy and autonomy. Thus, family involvement may be especially important to the outcome of the school-based prevention service.

Another example of services is Rotheram-Borus's (1988) effective assertiveness training program that is classroom based and teaches children social skills, coping skills, and behavioral interventions to prepare them for potentially risky situations. The program, described by Rotheram-Borus, could be implemented across several school years and could provide a strong base for prevention programs aimed at specific, high-risk behaviors found in junior high and high school students. This and similar prevention efforts easily fit within the educational services provided by the school.

Life skills training as an approach to preventing substance abuse in adolescents was demonstrated to be effective by Botvin and Tortu (1988). They found that through such training, junior high school students could be taught to resist the temptation or pressure to use cigarettes, alcohol, and drugs. Furthermore, the students learned social skills, how to cope with anxiety, and how to have successful relationships. Botvin and Tortu strongly recommended that prevention programs address the causal factors associated with the problem behaviors (see also Botvin, 1982; Swisher, 1979).

Prevention efforts also have been successful in assisting children with transitions from one school to another. Most children change schools at some point in their lives, and transitions often require significant adjustment, leaving children vulnerable to psychological or academic problems. For many children, changing schools can cause a decrease in academic performance, as well as increases in absenteeism, significant declines in psychological health, and increased potential for substance abuse problems, delinquent behavior, and other social difficulties (Felner & Adan, 1988; see also Felner, Ginter, & Primavera, 1982; Felner, Primavera, & Cauce, 1981). The School Transitional Environment Project (Felner & Adan, 1988) and the Transition Project (Felner et al., 1982) both reported success in helping children to adapt to their new schools, thus increasing their chances of academic success. Both programs were inexpensive and were easily integrated into a school's existing organizational structure. Felner and his colleagues noted that school administrators' and teachers' awareness and participation were crucial to the success of the prevention service.

In the event that children's problems require direct treatment, the schools also may provide an environment conducive to intervention services for children and adolescents. Although there are many approaches to intervening in the problems that children experience, a few of the most common intervention methods are the cognitive-behavioral, the solution-oriented, and the systemic-structural models. The cognitive-behavioral model attempts to combine cognitive and behavioral theories with therapy. This model may be particularly appropriate for use within the schools due to the fact that most school psychologists and counselors are typically familiar with aspects of the approach. It assumes that system members' attitudes, desires, and characteristics regarding their relationships and the child in question will affect their behavior toward the child and toward others who relate to themselves and the child (Carlson, 1992). Daily exposure to the child's problems and ability to observe and clearly define the child's difficulties make the teacher or counselor a valuable contributor to the success of programs employing the cognitive-behavioral model.

The solution-oriented model also has been effective when delivered within the school setting (Kral, 1986). Carlson (1992) asserted that this approach has several advantages, such as brevity and an emphasis on collaboration and positive solutions. When utilizing the solution-oriented model, the mental health professional and the child can concentrate on constructive aspects of the child's situation and together develop solutions that are suitable to all involved.

The systemic-structural model as discussed by Carlson (1992) is based on the structural family therapy approach (Minuchin, 1974; Minuchin & Fishman, 1981; Minuchin, Montalvo, Guerney, Rosman, & Schumer, 1967; Minuchin, Rosman, & Baker, 1978) and is considered to be applicable to the school system due to the similar structural nature of schools and families. The primary strength of this model is its integrated nature (Quirk, Fine, & Roberts, 1992). Research (Donovan, 1992) indicates that family systems intervention may be more effective in improving family communication than other forms of family intervention such as insight-oriented family therapy and didactic family group discussions. Donovan also asserted that family systems models, such as Everett's (1976) family assessment and intervention model, not only are suitable for use in the schools but also may be more productive and economical than other traditional services.

All approaches to mental health treatment for children, whether focused on assessment, prevention, or intervention, should involve both families and schools in the information-gathering and healing processes. Families play a critical role in the development of the child, as do schools, and their knowledge and influence are essential factors in the success of any school-based psychological service.

Policy Issues

The trend toward school-based mental health services, despite the positive implications, continues to be beset with challenges in the policy arena that hinder the implementation of such programs.

Although Public Law 94-142, the Education of the Handicapped Act of 1975 (EHA), now the Individuals With Disabilities Education Act of 1990 (IDEA), set the precedent for schools to be responsible for the educational as well as related service needs of students who are severely emotionally disturbed (SED), this legislation did not intend to serve the mental health and developmental needs of all children. In this era of limited resources, these funds are directed to the most severely affected children in the public school system. Nonetheless, the issues encountered in implementing this policy reflect current barriers and warrant close consideration when developing a comprehensive school-based system of services. An exhaustive analysis of policy issues in this area is beyond the scope of this chapter; therefore, discussion is limited to four of the primary topics of controversy at the policy level that have serious implications for the delivery of services.

Accurate Identification

Perhaps the most rudimentary issue with which policy makers grapple is the question of whom to serve. This confusion exists as a by-product of limited resources and the accompanying philosophical orientation toward tertiary treatment of those in greatest need of service (see Feltman, 1990). This approach is reflected in the language of the landmark legislation, the EHA of 1975, which mandated public schools' provision of educational and related services for children with SED. The eligibility criteria set forth in this document are open to subjective judgment (Cline, 1990); exclude arbitrarily many children who, according to our current understanding of emotional disturbance, may be considered in comparably greater need of services (Epanchin, 1990; Weinberg, 1992); and are inconsistently applied at the state and local level across the country (Forness & Knitzer, 1992; Koyanagi & Weintraub, 1990).

The language of the original legislation (Pub. L. No. 94-142) includes SED children, but excludes from services children who are "socially maladjusted" unless those children are also severely emotionally disturbed. However, the definition of SED is sufficiently vague to permit differential application of the criteria. Cross-state and cross-district differences in definition result in wide variations in the rate of identification of children with SED (Kukic, Reavis, Scott, Phillips, & Staib, 1990), as well as in the types of problems exhibited by the children so identified (Forness & Knitzer, 1992; Silver, 1991; Tharanger, Laurent, & Best, 1986). One of the most commonly cited weaknesses in the definition of SED is the contradictory inclusion of the criterion, "inability to build or maintain satisfactory relationships with peers and teachers," and the exclusion of the criterion, "socially maladjusted." This discrepancy has led to frequent exclusion of children with conduct disorder, behavioral disorders, and even externalizing disorders (Forness & Knitzer, 1992; Skiba & Grizzle, 1991). These inconsistencies have serious implications for equity in the distribution of limited resources among a needy population. In addition, these discrepancies violate the original intent of the legislation to serve all children with severe emotional disturbance (Cline, 1990; Forness & Knitzer, 1992).

A great deal of support exists for changing the definition of SED within the legislation (American Psychological Association, 1990; Cline, 1990; Mattison, Morales, & Bauer, 1992). A movement to pass legislation modifying the original criteria for SED to include "emotional or behavioral disorder" is currently led by the Council for Children With Behavioral Disorders (Forness & Knitzer, 1992). This proposal is intended to clarify the definition of eligible children and firmly reestablish the inclusion and exclusion criteria originally intended by the legislation.

Interagency Coordination

Inherent to consideration of a multiagency, comprehensive, school-based system of services are collaborative relationships among the various agencies involved. This component of mental health service delivery in the schools has been a significant barrier to the successful implementation of many existing services (Knitzer et al., 1991; Knoff & Batsche, 1990; Koyanagi & Weintraub, 1990; Saxe et al., 1988). Traditionally, departments of education and mental health have not developed partnerships for collaboration for a variety of reasons (Feltman, 1990; Kukic et al., 1990), such as divergent goals, distinct administrative structures, and poor interagency communication (Knoff & Batsche, 1990; Kukic et al., 1990; Tuma, 1989). It is encouraging, however, to see the continuing efforts at coordinating systems of care, centered within or including the education system (see Bobbitt, Dailey, Reed, Mattessich, & Heiserman, 1992; Feltman, 1990; Fox et al., 1992; Ignelzi, Tucker, De Carolis, Broer, & Sturtevant, 1990). The school is an integral part of the comprehensive individualized system of care being developed in La Grange, Illinois. The local department of special education has implemented Project WRAP, a program designed to meet the complex needs of children with SED and their families (Eber & Stieper, 1992). Individualized and tailored to the child and family's needs, WRAP offers a model for collaborative service delivery of mental health, education, and social services that are "wrapped around" each family, given their unique circumstances. Though not providing direct service, the WRAP program facilitates access to and coordination of the multiple services needed by children with SED and their families.

Several localities have applied creative administrative and funding mechanisms to facilitate the delivery of mental health services within school buildings (see Bobbitt et al., 1992; Fox et al., 1992). The state of Vermont has set a goal to educate all children in regular public school classrooms and to provide the services for children with severe emotional disorders so that they too will have the opportunity to succeed in a regular school setting. To meet this goal, schools establish school-wide planning teams and individual student planning teams. The school-wide team is responsible for regularly evaluating and modifying existing organizational structures and service delivery mechanisms for the improvement of education services for all students. For every child, the student planning team, made up of parents, teacher, counselor, principal, and other providers, identifies needs and prepares individualized educational plans (Fox et al., 1992).

In other regions, the network of service delivery agencies has been modified to increase interagency collaboration in the delivery of mental health and other services to children and adolescents. The Ventura County planning model has approached the challenge of interagency coordination by distributing mental health staff and services among other service agencies—education, juvenile justice, child welfare, and so forth (Jordan & Hernandez, 1990). This model allows for multiple points of entry to the system, while maintaining singular responsibility for mental health services. As Feltman (1990) illustrated, a primary goal of the model is to help children and adolescents remain in their natural school and home environment while receiving the mental health services they need. The mental health department has adopted the goals of the related service agencies and has organized its program of service delivery to achieve these mutual goals. The mental health agency views itself as supportive to the other agencies, and without legal responsibility for individual children. This system thereby treats children as members of the Ventura community, rather than placing them under the auspices of a single service agency.

A clustering approach has been initiated within the state of Ohio through which innovative administrative and financial arrangements have been established to serve children and adolescents with multiple needs (Ignelzi et al., 1990; Segal & McCreight, 1992). Clusters comprise representatives from each of seven agencies serving children and adolescents; local clusters and a single state-level cluster meet weekly to review cases of children with multiple service agency needs. Unlike the Ventura model, the clustering system revolves around centralized assessment and case planning. Funding for cluster operations is derived from equal contributions from each of the participating agencies (Ignelzi et al., 1990).

Parent Involvement

To date, the concept of parent participation in children's services has been further developed and implemented in the area of education, particularly in the areas of special education for children with developmental or learning disabilities, than in the area of children's mental health services. The EHA was a clear catalyst toward this goal. The legislation mandated parental participation in the process of obtaining and providing educational and related services. However, as Butler, New, and Isaacs (1990) suggested, more work needs to be done in this area because there are varying degrees of compliance with the legislated level of parent involvement in the Individual Educational Plan (IEP) process among the school districts (Institute of Medicine, 1989; Knitzer et al., 1990).

Even with these difficulties, parent involvement with the educational system far outshines that in the mental health service system. In fact, the status of parent involvement in mental health policy resembles that of the education arena approximately 30 years ago, prior to the legal impetus for education professionals to consider parents as collaborators in children's education. Educators were often viewed as the authorities regarding the child, whereas parents were seen merely as the recipients of that information, so mental health professionals today may see themselves (and may be perceived by parents) as experts regarding the child and the parents as the ones to be instructed about the child (Vaughn, Bos, Harrell, & Lasky, 1988). Much of the research that has been conducted in attempts to understand the current status of parent involvement in special education unfortunately suggests that Public Law 94-142 has fallen short of its original goal (Knitzer et al., 1990; Witt, Miller, McIntyre, & Smith, 1984). However, the current expectation for parent participation and the existing legal mandate for such involvement within the education community can be used to accelerate the development of this principle in the area of mental health services if the school is considered the center of services.

Although some uncontrolled studies and surveys have suggested that parents are dissatisfied with the limited or sometimes perfunctory participation they are offered by school programs (Knitzer et al., 1990; Tarico et al., 1989), results of other studies indicate that parents' overall satisfaction with services for their children is related to variables other than amount of parental participation (Goldstein, Strickland, Turnbull, & Curry, 1989; Vaughn et al., 1988; Witt et al., 1984). Some research suggests that characteristics of the teachers and the school itself influence the amount and nature of parent participation in children's services (Hoover-Dempsey et al., 1987; Swick & McKnight, 1989). In addition, families of children with SED are frequently overwhelmed with multiple stressors and few resources (Jenson & Whittacker, 1987; Mattison et al., 1992; Silver, 1991). These findings suggest that before parent or family participation is mandated, more research should be conducted to determine (a) how such participation can best meet the needs of families and children, and (b) how patterns of parental participation and family involvement might affect the clinical and educational outcomes of children, and which patterns are beneficial to the treatment process. The balance of providing necessary information, support, and consultation without further taxing an already overwhelmed family will vary across families, highlighting the need for individual evaluation of family circumstances for all SED children.

Financing

Perhaps the fundamental challenge to the provision of mental health services to children through the schools is the lack of sufficient funding to meet existing needs. The EHA established requirements for the provision of not only educational but also related services for children with SED (such as, speech pathology, audiology, psychological services, physical and occupational therapy, recreational services, and medical services (Butler et al., 1990). Psychological services for both parents and children are included in the legislation; however, emphasis is placed on assessment rather than treatment. Schools are not intended to be solely responsible for the financial support of these services, and Part H of the Individuals With Disabilities Education Act specifically indicates that related agencies are to be involved in cost sharing. However, education agencies are generally held liable by the courts as the ultimate source of funding when pushed to the letter of the law (Butler et al., 1990). In terms of legal enforcement of the cost-sharing principle, there is no precedent for the school district to pay for all of the services, nor is it found that the mental health system is solely responsible. Some litigation finds the school responsible and other litigation does not; medically necessary and physician-provided services are among those deemed beyond the responsibility of the school. In their national review of five school districts nationwide, Butler et al. (1990) found that, on average, children labeled SED represented approximately average costs to schools when compared to other handicapped children; they incurred more costs than learning disabled, mentally retarded, or speech impaired children, but less than hearing impaired, physically handicapped, and multiply handicapped children. Within the districts studied, only 7% of the per-pupil expenditure was spent on related services, suggesting that schools do not spend much on counseling and psychological services for SED children.

Several states are experimenting with creative financing arrangements. Wraparound monies, interagency personnel swapping, expansion of state Medicaid guidelines, interdepartmental pooling of funds, and a redirection of resources away from expensive care facilities to community-based services are some of the efforts currently being initiated to better meet the needs of SED children given the limited funding (Butler et al., 1990; Eber, 1991; Feltman, 1990). Behar's chapter in this book (Chapter 2) describes how the state of North Carolina is financing some of its programs. However, some states still resort to methods that have detrimental effects on the families of children with SED. Specifically, many states require parents to relinquish custody of their children to provide the needed services (Cohen, Harris, & Gottlieb, 1990).

The developers of the Ventura County planning model, recognizing the California legislature's responsibility to reduce expenditures, proposed a model for coordinated mental health service delivery that could demonstrate substantial "cost avoidance" (Feltman, 1990; Jordan & Hernandez, 1990). The Ventura model implemented three of the five innovations in funding mentioned above: interagency personnel swapping, interdepartmental pooling of funds, and decreased utilization of costly residential services when less restrictive, less costly alternatives were appropriate. In addition, the Ventura leaders invited individual members of the community as well as for-profit providers to support some of the needs of the children in the system through either financial contributions or in-kind service offerings (Feltman, 1990). Cost avoidance was measured as savings in AFDC group home, state hospitalization, private residential school placements, incarceration, and special education costs (Jordan & Hernandez, 1990). Although these indices of outcome are evidence of implementation of program goals to consolidate costs, yet to be demonstrated are individual-level mental health status outcomes more positive than in the "services as usual" system. Through the reduction of costs to agencies other than mental health, the Ventura system has provided the evidence necessary for the legislature to support future funding for this cost-offsetting system (Jordan & Hernandez, 1990).

Wraparound monies (Butler et al., 1990) are discretionary funds pooled for acquiring goods or services that otherwise would not be accessible to facilitate a family's obligation to meet the needs of their child. Wraparound money is commonly used for securing respite care, transportation, or individually tailored services that are not typically reimbursable through third parties. This pool of funds is made available either directly to families of children with SED or to case managers working with families.

Another innovative approach to financing the multiple needs of children with mental health problems across community settings including schools is expansion of state Medicaid guidelines. In her nationwide review of state Medicaid policies, Fox (1988) identified a range in the degree to which policies relevant to child and adolescent mental health services adequately served the population. She noted the relative discretion each state has in defining the parameters of reimbursement. Vermont, for example, employs an innovative "home- and community-based service waiver" for children with serious emotional disturbance. These waivers can be used to secure services not authorized under the state's Medicaid plan. The objective of these waivers is to provide noninstitutionalized community-based ser- vices to children who would otherwise be in costly out-of-home placements (Fox, 1988). Kentucky has broadened its Medicaid guide- lines as well, allowing mental health professionals to claim Medicaid reimbursement for services provided on site at schools, as well as in other nonclinic settings (Kukic et al., 1990).

Service providers, school personnel, administrators, and policy makers have struggled with the challenges discussed here as well as numerous other obstacles at the federal, state, local, and individual case level. After reviewing these four policy issues, it may be useful to highlight the organizational level at which changes may have the most impact. The first issue raised, accurate identification, is criti- cal to the equitable distribution of resources among the population in need. Consensus regarding who will be served should be achieved at the federal level, making clear inclusionary and exclusionary cri- teria that minimize the risk of variations in state and local interpre- tations. Both interagency coordination and financing may be most effectively directed at the state and local levels. The variable nature of existing agency linkages and organizational and leadership structures across states and districts requires flexibility in approaches to the systems coordination necessary for the provision of school-based mental health services.

As noted above, the lack of sufficient federal monies allocated for these services is likely to persist. Innovative financial practices, aggressive application for competitive (private and public) funds, and interagency agreements at the state and local levels may be viable alternative approaches to the funding challenges encountered when providing school-based services.

The fundamental value of parent involvement has been recognized and mandated at the federal level. However, individual differences among families of children with SED, as well as their varying needs, call for flexibility in defining the specific nature and extent of parent involvement in their children's services. Therefore, a general federal policy should be established that invites complete partnership with parents in the services their children receive and allows for individual case-by-case application of the process.

Conclusion and Recommendations

This chapter has discussed the appropriateness of the school setting for the delivery of mental health services needed by children. Because children are required by law to attend school for a certain number of years, they are a "captive" population (Powell, 1991); schools thus are a familiar setting where children are expected to spend their days and where services could be provided more efficiently. Furthermore, the school and its personnel are equipped to furnish mental health professionals with valuable information regarding children's behavior. This can clearly help in the assessment and treatment of children's problems. The many benefits to providing mental health services through the schools, based on the reports of success for many programs, overall outweigh the acknowledged difficulties often affecting the provision of mental health services through the schools.

Several principles should be considered when contemplating school-based mental health services:

1. Whenever possible, services offered through the schools should be based on the principle that mental health is a normal and desirable developmental goal; further, services should be based on an understanding that educational processes will be employed in ways that enable child and adolescent clients, as well as their families, to take an active role in returning the child to developmentally appropriate social, emotional, and intellectual functioning. Toward this end, preventive services should receive significant attention.

2. School-based mental health programs should be made universally available to children and adolescents within school settings, without means testing or other unnecessarily stigmatizing program entry criteria. Explicit and vigorous efforts should be made to minimize stigmatization of clients and maximize both client and program integration into regular, ongoing school programming. Mental health services should be considered by school and mental health personnel as a normal part of regular school services.

3. Local input concerning recommendations for the content, focus, and priorities of mental health programs based in the schools should be gathered systematically from parents, school professionals, mental health professionals, and a range of other community leaders.

4. A systems perspective should form the core of school-based mental health services for children and adolescents. Families, especially parents, must be involved in many programming options. It should be assumed, unless proven otherwise, that parents want an active and effective role in helping their children (return) to full mental health. Whenever possible, families should play an active role in shaping service options, making choices for child and adolescent treatment options, having full access to relevant information when their children are receiving services, and evaluating programs.

5. School-based mental health programs, once in place, must be reliably available, accessible, and well advertised so that professionals and families may plan effectively for service utilization when needs arise.

6. Mental health programs and related treatment should be made available in the least restrictive setting possible and in a range of settings beyond, but coordinated through, the school-based program (e.g., specialized outpatient programs, inpatient treatment) for those children and adolescents whose needs are more intense (chronically or periodically) than can be dealt with effectively in the school setting.

7. A systematic approach to the evaluation of services must be developed and conducted on an ongoing basis to ascertain which treatments and approaches are more effective with varied populations and presenting problems or needs.

This chapter demonstrates that schools are an appropriate and potentially effective location for the provision of most mental health services for children and adolescents. Many principles, noteworthy programs, and policy issues culled from the extant literature in mental health and education offer support for efforts to increase school-based mental health services to children.

References

American Psychological Association. (1990). Special education and related services for children with conduct disorders. *American Psychologist, 45,* 843.

Bobbitt, B. L., Dailey, B. R., Reed, M. K., Mattessich, P. W., & Heiserman, M. (1992). Child mental health: The nature and impact of collaboration between the Amherst H. Wilder Foundation and the St. Paul public schools. In K. Kutash, C. J. Liberton, A. Algarin, & R. M. Friedman (Eds.), *A system of care for children's mental health: Expanding the research base. Fifth annual research conference proceedings* (pp. 287-294). Tampa: Florida Mental Health Institute.

Botvin, G. J. (1982). Broadening the focus of smoking prevention strategies. In T. Coates, A. Peterson, & C. Perry (Eds.), *Promoting adolescent health: A dialogue on research and practice* (pp. 137-148). New York: Academic Press.

Botvin, G. J., & Tortu, S. (1988). Preventing adolescent substance abuse through life skills training. In R. H. Price, E. L. Cowen, R. P. Lorion, & J. Ramos-McKay (Eds.), *Fourteen ounces of prevention: A casebook for practitioners* (pp. 98-110). Washington, DC: American Psychological Association.

Butler, J., New, F., & Isaacs, M. (1990). Financing options for collaboration. In A. Duchnowski, A. Algarin, R. Friedman, & E. Henderson (Eds.), *Mental health and education: Partners in serving children with serious emotional disturbances. Conference proceedings* (pp. 23-33). Tampa: University of South Florida, Research and Training Center for Children's Mental Health.

Carlson, C. (1987). Family assessment and intervention in the school setting. In T. R. Kratochwill (Ed.), *Advances in school psychology* (Vol. 7, pp. 81-130). Hillsdale, NJ: Lawrence Erlbaum.

Carlson, C. (1991). Assessing the family context. In R. Kampaus & C. R. Reynolds (Eds.), *Handbook of psychological and educational assessment of children: Vol. 2. Personality behavior and context* (pp. 546-575). New York: Guilford.

Carlson, C. (1992). Models and strategies of family-school assessment and intervention. In M. J. Fine & C. Carlson (Eds.), *The handbook of family-school intervention: A systems perspective* (pp. 18-44). Boston: Allyn & Bacon.

Cline, D. H. (1990). A legal analysis of policy initiatives to exclude handicapped/disruptive students from special education. *Behavioral Disorders, 15,* 159-173.

Cohen, R., Harris, R., & Gottlieb, S. (1990). Assessing the use of transfer of custody as a requirement for families to receive services for children with serious emotional disturbance. In A. Algarin & R. Friedman (Eds.), *A system of care for children's mental health: Expanding the research base. Third annual research conference proceedings* (pp. 257-266). Tampa: Florida Mental Health Institute.

Cowen, E. L., Trost, M. A., Lorion, R. P., Door, D., Izzo, L. D., & Isaacson, R. V. (1975). *New ways in school mental health: Early detection and prevention of school maladaption.* New York: Human Science Press.

Craig, R. T. (1990). *What legislators need to know about children's mental health.* Washington, DC: National Conference of State Legislators.

Dokecki, P. R., & Moroney, R. M. (1983). To strengthen all families: A human development and community value framework. In R. Haskins & D. Adams (Eds.), *Parent education and public policy* (pp. 40-64). Norwood, NJ: Ablex.

Donovan, A. (1992). The efficacy of family systems intervention: A critical analysis of research. In M. J. Fine & C. Carlson (Eds.), *The handbook of family-school intervention: A systems perspective* (pp. 440-463). Boston: Allyn & Bacon.

Dougherty, D. (1988). Children's mental health problems and services: Current federal efforts and policy implications. *American Psychologist, 43,* 808-812.

Eber, L. (1991). The challenge of including students with emotional and behavioral disabilities in normalized school settings. In A. Algarin & R. Friedman (Eds.), *A system of care for children's mental health: Expanding the research base. Fourth annual research conference proceedings* (pp. 297-302). Tampa: Florida Mental Health Institute.

Eber, L., & Stieper, C. (1992). Designing and implementing a comprehensive system of education and support for children with serious emotional disturbance: Project WRAP. In K. Kutash, C. J. Liberton, A. Algarin, & R. M. Friedman (Eds.), *A system of care for children's mental health: Expanding the research base. Fifth annual research conference proceedings* (pp. 295-301). Tampa: Florida Mental Health Institute.

Entwisle, D. R., & Stevenson, H. W. (1987). Schools and development. *Child Development, 58,* 1149-1150.

Epanchin, B. C. (1990). Research in education: Where are we going now and where should we be going? In A. Algarin & R. Friedman (Eds.), *A system of care for children's mental health: Expanding the research base. Third annual research conference proceedings* (pp. 227-235). Tampa: Florida Mental Health Institute.

Everett, C. (1976). Family assessment and intervention for early adolescent problems. *Journal of Marriage and Family Counseling, 2,* 155-165.

Felner, R. D., & Adan, A. M. (1988). The school transitional project: An ecological intervention and evaluation. In R. H. Price, E. L. Cowen, R. P. Lorion, & J. Ramos-McKay (Eds.), *Fourteen ounces of prevention: A casebook for practitioners* (pp. 111-122). Washington, DC: American Psychological Association.

Felner, R. D., Ginter, M. A., & Primavera, J. (1982). Primary prevention during school transitions: Social support and environmental structure. *American Journal of Community Psychology, 10,* 227-240.

Felner, R. D., Primavera, J., & Cauce, A. M. (1981). The impact of school transitions: A focus for preventive efforts. *American Journal of Community Psychology, 9,* 449-459.

Feltman, R. (1990). The Ventura County model of interagency collaboration. In A. Duchnowski, A. Algarin, R. Friedman, & E. Henderson (Eds.), *Mental health and education: Partners in serving children with serious emotional disturbances. Conference proceedings* (pp. 107-119). Tampa: University of South Florida, Research and Training Center for Children's Mental Health.

Fine, M. J., & Carlson, C. (Eds.). (1992). *The handbook of family-school intervention: A systems perspective.* Boston: Allyn & Bacon.

Forness, S. R., & Knitzer, J. (1992). A new proposed definition and terminology to replace "serious emotional disturbance" in Individuals With Disabilities Act. *School Psychology Review, 21,* 12-20.

Fox, H. B. (1988). An analysis of Medicaid coverage policies affecting access to children's mental health services. In *The financing of mental health services for children and adolescents. Conference proceedings, February 1988* (pp. 57-63). Washington, DC: National Center for Education in Maternal and Child Health.

Fox, W. L., Hamilton, R. W., Broer, S., Friedman, C., Topper, K., & Yuan, S. (1992). Best practices for educating students with serious emotional disturbance in their local public schools and communities. In K. Kutash, C. J. Liberton, A. Algarin, & R. M. Friedman (Eds.), *A system of care for children's mental health: Expanding the research base. Fifth annual research conference proceedings* (pp. 303-306). Tampa: Florida Mental Health Institute.

Goldstein, S., Strickland, B., Turnbull, A. P., & Curry, L. (1989). Assessing parent participation: The parent/family involvement index. *Exceptional Children, 46,* 278-286.

Good, T. L., & Weinstein, R. S. (1986). Schools make a difference: Evidence, criticisms and new directions. *American Psychologist, 41,* 1090-1097.

Grotevant, H. D., & Carlson, C. I. (1989). *Family assessment: A guide to methods and measures.* New York: Guilford.

Hamilton, S. F. (1983). The social side of schooling: Ecological studies of classrooms and schools. *Elementary School Journal, 83,* 313-334.

Hobbs, N. (1975). *The futures of children: Recommendations of the Project on the Classification of Exceptional Children.* San Francisco: Jossey-Bass.

Hobbs, N., Dockeki, P. R., Hoover-Dempsey, K. V., Moroney, R. M., Shayne, M. W., & Weeks, K. H. (1984). *Strengthening families.* San Francisco: Jossey-Bass.

Hoover-Dempsey, K. V., Bassler, O. C., & Brissie, J. S. (1987). Parent involvement: Contributions of teacher efficacy, school socioeconomic status, and other school characteristics. *American Educational Research Journal, 24,* 417-435.

Ignelzi, S., Tucker, D., De Carolis, G., Broer, S., & Sturtevant, J. (1990). Meeting individual needs through interagency collaboration. In A. Duchnowski, A. Algarin, R. Friedman, & E. Henderson (Eds.), *Mental health and education: Partners in serving children with serious emotional disturbances. Conference proceedings* (pp. 55-63). Tampa: University of South Florida, Research and Training Center for Children's Mental Health.

Individuals With Disabilities Education Act of 1990, 20 U.S.C. § 1400 *et seq.*

Institute of Medicine. (1989). *Research on children and adolescents with mental, behavioral and developmental disorders: Mobilizing a national initiative.* Washington, DC: National Academy Press.

Jenson, J. M., & Whittacker, J. K. (1987). Parental involvement in children's residential treatment: From preplacement to aftercare. *Children and Youth Services Review, 9*(2), 81-100.

Johnson, D. L. (1988). Primary prevention of behavior problems in young children: The Houston Parent-Child Development Center. In R. H. Price, E. L. Cowen, R. P. Lorion, & J. Ramos-McKay (Eds.), *Fourteen ounces of prevention: A casebook for practitioners* (pp. 44-52). Washington, DC: American Psychological Association.

Jordan, D. D., & Hernandez, M. (1990). The Ventura planning model: A proposal for mental health reform. *Journal of Mental Health Administration, 17,* 26-47.

Kagan, S. L. (1987). Home-school linkages: History's legacy and the family support movement. In S. L. Kagan, D. R. Powell, B. Weissbourd, & E. F. Zigler (Eds.),

America's family support programs: Perspectives and prospects (pp. 161-181). New Haven, CT: Yale University Press.

Knitzer, J. (1982). *Unclaimed children: The failure of public responsibility to children and adolescents in need of mental health services.* Washington, DC: Children's Defense Fund.

Knitzer, J., Steinberg, Z., & Fleisch, B. (1990). *At the schoolhouse door: An examination of programs and policies for children with behavioral and emotional problems.* New York: Bank Street College of Education.

Knitzer, J., Steinberg, Z., & Fleisch, B. (1991). Schools, children's mental health, and the advocacy challenge. *Journal of Clinical Child Psychology, 20,* 102-111.

Knoff, H. M., & Batsche, G. M. (1990). The place of the school in community mental health services for children: A necessary interdependence. *Journal of Mental Health Administration, 17,* 122-130.

Koyanagi, C., & Weintraub, F. (1990). The special education-mental health coalition. In A. Duchnowski, A. Algarin, R. Friedman, & E. Henderson (Eds.), *Mental health and education: Partners in serving children with serious emotional disturbances. Conference proceedings* (pp. 77-81). Tampa: University of South Florida, Research and Training Center for Children's Mental Health.

Kral, R. (1986). *Strategies that work: Techniques for solution in the schools.* Milwaukee, WI: Brief Therapy Center.

Kukic, S., Reavis, K., Scott, W., Phillips, V., & Staib, C. (1990). Issues in identification: Two states' experiences. In A. Duchnowski, A. Algarin, R. Friedman, & E. Henderson (Eds.), *Mental health and education: Partners in serving children with serious emotional disturbances. Conference proceedings* (pp. 83-96). Tampa: University of South Florida, Research and Training Center for Children's Mental Health.

Linney, J. A., & Seidman, E. (1989). The future of schooling. *American Psychologist, 44,* 336-340.

Linney, J. A., & Vernberg, E. (1983). Changing patterns of parental employment and the family-school relationship. In C. D. Hayes & S. B. Kamerman (Eds.), *Children of working parents: Experiences and outcomes* (pp. 73-99). Washington, DC: National Academy Press.

Mattison, R. E., Morales, J., & Bauer, M. A. (1992). Distinguishing characteristics of elementary schoolboys recommended for SED placement. *Behavioral Disorders, 17,* 107-114.

Melaville, A. I., & Blank, M. J. (1991). *What it takes: Structuring interagency partnerships to connect children and families with comprehensive services.* Washington, DC: Education and Human Services Consortium.

Merrill, M. A., Clark, R. J., Varvil, C. D., Van Sickle, T. R., & McCall, L. J. (1992). Family therapy in the schools: The pragmatics of merging systemic approaches into educational realities. In M. J. Fine & C. Carlson (Eds.), *The handbook of family-school intervention: A systems perspective* (pp. 400-413). Boston: Allyn & Bacon.

Meyers, J. C. (1985). Federal efforts to improve mental health services for children: Breaking the cycle of failure. *Journal of Clinical Child Psychology, 14,* 182-187.

Minuchin, S. (1974). *Families and family therapy.* Cambridge, MA: Harvard University Press.

Minuchin, S., & Fishman, H. C. (1981). *Family therapy techniques.* Cambridge, MA: Harvard University Press.

Minuchin, S., Montalvo, B., Guerney, B., Rosman, B., & Schumer, F. (1967). *Families of the slums.* New York: Basic Books.

Minuchin, S., Rosman, B., & Baker, L. (1978). *Psychosomatic families*. Cambridge, MA: Harvard University Press.

Powell, D. R. (1991). How schools support families: Critical policy tensions. *Elementary School Journal, 91,* 307-319.

Powers, S. I., Hauser, S. T., & Kilner, L. A. (1989). Adolescent mental health. *American Psychologist, 44,* 200-208.

Price, R. H., Cowen, E. L., Lorion, R. P., & Ramos-McKay, J. (Eds.). (1988). *Fourteen ounces of prevention: A casebook for practitioners.* Washington, DC: American Psychological Association.

Quirk, J. P., Fine, M. J., & Roberts, L. (1992). Professional and ethical issues and problems in family-school systems interventions. In M. J. Fine & C. Carlson (Eds.), *The handbook of family-school intervention: A systems perspective* (pp. 414-427). Boston: Allyn & Bacon.

Ramey, C. T., Bryant, D. M., Campbell, F. A., Sparling, J. J., & Wasik, B. H. (1988). Early intervention for high-risk children: The Carolina early intervention program. In R. H. Price, E. L. Cowen, R. P. Lorion, & J. Ramos-McKay (Eds.), *Fourteen ounces of prevention: A casebook for practitioners* (pp. 32-43). Washington, DC: American Psychological Association.

Rog, D. J. (1990). *The status of children's mental health.* Alexandria, VA: National Mental Health Association.

Rotheram-Borus, M. J. (1988). Assertiveness training with children. In R. H. Price, E. L. Cowen, R. P. Lorion, & J. Ramos-McKay (Eds.), *Fourteen ounces of prevention: A casebook for practitioners* (pp. 83-97). Washington, DC: American Psychological Association.

Rubin, V. (1983). Family work patterns and community resources: An analysis of children's access to support and services outside school. In C. D. Hayes & S. B. Kamerman (Eds.), *Children of working parents: Experiences and outcomes* (pp. 100-129). Washington, DC: National Academy Press.

Rutter, M. (1983). School effects on pupil progress: Research findings and policy implications. *Child Development, 54,* 1-29.

Sarason, S. (1971). *The culture of the school and the problem of change.* Boston: Allyn & Bacon.

Saxe, L., Cross, T., & Silverman, N. (1988). Children's mental health: The gap between what we know and what we do. *American Psychologist, 43,* 800-807.

Schlossman, S. L. (1983). The formative era in American parent education: Overview and interpretation. In R. Haskins & D. Adams (Eds.), *Parent education and public policy* (pp. 7-39). Norwood, NJ: Ablex.

Segal, E. A., & McCreight, M. J. (1992). Collaborative community-based services for multi-need youth: A clustering approach. In K. Kutash, C. J. Liberton, A. Algarin, & R. M. Friedman (Eds.), *A system of care for children's mental health: Expanding the research base. Fifth annual research conference proceedings* (pp. 153-157). Tampa: Florida Mental Health Institute.

Shore, M. F., & Mannino, F. V. (1976). Mental health services for children and youth: 1776-1976. *Journal of Clinical Child Psychology, 5,* 21-25.

Silver, A. A. (1991). Children in SED classes. In A. Algarin & R. Friedman (Eds.), *A system of care for children's mental health: Expanding the research base. Fourth annual research conference proceedings* (pp. 303-310). Tampa: Florida Mental Health Institute.

Skiba, R., & Grizzle, K. (1991). The social maladjustment exclusion: Issues of definition and assessment. *School Psychology Review, 20*, 580-598.

Stroul, B. A., & Friedman, R. (1986). *A system of care for severely emotionally disturbed children and youth.* Washington, DC: Child and Adolescent Service System Program Technical Assistance Center.

Swick, K. J., & McKnight, S. (1989). Characteristics of kindergarten teachers who promote parent involvement. *Early Childhood Research Quarterly, 4*, 19-29.

Swisher, J. D. (1979). Prevention issues. In R. I. Dupont, A. Goldstein, & J. O'Donnell (Eds.), *Handbook on drug abuse* (pp. 49-62). Washington, DC: National Institute on Drug Abuse.

Tarico, V. S., Low, B. P., Trupin, E., & Forsyth-Stephens, A. (1989). Children's mental health services: A parent perspective. *Community Mental Health Journal, 25*, 313-326.

Tharanger, D. J., Laurent, J., & Best, L. R. (1986). Classification of children referred for emotional and behavioral problems: A comparison of Pub. L. No. 94-142 SED criteria, DSM III, and the CBCL system. *Journal of School Psychology, 24*, 111-121.

Tuma, J. M. (1989). Mental health services for children: The state of the art. *American Psychologist, 44*, 188-199.

Vaughn, S., Bos, C. S., Harrell, J. E., & Lasky, B. A. (1988). Parent participation in the initial placement/IEP conference ten years after mandated involvement. *Journal of Developmental Disabilities, 21*, 82-89.

Weinberg, L. A. (1992). The relevance of choice in distinguishing seriously emotionally disturbed from socially maladjusted students. *Behavioral Disorders, 17*, 99-106.

Weiss, H. (1989). State family support and education programs: Lessons from the pioneers. *American Journal of Orthopsychiatry, 59*, 32-48.

Weissbourd, B. (1987). A brief history of family support programs. In S. L. Kagan, R. Powell, B. Weissbourd, & E. F. Zigler (Eds.), *America's family support programs: Perspectives and prospects* (pp. 38-56). New Haven, CT: Yale University Press.

Will, M. (1990). Special address. In A. Duchnowski, A. Algarin, R. Friedman, & E. Henderson (Eds.), *Mental health and education: Partners in serving children with serious emotional disturbances. Conference proceedings* (pp. 1-7). Tampa: University of South Florida, Research and Training Center for Children's Mental Health.

Witt, J. C., Miller, C. D., McIntyre, R. M., & Smith, D. (1984). Effects of variables on parental perceptions of staffings. *Exceptional Children, 51*, 27-32.

Zigler, E. F. (1989). Addressing the nation's child care crisis: The school of the twenty-first century. *American Journal of Orthopsychiatry, 59*, 484-491.

Juvenile Justice:

Once and Future
Gatekeeper for a System of Care

KATHLEEN A. MALOY

The only institution that can reasonably exercise leadership on behalf of the society and the children is the juvenile court. The reason is simply that no other institution can claim to have an equally broad view of all the interests at stake, to have as wide a range of action, or to be able to make decisions that are designed to reflect the values of the society as expressed in its laws and constitution.

Mark Harrison Moore (1987)

The juvenile justice system holds a unique position in the delivery of mental health as well as social services to children and adolescents. The fact that the first child guidance clinic in the United States was founded to aid the juvenile court in Chicago indicates an early recognition that many children who became involved in the juvenile justice system had mental health problems (Shanok & Lewis, 1977). Fundamental precepts of the juvenile justice system were, and still are, a priority emphasis on individualized treatment and rehabilitation as opposed to the punitive orientation of adult criminal justice and on a protective cloak of care and supervision for neglected, dependent, and delinquent children (Towberman, 1992). The historical intertwining of juvenile and family law with the mental health professions was premised on the belief that the mental health professionals had the knowledge and expertise to rehabilitate young offenders and support family reintegration and cohesion (Aber & Reppucci, 1987).

Socioeconomic facts of life indicate that juvenile courts are frequently the repository of children and adolescents with a wide variety of needs, ranging from extremely disturbed children (Shanok & Lewis, 1977) to juveniles accused of serious offenses. Troubled youth and their families who come to the attention of the state are usually served by one of three systems: child welfare, mental health, or juvenile justice (National Conference of State Legislatures Health and Mental Health Program, 1989). Research shows that the children and families served by these three systems are remarkably alike, with similar characteristics and services needs (National Council of Juvenile and Family Court Judges, 1984; Shanok & Lewis, 1977). The primary characteristics of high-need, high-risk juvenile offenders have been identified as substance abuse problems, dysfunctional home environments, histories of abuse and neglect, and serious learning problems (Towberman, 1992). As a result, juvenile courts often function as the catalysts for access to services for troubled families facing custody issues, troubled children struggling with emotional and/or environmental deficits, and troubled adolescents facing probation or detention. For example, in Tennessee, as in most other states, juvenile court judges make dispositions on custody and dependent/neglect cases contingent on specific directives to the human services/child welfare and mental health systems for the provision of services to children and their families. Moreover, there is a growing awareness that an inadequate system of financing for services for children with serious emotional disorders frequently makes it necessary for parents to give up custody of their children through the juvenile court so that the children can be eligible for publicly funded services (Cohen et al., 1993). Increasingly, the juvenile courts are becoming the gatekeepers for children and adolescents in need of mental health services.

Much has been written about the juvenile justice system in the United States, addressing such issues as the evolutionary history of this separate court for youth (Hawes, 1971; Mack, 1909; Pickett, 1969),

the informality of these courts during most of the 20th century and
the popularity of the rehabilitation/training school approach to dispositions (Empey, 1982; Street, Vinter, & Perrow, 1966); the federally
driven push for procedural and substantive reforms in juvenile justice during the 1960s and 1970s (Kobrin & Klein, 1983; National Advisory Commission on Criminal Justice Standards and Goals, 1976);
the various social and political theories underlying the modern reform movements in juvenile justice (Cloward & Ohlin, 1960; Lemert,
1967; Miller & Ohlin, 1985; Miller, Ohlin, & Coates, 1977); to the im-
position of the more punitive, "just deserts" approach to juvenile
justice of the 1980s (Krisberg, Schwartz, Litsky, & Austin, 1986; Rubin,
1985). The primary focus of this chapter is to examine the role of the
juvenile justice system within the context of current efforts to reform,
improve, and expand systems of care for children and adolescents.
This chapter does not examine substantive or procedural aspects of
juvenile law; nor does it examine the legal rights of children except
where necessary to understand the functions of the juvenile court as
a quasi-social service agency as opposed to a strictly legal institution.[1]

    This chapter first briefly reviews the major historical develop-
ments in juvenile justice to identify and discuss the broad social policy issues that have affected this institution. Second, it examines the
intersection of the juvenile justice and mental health arenas in order
to define the particular problems and issues that both systems must
address collaboratively. Third, it reviews the state of research-based
knowledge about the therapeutic outcomes for mental health interventions that juvenile courts may rely upon for meeting their rehabilitative mandates. Finally, it draws conclusions about the
continuing viability of juvenile court as the *de facto* gatekeeper for
many youth needing mental health services and the implications of
this role for developing, implementing, and evaluating comprehensive systems of care for children and adolescents. Given the emphasis
on systems of care for children, this examination broadens to discuss
the arenas of child welfare, health, education, and social services and
delineates questions for future services research and evaluation projects on the feasibility of state-level, multiagency service delivery for
children and the role for juvenile justice in such a service delivery
system.

Historical, Political, and
Social Issues in Juvenile Justice

The beginnings of juvenile courts in the United States were tied to the advent of industrialization and compulsory education during the late 19th century. There was a need to ensure that the majority of young people were effectively socialized to fit in and contribute to the new social order. The juvenile justice system was basically a sociolegal institution for regulating the behavior of juveniles and for strengthening the authority of both the family and the school (Ferdinand, 1991). The term traditionally used to define and describe the function of the juvenile court—*parens patriae*, or the authority to protect those who cannot protect themselves—has historically meant that the court's goals are rehabilitative and protective as opposed to punitive when dealing with delinquent youth/juvenile offenders (Empey, 1982).

The legislation that established the first formal juvenile court in Chicago in 1899 extended the court's jurisdiction to cover virtually all juveniles, including status offenders, such as runaways and neglected and dependent children (Ferdinand, 1991). The broad scope of this legal authority recognized the primary function of the juvenile courts as caretaking and rehabilitation and established the full responsibility of these courts for child guidance and child welfare (Levine & Levine, 1970). As noted above, the first child guidance clinic in the United States—the Juvenile Psychopathic Institute of Chicago—was established in response to requests for assistance from the juvenile judge. This event forecast the prevailing social and political presumptions that benevolent juvenile judges, informed and guided by mental health professionals, could effectively rehabilitate, caretake, and socialize all categories of delinquent or neglected youth (Levine & Levine, 1970). The political and social implications of this broadened role for juvenile courts were frequently evidenced in the so-called "turf wars" between juvenile courts and the more traditional social service agencies (Block & Hale, 1991).

By 1945 all 50 states had established separate juvenile justice systems premised on the *parens patriae* philosophy, which promoted an informal atmosphere in the courtroom and gave juvenile judges considerable leeway in making decisions about the youth coming before them (Ferdinand, 1991). By the 1960s, however, it was becoming apparent that the state juvenile justice systems were seriously flawed in two respects. First, the informality of the legal proceedings had led to systematic and serious due process failures, with the result that (a) so-called therapeutic measures (i.e., excessive and extended use of infamous training schools) were much worse than punishments, and (b) the dispositions of cases were marked by flagrant race and gender discrimination (Allen, 1964; Cohen, 1976; National Council of Juvenile and Family Court Judges, 1990; Rubin, 1985; Westendorp, Brink, Roberson, & Ortiz, 1986). Second, the development of appropriate programs and services necessary to guide and support the rehabilitation goals of juvenile court was haphazard, inadequately funded, and largely unresponsive to the decision-making needs of juvenile judges and the services needs of youth (Ferdinand, 1991).

Beginning in the middle 1960s, the federal response to these state-level problems was developed along three strategies (Binder & Polan, 1991). First, due process standards for juvenile court proceedings were codified and disseminated to the states, with receipt of certain federal revenue-sharing funds contingent upon compliance with these standards. Second, the availability of additional, more discretionary federal funds was contingent on program development to promote the diversion of youth from the traditional juvenile justice institutions (e.g., training schools) to community-based rehabilitative programs. Third, the dissemination and application of new sociologically based theories about the causes of juvenile delinquency were supported by the Justice Department and the Department of Health, Education and Welfare (Binder & Polan, 1991). The purpose of these three strategies was to ensure consistent and just treatment of delinquent youth and dependent and neglected youth, facilitate the development of innovative community-based programs for delinquent youth derived from a different perspective on how to address delinquency, and encourage the states to allocate more resources for the establishment of such programs.

The consequences of these federal efforts, perhaps predictably, were, and continue to be, rather mixed. Although the emphasis on deinstitutionalization resulted in a reduction of youth in juvenile justice system and public institutions such as training schools during the 1970s and early 1980s, there is evidence that a "hidden system" for institutionalizing and controlling children emerged in response (Jackson-Beeck, Schwartz, & Rutherford, 1987; Schwartz, Jackson-Beeck, & Anderson, 1984). This system comprises private psychiatric hospitals, residential treatment centers, and chemical dependency units; the use of these types of institutions was fueled in part by the increasing tendency to medicalize deviant behavior for social control purposes (Staples & Warren, 1988) and by the sociological theories of the 1960s labeling delinquent youth as "sick" rather than "bad" (Binder & Polan, 1991). The availability of health insurance, both public and private, also facilitated this process of "transinstitutionalization" (Brown, 1985). The ability to divert youth to private institutions effectively bypassed many of the due process guarantees mandated by federal agencies for the treatment of delinquent youth (Schmidt, 1985). This continued reliance on very restrictive settings for dispositions raises serious questions about the adequacy and appropriateness of the juvenile justice system's approach to rehabilitation for youth (Staples & Warren, 1988). Moreover, the number of youth in public and private facilities and institutions has been steadily increasing since the mid-1980s (U.S. Department of Justice, Office of Juvenile Justice and Delinquency Prevention, 1991). This phenomenon is probably related to the significant increase during the 1980s in the numbers of youth living in poverty and unstable social environments combined with significant reductions in resources for social service programs (Center for the Study of Social Policy, 1990; Children's Defense Fund, 1991; Fordham Institute for Innovation in Social Policy, 1990).

In fact, state juvenile justice systems have been and continue to be severely criticized for failing to meet their *parens patriae*/rehabilitation mandate properly (National Council of Juvenile and Family Court Judges, 1984). A case can be made that the failure to rehabilitate juvenile offenders and ensure appropriate placements for dependent children is probably due in large measure to the failure of state agencies to provide solid support for community and institutional treatment programs necessary to facilitate the rehabilitative functions of juvenile court (Ferdinand, 1991). Despite their traditional rehabilitative and treatment responsibilities vis-à-vis delinquent and dependent youth, juvenile courts have never had much influence over the availability or content of treatment programs, whether institutional or community based. Consequently and predictably, research suggests that many children and adolescents experiencing mental health problems within the juvenile justice system are not formally diagnosed or referred for appropriate treatment (Institute of Medicine, 1989). Another factor contributing to the apparent failure of the juvenile courts is the difficulty inherent in meeting the service needs of two very different populations in the juvenile justice system: serious offenders and status offenders/dependent and neglected youth. There is a growing concern that the increasingly serious offenses of older juveniles, such as rape, aggravated assault, and murder, will result in the criminalization of juvenile court proceedings and inappropriate dispositions for the usually younger status offenders, such as runaways and truants, and dependent and neglected youth (Ferdinand, 1991).

The complexity of the historical, social, and political issues associated with the juvenile justice system is evident from this very cursory review of the literature and provides an essential context for examining the relationship between the mental health and related social service systems and the juvenile justice system. The multidimensional and often conflicting expectations about regulating and rehabilitating youth subject to the authority of the juvenile courts have certainly contributed to the seemingly insurmountable barriers associated with efforts to create a good fit between service needs of the court; youth and their families; and the fiscal, conceptual, and ideological constraints of the service programs and providers. The next section examines the particular characteristics and dynamics of the intersection between mental health and juvenile justice to specifically discuss the problems and issues that both systems must address collaboratively.

Intersection of
Mental Health and Juvenile Justice

As noted above, troubled youth and their families who become involved in the juvenile justice system present characteristics very similar to youth and families served by the mental health and child welfare/social service agencies (National Conference of State Legislatures Health and Mental Health Program, 1989; Shanok & Lewis, 1977). The empirical evidence documenting the growing numbers of youth with serious emotional disorders who come into contact with the juvenile justice system continues to grow (Friedman & Kutash, 1992). Consequently, juvenile judges expect that mental health professionals in particular can assist them in two distinct, but somewhat overlapping, ways: (a) designing, developing, and implementing a range of innovative and effective services for youth; and (b) advising and guiding juvenile judges in fashioning dispositions that will address and redress the individual rehabilitation needs of delinquent youth and their families.

Notwithstanding the fact that the first child guidance clinic in the United States was founded to aid the first juvenile court, there is significant skepticism about the utility of mental health participation in juvenile and family law (Aber & Reppucci, 1987). Mental health professionals have demonstrated limited clinical abilities to determine a juvenile's amenability to treatment (Mulvey, 1984) or to determine the best interests of children in abuse/neglect and custody dispositions (Reppucci, 1984). On the one hand, reliance upon the social and behavioral sciences to inform judicial decision making has been characterized as creating an inappropriate tension between the juvenile court as objective trier of fact and the juvenile courts as a social service provider (Mulvey, 1982). On the other hand, continued reliance on mental health expertise reflects the historical and political assumption that objective scientific information will protect against the subjective exercise of the juvenile court's parens patriae authority to rehabilitate juveniles (Aber & Reppucci, 1987).

Consequently, given this existing state of mental health knowledge, expertise, and resources, it is questionable whether mental health systems have the capacity and capability to meet these two frequently conflicting needs of the juvenile justice system. Practically speaking, it is frequently difficult for mental health professionals to distinguish between the role of adviser/guide to the court and the role of program developer and service provider, and to fashion their responses accordingly. Few efforts have been made either to develop professional and ethical standards for providing this usually very influential information to juvenile courts or to critically review and assess the existing scientific knowledge so that these decision makers are given the best available tools for determining the best interests of children and ordering the provision of appropriate services.

The National Council of Juvenile and Family Court Judges (1984) published 38 recommendations designed to improve juvenile court dispositions for juvenile offenders. These recommendations for changes in the operation and activities of juvenile judges and courts are instructive with respect to the propriety and necessity of juvenile courts' ability to call upon mental health expertise in making dispositions for children and adolescents and their families. Highlights from the Council's recommendations include dispositions that emphasize the need for individualized treatment, ranging from secure institutional facilities to open community-based programs; court referrals to programs that strengthen social institutions such as family and schools and that include transitional services to support rehabilitation and return to the community; court demands for effective treatment and intervention programs for adolescent substance abuse; and judicial activism regarding the development of resources for children and adolescents in their communities.

It is clear that underlying these recommendations is the assumption that juvenile judges will seek and actually have access to expert advice to inform their broad-ranging and relatively discretionary dispositions. These assessments from individual mental health professionals frequently involve services and programs beyond the control of the mental health system and, as a result, provide an informative window for juvenile judges into the larger service system for children and their families. This dynamic highlights the potential for the mental health-juvenile justice intersection to illustrate the broad system of care issues (Macro International Inc., 1992). It also recalls the historic tensions over who should control social service resources and determine social policy that have shaped the relations between juvenile justice and social services (Block & Hale, 1991). Given the historic limitations in public resources and private insurance for mental health services and the tradition of inattention to interagency collaboration, the increasingly common gatekeeper actions of juvenile courts in mandating particular services for children and their families have frequently served to exacerbate these historic turf- and resource-related tensions between the mental health and juvenile justice systems.

The foregoing discussion presumes the ability of mental health professionals to inform and guide juvenile court decision making and the advisability of juvenile judges' relying on such guidance. Thus, the next section reviews the state of empirically based knowledge about the effectiveness of mental health interventions for children and adolescents to assess the capacity of mental health professionals to recommend, evaluate, or create the types of services and programs needed to facilitate appropriate dispositions by juvenile judges.

Effectiveness of Mental Health Interventions for Troubled Youth and Juvenile Offenders

A discussion of the issues related to the effectiveness of mental health treatment as well as the importance of mental health services to juvenile court decision making must differentiate between the two broad categories of youth who come within the jurisdiction of juvenile court: (a) dependent and neglected children and status offenders, and (b) juvenile offenders/juvenile delinquents. Some of the main distinguishing characteristics of these two groups were discussed above; the important point to understand here is that the substance of the research literature vis-à-vis these two groups is quite different.

Empirically based knowledge about the effectiveness and appropriate use of mental health interventions for dependent and neglected children/status offenders is drawn from the general research literature on the effectiveness of mental health treatment for children and adolescents. Researchers have been hampered by the fact that, historically and to date, mental health services for children have been poorly funded, fragmented, inaccessible, and narrowly focused (Knitzer, 1982; Maloy, 1991; Saxe, Cross, Silverman, Batchelor, & Dougherty, 1987), with most resources going for institutional placement and inpatient treatment (Dougherty, 1988). The lack of empirically based knowledge about the effectiveness and outcomes of mental health services in general is a significant problem for policy makers and service providers in the adult as well as child arena (Maloy, 1992). Not only is there insufficient evidence of the effectiveness of institutionally based treatment for children and adolescents with mental disorders (Burns & Friedman, 1990), but the evidence concerning the effectiveness of alternative, community-based mental health services, though promising, is based on limited data (Rog, 1992). There is also a growing awareness among service providers and researchers that the interventions must address family issues as well if the intervention is to be effective for the child (Stroul & Friedman, 1986; Vossler-Hunter, 1989); the research literature on these interventions, however, is also nascent (Rog, 1992).

Consequently, juvenile judges trying to make decisions about treatment and related services for dependent and neglected children cannot find much reassuring advice from this literature. The consequences of limited knowledge and choices can seriously undermine how children are "taken care of" by the juvenile courts, as it is reasonable to assume that the orders and directives of juvenile judges are the primary determinants of the mental health services received by children and adolescents in state custody. For example, the numbers of children placed in inpatient and residential settings, as well as the costs associated with such placements, have increased significantly during the 1980s (Saxe, Cross, & Silverman, 1988; Zeigler-Dendy, 1989). Many explanations have been proposed for this growing rate of utilization, including the lack of suitable alternatives in the community and the availability of fiscal incentives to use hospitals for a treatment setting. A significant portion of these fiscal incentives is absorbed by states for children in state custody whose disposition is overseen by the juvenile courts (Zeigler-Dendy, 1989).

Although there has been more concentrated policy and research interest in mental health/treatment intervention for juvenile offenders/juvenile delinquents, the state of the empirically based knowledge about the effectiveness of these programs is not much better. The development of effective intervention strategies has been an extremely difficult task from conceptual, methodological, and practical perspectives (Lipsey, 1988). Although researchers have identified the levels of psychopathology among serious delinquents (McManus, Alessi, Grapentine, & Brickman, 1984; Shanok & Lewis, 1977), connections between substance abuse and psychopathology among serious delinquents (Milin, Halikas, Meller, & Morse, 1991), and the conceptual promise of family therapy (Tolan, Cromwell, & Brasswell, 1986) and community-based programs (Barton & Butts, 1990) as effective interventions for juvenile delinquents, the gap between theory and practice remains wide (Mulvey, 1984; Niarhos & Routh, 1992), and the abundance of unaddressed methodological problems and of poorly designed and inconsistently executed research is daunting (Aber & Reppucci, 1987).

In a meta-analytic review of 443 separate outcome studies of interventions for juvenile delinquents, Lipsey (1991) attempted to address methodological flaws related to small study populations, inconsistent variable definitions, and broad diversity of intervention programs and study populations. Although this work is still in the early stages due to the complexities of dealing with numerous variables and enormous variation, he found that overall these interventions did have a small positive effect on recidivism: That is, recidivism declined slightly. He also noted that it is much too early in the meta-analytic process to determine what types of programs "work" for what types of delinquent youth. It is telling that the impetus for Lipsey's meta-analysis is the fact that, when examined individually, these studies provide almost no empirical evidence for the effectiveness of these intervention programs.

Recently, researchers have reported some progress with a particular intervention approach with juvenile delinquents. Consistent with findings from causal modeling studies that show multiple factors associated with delinquent behavior, a multisystemic treatment model has been applied to serious juvenile offenders and their families (Henggler et al., 1986). Multisystemic interventions attempt to change interactions within and among systems relevant to the juvenile's behaviors such as school, peers, and family (Henggler & Borduin, 1990). The structure of these interventions involves interdisciplinary, intensive, in-home work with juveniles and their families; communication and skills-building workshops with parents and teachers; and targeted interventions using peer groups such as athletic teams or the Boy Scouts. On a short-term and preliminary basis, these multisystemic interventions have shown decreases in conduct behaviors, improvements in family interactions, and reductions in delinquent associations and behaviors (Henggler & Borduin, 1990).

As discussed above, the intersection of juvenile justice and mental health inevitably raises intervention/treatment issues from a systems perspective: that is, the relationship between these agencies within the context of providing services. Consequently, the question of whether and how mental health interventions can be effective vis-à-vis the needs of the juvenile courts can be examined from the framework and perspective of the juvenile court: Considering the actual procedures and decision making of the juvenile judges, what is the empirical evidence for utility and perhaps necessity of an informed dynamic between juvenile justice and mental health systems? Unfortunately, few efforts have been made to examine carefully and systematically how juvenile courts deal with various types of youth and what effect these differences have on disposition decisions and ultimate outcomes for troubled youth and their families.

For example, there is little empirically based knowledge about the specific issues influencing decisions to place children and adolescents in the most restrictive mental health treatment settings. Studies are needed on the factors associated with utilization of institutional and outpatient mental health services in order (a) to more intelligently design alternative and less restrictive services and (b) to ensure that juvenile judges are fully informed about intervention choices. Although juvenile courts are often the primary agency intervening in the lives of troubled youth and their families, empirically based knowledge about the specific dynamics of these interventions and services utilization is limited. For example, what are the differences between youth served entirely within the social service system and those who come within the authority of the juvenile court? Do youth with similar characteristics receive substantively different interventions/treatment as a result of being in one system rather the other? A more precise understanding is needed of the process by which youth move through the juvenile justice system; only the most rigorously designed and carefully executed studies can generate this knowledge (Sechrest & Rosenblatt, 1987).

Moreover, little is known about the extent to which mental health problems are identified during the juvenile justice process, what the structural barriers to identification and treatment are, how effective the existing referral mechanisms and treatment programs are, and whether juvenile courts are more or less "successful" in dealing with troubled children and youth than with troubling juvenile delinquents and serious offenders. The conflicting goals of juvenile justice (rehabilitation and retribution) the constant tension between caretaking and the rights of children, and complex issues of confidentiality and informed consent all mean that researchers must be very aware of their ethical and professional responsibilities when working in this area (Mulvey & Phelps, 1988).

Difficulties notwithstanding, however, additional research-based knowledge is needed about these specific issues vis-à-vis the appropriate parameters for the interaction between mental health and juvenile justice:

1. What are the characteristics of children and adolescents coming through juvenile court, including apparent services needs, prior services utilization, family characteristics, and school history?
2. How well are existing linkages working to implement referrals between juvenile courts and various mental health services agencies?
3. What are the specific treatment and intervention program needs of juvenile court judges vis-à-vis their dispositional rehabilitation responsibilities?
4. What are the differences in terms of services utilization, mental health outcomes, and recidivism to juvenile court that can be attributed to increased availability of mental health services and programs to juvenile judges?
5. To what extent are the two general populations (i.e., dependent children/status offenders and juvenile delinquents/serious offenders) distinguished and treated differently in terms of identifying mental health problems and meeting services needs?
6. Can the advances in multisystemic treatment and family therapy be effectively operationalized and make a difference in the functioning of the juvenile court?

Juvenile Court as a Gatekeeper for a System of Care

As discussed above, the origins and evolution of the juvenile court in the United States have been intertwined with the development of a public system of social services for troubled youth and their families. Although juvenile court is obviously not the only avenue for children and adolescents to access needed services, these courts have clearly been a vehicle to allocate limited public resources to youth arguably most at risk and most in need of services. The realities of the emotional disorders and mental health problems demonstrated by juvenile delinquents and dependent children are well documented. Within the constellation of the publicly funded social service agencies responsible to help children and their families put disrupted lives back together, time and again the juvenile court is characterized as the all-important catalyst for access to (i.e., the *de facto* gatekeeper for) services and resources (Bane, 1991; Macro International Inc., 1992; National Conference of State Legislatures Health and Mental Health Program, 1989; Soler & Shauffer, 1990).

Children living in poverty, stressful socioeconomic environments, and abusive families are likely to be most at risk for emotional disorders and most in need of mental health services (Knitzer, 1993). These situations are also the ones in which the juvenile justice system is most likely to intervene, due to either custody issues associated with dependent and neglected children or juvenile delinquency issues associated with youth who are emotionally disordered or acting out. In most states, juvenile judges have the jurisdictional authority and legal responsibility by virtue of the permanency planning process to order and enforce the provision of services necessary to ensure stable and therapeutic environments for youth (Hardin, 1992). Consequently, juvenile courts are frequently in the position of determining as well as ensuring access to the services that will allow a child to return to his or her family, be diverted from an institutional setting, or receive care that he or she would probably otherwise not receive (Soler & Shauffer, 1990).

Moreover, due to the absence of an appropriately structured and adequately financed service system for children with serious emotional disorders, it is frequently necessary for parents to give up legal custody of their children to the state to receive publicly funded services. In general, transfers of legal custody must be reviewed and approved by the juvenile court and are usually contingent upon the provision of service designed to reunite the family. Although few state agencies will formally acknowledge or endorse this practice and many states have laws prohibiting such custody transfers, there is significant evidence that many parents agree to custody transfers to gain access to services (Cohen et al., 1993). The effects of this reality may be evident in Tennessee, where current efforts to reform the service delivery system for children by targeting services to children in state custody—ostensibly to reunite these children with their families—may initially be increasing the number of children in state custody (personal communication, K. Edwards, Executive Director, Tennessee Select Committee on Children and Youth, Tennessee House of Representatives, May 1993). Thus, notwithstanding the lack of empirical evidence concerning the utility of treatment interventions for juvenile delinquents, the frequently hostile and uninformed interactions between juvenile justice and other social service agencies, and the questionable ability of the existing juvenile justice system either to take care of or to rehabilitate troubled youth, there can be little argument that the juvenile justice system has a singularly powerful role to play in the lives of most children and adolescents who need mental health services.

The utility and viability of the gatekeeper role for the juvenile courts are also consistent with much of the mental health treatment and services research literature reviewed above. The clear conclusion to be drawn from that discussion concerns the need for multisystemic, collaborative, interagency approaches to providing services in order to fully address the needs of troubled children and adolescents and their families (Friedman & Kutash, 1992; Knitzer, 1993). The juvenile court is the only agency involved with these youth that has the authority to order/demand the participation of agencies and mandate the commitment of resources necessary for services delivery (Hardin, 1992; Soler & Shauffer, 1990). Consequently, state officials and program developers must recognize and act on the need to capacity-build with the juvenile courts. This means that juvenile judges and court staff must be made aware of the full range and types of services potentially available for children and adolescents, such as home-based services (AuClaire & Schwartz, 1987), therapeutic foster care (Stroul, 1989), and individualized wraparound services (Burchard & Clarke, 1990), and the types of children, adolescents, and families for whom these services are appropriate. The courts also have a key role to play in the increasingly important policy areas of delivering individualized, case-managed services to children and their families (*Integrating Human Services*, 1992) and avoiding "revolving-door" families in juvenile court. Children often move back and forth between the juvenile justice system and the mental health system with little joint monitoring or planning (Fagan, 1991).

This *de facto* gatekeeper role also means that mental health services researchers and policymakers must recognize juvenile courts as an integral component of a system of care for children and adolescents. Juvenile courts are frequently not included in evaluation research of comprehensive systems of care because they do not fit the traditional notion of a social service agency. It is clear from the foregoing discussion that these courts play a key role in the implementation and ongoing functioning of mental health service systems for children and adolescents; an evaluation of a system of care for children and adolescents that does not include an examination of the role played by the juvenile court is incomplete and insufficient. In conceptualizing and designing their studies, researchers should think about the particular questions and types of outcomes vis-à-vis services for children that will be meaningful to juvenile judges and that will guide them in their efforts to mandate agencies services. This type of knowledge is particularly essential when the court must distinguish between needs of adolescent offenders and the needs of troubled children and families. Examples of these types of questions were provided above in the discussion of future research needs. Finally, child mental health services researchers must also measure and account for the operation of the juvenile justice system when they are investigating the effects of service system change/reform on outcomes for children and their families.

Conclusion

Policy makers and researchers are asserting the advent of a new paradigm for children's mental health. This new paradigm is premised on a shift from the traditional approach of treating children in institutional environments, away from family and without the involvement of other systems such as education, to an approach emphasizing individualized, family-based services delivered by a broadly defined, community-based system of care with enhanced cultural sensitivities (Knitzer, 1993). There are several key underpinnings for the effective operationalization of this new paradigm; these include changes in the financing structures, carefully structured interagency collaboration, and coordinated and cohesive locally controlled programs designed to address multiple needs of children and families (Friedman & Kutash, 1992; Maloy, 1991).

There are two reasons that the juvenile justice system has a critical—in fact, essential—role to play in making this new paradigm a reality for children and adolescents and their families. First, to meet their parens patriae responsibilities, juvenile justice must become, and be considered, an integral part of coordinated systems of care. Juvenile judges and court staff must strengthen collaborative linkages with state agencies responsible for treatment and intervention programs to make informed and appropriate dispositions for delinquent and troubled youth. At the same time, appropriate diagnostic, treatment, rehabilitation, and family reunification programs must be available to juvenile judges so that they effect a balance between treatment and rehabilitation goals in their dispositional recommendations for probation, detention, custody, and institutional treatment.

Second, the juvenile courts can use their judicial authority to support and enforce the demands of children and their families, as well as of agencies, for comprehensive services and the resources to ensure the availability of such services. As discussed above, through judicial orders the juvenile justice system is empowered both to ensure the availability of mental health and other social services and to enforce these orders with judicial hearing procedures that effectively monitor the ongoing accessibility of services. Moreover, the juvenile court procedures for permanency planning can serve as instructive case planning models for agencies providing individualized care. Thus, given its traditional and *de facto* gatekeeper function as well as its ability to enforce the operation of systems of care, the juvenile justice system should continue to be understood and appreciated as an essential tool for policy makers, researchers, and providers working to understand and implement integrated and comprehensive children's mental health service systems.

Note

1. There are numerous sources for comprehensive discussions and examinations of legal issues vis-à-vis the juvenile justice system and the rights and treatment of

children. For example, see Davis, 1983; Goldstein, Freud, and Solnit, 1973, 1979; Grisso and Conlin, 1984; Henning, 1982; Mnookin, 1979; National Advisory Committee on Criminal Justice Standards, 1980; National Juvenile Justice Assessment Center, 1980; Reppucci and Crosby, 1993; and Wadlington, Whitebread, and Davis, 1983.

References

Aber, M., & Reppucci, N. (1987). The limits of mental health expertise in juvenile and family law. *International Journal of Law and Psychiatry, 10,* 167-184.

Allen, F. A. (1964). *The borderland of criminal justice.* Chicago: University of Chicago Press.

AuClaire, P., & Schwartz, I. M. (1987). Are home-based services effective? A public child welfare agency's experiment. *Children Today, 16,* 6-9.

Bane, M. (1991). *Paying attention to children services setting and systems.* Unpublished working paper, Harvard University, John F. Kennedy School of Government, Malcolm Wiener Center for Social Policy.

Barton, W. H., & Butts, J. A. (1990). Viable options: Intensive supervision programs for juvenile delinquents. *Crime and Delinquency, 36,* 238-256.

Binder, A., & Polan, S. (1991). The Kennedy-Johnson year, social theory, and federal policy in the control of juvenile delinquency. *Crime and Delinquency, 37,* 242-261.

Block, K., & Hale, D. (1991). Turf wars in Progressive Era juvenile justice: The relationship of private and public child care agencies. *Crime and Delinquency, 37,* 225-241.

Brown, P. (1985). *The transfer of care: Psychiatric deinstitutionalization and its aftermath.* London: Routledge & Kegan Paul.

Burchard, J., & Clarke, R. (1990). The role of individualized care in a service delivery system for children and adolescents with severely maladjusted behavior. *Journal of Mental Health Administration, 17,* 48-60.

Burns, B. J., & Friedman, R. M. (1990). Examining the research base for child mental health services and policy. *Journal of Mental Health Administration, 17,* 87-98.

Center for the Study of Social Policy. (1990, January). *Kids count: Data book—state profiles of child well-being.* Washington, DC: Author.

Children's Defense Fund. (1991). *The status of America's children.* Washington, DC: Author.

Cloward, R., & Ohlin, L. (1960). *Delinquency and opportunity: A theory of delinquent gangs.* New York: Free Press.

Cohen, L. E. (1976). *Delinquency dispositions: An empirical analysis of processing decisions in three juvenile courts* (National Criminal Justice Information and Statistics Services, Law Enforcement Assistance Administration). Washington, DC: Government Printing Office.

Cohen, R., Prieser, L., Gottlieb, S., Harris, R., Baker, J., & Sonenklar, N. (1993). Relinquishing custody as a requisite for receiving services for children with serious emotional disorders. *Law and Human Behavior, 17,* 121-134.

Davis, S. (1983). *Rights of juveniles: The juvenile justice system.* New York: Clark Boardman.

Dougherty, D. (1988). Children's mental health problems and services: Current federal efforts and implications. *American Psychologis, 43,* 808-812.

Empey, L. T. (1982). *American delinquency.* Homewood, IL: Dorsey.

Fagan, J. (1991). Community-based treatment for mentally disordered juvenile offenders. *Journal of Clinical Child Psychology, 20,* 42-50.

Ferdinand, T. (1991). History overtakes the juvenile justice system. *Crime and Delinquency, 37,* 204-224.

Fordham Institute for Innovation in Social Policy. (1990). *The index of social health 1990: Focus: The social health of children.* Tarrytown, NY: Author.

Friedman, R., & Kutash, K. (1992). Challenges for child and adolescent mental health. *Health Affairs, 11*(3), 125-136.

Goldstein, J., Freud, A., & Solnit, A. (1973). *Beyond the best interest of the child.* New York: Free Press.

Goldstein, J., Freud, A., & Solnit, A. (1979). *Beyond the best interest of the child* (2nd ed.). New York: Free Press.

Grisso, T., & Conlin, M. (1984). Procedural issues in the juvenile justice system. In N. D. Reppucci, L. Weithorn, E. Mulvey, & J. Monahan (Eds.), *Children, mental health, and the law* (pp. 171-193). Beverly Hills, CA: Sage.

Hardin, M. (1992). *Establishing a core of services for families subject to state intervention: A blueprint for statutory and regulatory action.* Washington, DC: American Bar Association, Center on Children and the Law.

Hawes, J. M. (1971). *Children in urban society: Juvenile delinquency in nineteenth-century America.* New York: Oxford University Press.

Henggler, S. W., & Borduin, C. M. (1990). *Family therapy and beyond: A multisystemic approach to treating the behavior problems of children and adolescents.* Pacific Grove, CA: Brooks/Cole.

Henggler, S. W., Rodick, J. D., Borduin, C. M., Hanson, C. L., Watson, S. M., & Urey, J. R. (1986). Multisystemic treatment of juvenile offenders: Effects on adolescent behavior and family interaction. *Developmental Psychology, 22,* 132-141.

Henning, J. (Ed.). (1982). *The rights of children: Legal and psychological perspectives.* Springfield, IL: Charles C Thomas.

Institute of Medicine. (1989). *Research on children and adolescents with mental, behavioral, and developmental disorders: Mobilizing a national initiative.* Washington, DC: National Academy Press.

Integrating human services: Linking at-risk families with services more successful than system reform efforts. (1992). Report to the Chairman, Subcommittee on Children, Family, Drugs and Alcoholism, Committee on Labor and Human Resources, U.S. Senate (GAO/HRD-92-108). Washington, DC: Government Printing Office.

Jackson-Beeck, M., Schwartz, I. M., & Rutherford, A. (1987). Trends and issues in juvenile confinement for psychiatric and chemical dependency treatment. *International Journal of Law and Psychiatry, 10,* 153-165.

Knitzer, J. (1982). *Unclaimed children: The failure of public responsibility to children and adolescents in need of mental health services.* Washington, DC: National Academy Press.

Knitzer, J. (1993). Children's mental health policy: Challenging the future. *Journal of Emotional and Behavioral Disorders, 1*(1), 8-16.

Kobrin, S., & Klein, M. (1983). *Community treatment of offenders: The DSO experiments.* Beverly Hills, CA: Sage.

Krisberg, B., Schwartz, I., Litsky, P., & Austin, J. (1986). The watershed of juvenile justice reform. *Crime and Delinquency, 32,* 5-38.

Lemert, E. M. (1967). The juvenile court: Quest and realities in the President's Commission on Law Enforcement and Administration of Justice. *Task force report: Juvenile delinquency and youth crime*. Washington, DC: Government Printing Office.

Levine, M., & Levine, A. (1970). *A social history of helping services: Clinic, court, school, and community*. New York: Appleton-Century-Crofts.

Lipsey, M. W. (1988). Juvenile delinquency intervention. In H. S. Bloom, D. S. Cordray, & R. J. Light (Eds.), *Lessons from selected programs and policy areas* (pp. 63-84). San Francisco: Jossey-Bass.

Lipsey, M. W. (1991). Juvenile delinquency treatment: A meta-analytic inquiry into the variability of effects. In T. Cook, H. Cooper, D. Cordray, H. Hartmann, L. Hedges, R. Light, T. Louis, & F. Mosteller (Eds.), *Meta-analysis for explanation: A casebook* (pp. 83-127). New York: Russell Sage.

Mack, J. W. (1909). The juvenile court. *Harvard Law Review, 23*, 104-122.

Macro International Inc. (1992). *Final report: Community-based mental health services for children in the child welfare system* (3 vols., Assistant Secretary for Planning and Evaluation, Department of Health and Human Services, Contract No. HHS-100-91-0016-01).

Maloy, K. (1991). *Analysis: Mental health for children: Can we get there from here?* Washington, DC: Mental Health Policy Resource Center.

Maloy, K. (1992). *Effectiveness and outcomes: Implication for policymakers*. Washington, DC: Mental Health Policy Resource Center.

McManus, M., Alessi, N. E., Grapentine, W. L., & Brickman, A. (1984). Psychiatric disturbance in serious delinquents. *Journal of the American Academy of Child Psychiatry, 23*, 602-615.

Milin, R., Halikas, J. A., Meller, J. E., & Morse, C. (1991). Psychopathology among substance abusing juvenile offenders. *Journal of the American Academy of Child and Adolescent Psychiatry, 30*, 569-574.

Miller, A., & Ohlin, L. (1985). *Delinquency and community: Creating opportunities and controls*. Beverly Hills, CA: Sage.

Miller, A., Ohlin, L., & Coates, R. (1977). *A theory of social reform: Correctional change processes in two states*. Cambridge, MA: Ballinger.

Mnookin, R. (1979). *Child, family and state: Problems and materials on children and the law*. Boston: Little, Brown.

Mulvey, E. (1982). Family courts: The issue of reasonable goals. *Law and Human Behavior, 6*, 49-64.

Mulvey, E. P. (1984). Judging amenability to treatment in juvenile offenders. In N. D. Reppucci, L. Weithorn, E. Mulvey, & J. Monahan (Eds.), *Children, mental health and the law* (pp. 195-210). Beverly Hills, CA: Sage.

Mulvey, E. P., & Phelps, P. (1988). Ethical balances in juvenile justice research and practice. *American Psychologist, 43*, 65-69.

National Advisory Commission on Criminal Justice Standards and Goals. (1976). *A national strategy to reduce crime*. Washington, DC: Government Printing Office.

National Advisory Committee on Criminal Justice Standards. (1980). *Report of the National Advisory Committee for Juvenile Justice and Delinquency Prevention: Standards for the administration of juvenile justice*. Washington, DC: U.S. Department of Justice.

National Conference of State Legislatures Health and Mental Health Program. (1989). *Coordinating juvenile justice, mental health and child welfare systems* (Office for Treatment Improvement ADAMHA Contract No. 89MF65929901D). Denver: Author.

National Council of Juvenile and Family Court Judges. (1984, Summer). The juvenile court and serious offenders. *Juvenile and Family Court Journal, 35.*

National Council of Juvenile and Family Court Judges. (1990). Minority youth in the juvenile justice system: A judicial response. *Juvenile and Family Court Journal, 41*(3A).

National Juvenile Justice Assessment Center. (1980). *Reports of the National Juvenile Justice Assessment Center: Juveniles in detention centers and jails (an analysis of state variations during the mid-1970's).* Washington, DC: U.S. Department of Justice.

Niarhos, F., & Routh, D. (1992). The role of clinical assessment in the juvenile court: Predictors of juvenile dispositions and recidivism. *Journal of Clinical Child Psychology, 21,* 151-159.

Pickett, R. S. (1969). *House of refuge: Origins of juvenile reform in New York State, 1815-1857.* Syracuse, NY: Syracuse University Press.

Reppucci, N. D. (1984). The wisdom of Solomon: Issues in child custody determination. In N. D. Reppucci, L. A. Weithorn, E. P. Mulvey, & J. Monahan (Eds.), *Children, mental health and the law* (pp. 59-78). Beverly Hills, CA: Sage.

Reppucci, N. D., & Crosby, C. A. (1993). Law, psychology, and children: Overarching issues. *Law and Human Behavior, 17*(1), 1-9.

Rog, D. J. (1992). Child and adolescent mental health services: Evaluation challenges. In L. Bickman & D. J. Rog (Eds.), *Evaluating mental health services for children* (pp. 5-16). San Francisco: Jossey-Bass.

Rubin, H. T. (1985). *Juvenile justice: Policy, practice, and law* (2nd ed.). New York: Random House.

Saxe, L., Cross, T., & Silverman, N. (1988). Children's mental health: The gap between what we know and what we do. *American Psychologist, 43,* 800-807.

Saxe, L., Cross, T., Silverman, N., Batchelor, W. F., & Dougherty, D. (1987). *Children's mental health: Problems and services.* Durham, NC: Duke University Press.

Schmidt, W. (1985). Considerations of social science in a reconsideration of *Parham v. J.R.* and the commitment of children to public mental health institutions. *Journal of Psychiatry and Law,* 339-359.

Schwartz, I., Jackson-Beeck, M., & Anderson, R. (1984). The "hidden" system of juvenile control. *Crime and Delinquency, 30,* 371-385.

Sechrest, L., & Rosenblatt, A. (1987). Research methods. In H. C. Quay (Ed.), *Handbook of juvenile delinquency* (pp. 417-450). New York: John Wiley.

Shanok, S., & Lewis, D. (1977). Juvenile court versus child guidance referral: Psychosocial and parental factors. *American Journal of Psychiatry, 134,* 1130-1133.

Soler, M., & Shauffer, C. (1990). Fighting fragmentation: Coordination of services for children and families. *Nebraska Law Review, 69,* 278-297.

Staples, W., & Warren, C. (1988). Mental health and adolescent social control. *Research in Law, Deviance and Social Control, 9,* 113-126.

Street, D., Vinter, R., & Perrow, C. (1966). *Organization for treatment.* New York: Free Press.

Stroul, B. (1989). *Series on community-based services for children and adolescents who are severely emotionally disturbed: Vol. 3. Therapeutic foster care.* Washington, DC: Georgetown University Child Development Center.

Stroul, B., & Friedman, B. (1986). *A system of care for severely emotionally disturbed children and youth.* Washington, DC: Georgetown University, Child and Adolescent Service System Program Technical Assistance Center.

Tolan, P. H., Cromwell, R. E., & Brasswell, M. (1986). Family therapy with delinquents: A critical review of the literature. *Family Process, 25,* 619-649.

Towberman, D. B. (1992). National survey of juvenile needs assessment. *Crime and Delinquency, 38,* 230-238.

U.S. Department of Justice, Office of Juvenile Justice and Delinquency Prevention. (1991, January). *Public juvenile facilities—Children in custody 1989* (Juvenile Justice Bulletin #NCJ127189). Washington, DC: Author.

Vossler-Hunter, R. W. (1989). *Changing roles, changing relationships: Parent-professional collaboration on behalf of children with emotional disabilities.* Portland, OR: Families as Allies Project.

Wadlington, W., Whitebread, C. H., & Davis, S. M. (1983). *Children in the legal system: Cases and materials.* Mineola, NY: Foundation.

Westendorp, F., Brink, K. L., Roberson, M. K., & Ortiz, I. E. (1986). Variables which differentiate placement of adolescents into juvenile justice or mental health systems. *Adolescence, 21,* 23-37.

Zeigler-Dendy, C. (1989). *Invisible Children Project.* Alexandria, VA: National Mental Health Association.

PART IV

Evaluating Children's
Mental Health Service Systems:
Three Current Examples

Systems of care have been identified as the major innovation that can help solve the problems of fragmented systems. As systems of care start to be implemented across the states and communities, the need for evaluations of the implementation, process, and effectiveness of these systems is critical for the children's mental health field. Without this information, it will be difficult, as Saxe, Cross, Lovas, and Gardner (Chapter 10) suggest, to move beyond the rhetoric in the development of systems of care for children with mental disorders.

The chapters in this section describe the three pioneer system evaluations. All three were initiated in the late 1980s for systems of care stemming from the CASSP concept. All three are multisite evaluations. At the time the chapters were initially prepared for this volume, all three evaluations were still in progress. Therefore, all three chapters focus on the design and process of the evaluations.

Clifford Attkisson and his coauthors (Chapter 11) describe the framework of the evaluation of the implementation and effectiveness of the California system-of-care model for children. The evaluation involves a clinical epidemiological investigation in four counties in the state, in which the study examines the prevalence, incidence, and distribution of mental disorders of those children serviced by major agencies in the system. By examining the gap between the population estimates of need and data from the clinical epidemiological study, it will be possible to determine the level and nature of unmet need in each of the study communities. In addition, the evaluation is examining whether the study counties are successful in shifting from service-agency-driven systems to client-oriented systems by examining changes in organization, financing, and costs of care.

Leonard Saxe and his associates at Brandeis University describe the design of and midpoint findings from the evaluation of the Robert Wood Johnson Foundation Mental Health Services Program for Youth (MHSPY; Chapter 10). Of the three evaluations described in this volume, the MHSPY evaluation is examining the broadest program in scope, involving eight sites across the country. The program is considered the first major privately funded extension of CASSP and is designed to demonstrate the feasibility and effectiveness of providing comprehensive and coordinated mental health services to children with severe emotional disturbances. The evaluation will examine whether the organization and financing of mental health services can improve the services that are provided, and thus is measuring changes in the comprehensiveness and coordination of services and the appropriateness of treatment plans developed for clients of the system.

In Chapter 9, Leonard Bickman and Craig Anne Heflinger describe the Fort Bragg Evaluation, an independent evaluation of the Fort Bragg Child and Adolescent Mental Health Demonstration. The demonstration is testing a full continuum-of-care delivery system with services tailored to individual needs. The theory being tested is that a comprehensive, integrated, and coordinated continuum of services is more cost-effective than a fragmented service system with a limited variety of services. The evaluation involves a quasi-experimental design in which the children and families receiving services in the Fort Bragg treatment site are compared to children and families receiving traditional services in two other army bases. Bickman discusses the theory-driven focus of the evaluation, describing how the study must first rule out implementation and evaluation failures in order to test the systems theory underlying the demonstration.

Seeking Success by Reducing
Implementation and Evaluation Failures

LEONARD BICKMAN
CRAIG ANNE HEFLINGER

Evaluations frequently show that programs do not produce the positive effects anticipated by sponsors and other stakeholders. This result is often taken as evidence that the program failed—it just did not work. However, this conclusion is vague and needs to be clearer about *what* did not work. First, the theory underlying the program may be wrong. Program theory is "the plausible and sensible model of how the program is supposed to work" (Bickman, 1987, p. 5) or "a set of propositions regarding what goes on in the black box during the transformation of input to output, that is, how a bad situation is transformed into a better one" (Lipsey, 1990, p. 4). Program theory

AUTHORS' NOTE: We acknowledge the contributions made to this chapter and program of research by other members of the Center for Mental Health Policy—in particular, Ana Maria Brannan, Carolyn Breda, Debbie Bryant, Cathy Burciaga, Ken Davis, Pam Guthrie, Warren Lambert, and Tom Summerfelt. This research was supported by the U.S. Army Health Services Command (DA-DA10-89C-0013) as a subcontract from the North Carolina Department of Human Resources/Division of Mental Health, Developmental Disabilities, and Substance Abuse Services, and a grant to Leonard Bickman (RO1MH-46136-01) from the National Institute of Mental Health.

can describe how one could go about solving a social problem on the basis of certain assumptions. However, if these assumptions are wrong, then the evaluation may correctly show that the program did not have the desired effect. For example, if it is assumed that the impact of mental health services on children's mental health would be strengthened if the services were more coordinated, then improving the coordination should result in better mental health outcomes. But if in fact coordination bears no relationship to mental health outcomes, then no effect should be found on mental health status. Theories can be based on what stakeholders believe to be important factors, social science data, or both. Testing the program theory is the most important function of an evaluation. But, faced with no effects, the evaluator must rule out other reasons for the null effects before he or she can conclude that the theory was incorrect. In planning an evaluation, it is important for the evaluator to anticipate these other factors and reduce the possibility that they are affecting the evaluation.

Two additional reasons that an evaluation may indicate that the intervention had no effect are (a) the failure to properly implement the program and (b) the failure to conduct an appropriate evaluation. The latter two reasons prevent a valid test of the program theory. This chapter uses our experience with the Fort Bragg Evaluation to clarify the relationships between these three factors: *theory, implementation,* and *evaluation failure.* In particular, we describe the actions the evaluators have taken to document the implementation of the demonstration and help guard against evaluation failure. First, we describe the Fort Bragg Demonstration and Evaluation.

Children's Mental Health Service System Issues

As Debra J. Rog (Chapter 1) and others have discussed, a strong consensus exists concerning the problematic manner in which mental health services are typically provided to children. Many children do not receive any services, and others receive inappropriate services. In the past two decades, many experts (Hobbs, 1982; Knitzer, 1982; Stroul & Friedman, 1986) have highlighted the vast discrepancy between the number of children and youth in need of mental health services and the number who receive appropriate services. It is estimated that 11% to 19% of children and adolescents are in need of mental health services (Saxe, Cross, & Silverman, 1988). More than half of these children receive no treatment, and many who are treated receive inappropriate care (Saxe et al., 1988). Senator Inouye (1988) maintained that 80% of the children who need services were receiving inappropriate care or none at all.

There is also agreement that unnecessarily restrictive treatment settings are overutilized (Dorwart, Schlesinger, Davidson, Epstein, & Hoover, 1991; Weithorn, 1988; Zeigler-Dendy, 1989). It is believed that children with emotional problems are best treated in the least restrictive, most normative environment that is clinically appropriate (Stroul & Friedman, 1986). However, the number of private psychiatric hospitals showed continued growth during the 1980s (Bickman & Dokecki, 1989). The best estimate to date (Burns, 1990) is that more than 70% of the funding for children's mental health services nationwide is spent on institutional care. The extent of residential mental health treatment is much greater than even those figures suggest once a broader system perspective is considered (Kiesler & Simpkins, 1991, 1993).

Contributing to the problem of unnecessary restrictive treatment is the fact that alternative treatment settings are generally unavailable. Knitzer (1982), Behar (1985), and Silver (1984) all reported that approximately 40% of inpatient placements were inappropriate because either the children could have been treated in less restrictive settings or the placements that were initially appropriate were no longer appropriate, but less restrictive treatment settings were not available. This remains the situation despite the strongly held belief that even severely emotionally disturbed children can receive treatment while living in their own homes when a comprehensive system of care is present in the community (Behar, 1985).

Even where services are available, the lack of coordination between programs compromises the effectiveness of the interventions (Saxe, Cross, Silverman, Batchelor, & Dougherty, 1987; Soler & Shaffer, 1990; Stroul & Friedman, 1986). Given the developmental complexity and multiple needs of children and adolescents, services should be both available and coordinated if they are to address the needs of these children effectively (Behar, 1985).

The continuum-of-care approach has been developed in response to the problems characterizing mental health service delivery systems for children and adolescents. The term *continuum of care* refers to a comprehensive and coordinated range of services required to treat severely disturbed children and adolescents that includes both nonresidential and residential services (Stroul & Friedman, 1986). Moreover, an emphasis on midrange or intermediate-level services is also emerging. This approach attempts to deliver needed services on an individualized basis and in a coordinated manner, relying on case management and interdisciplinary treatment teams to integrate treatment programs and facilitate transitions between services. It also is designed to be community based, involving various agencies pertinent to children's developmental, social, medical, and mental health needs.

The Fort Bragg Continuum of Care

The Fort Bragg Demonstration was based on the continuum-of-care approach and will be used to illustrate the concerns about theory, implementation, and evaluation failure. Before describing in greater detail the Fort Bragg Demonstration, however, we give background information about the typical services that are provided to dependents insured under the Civilian Health and Medical Program of the Uniformed Services, commonly known as CHAMPUS and similar to most third-party payer systems.

Traditional CHAMPUS Services

The high cost of providing mental health services to the children and adolescents of military personnel stimulated CHAMPUS to consider alternatives to the existing delivery system. Between 1985 and 1989, mental health costs for both children and adults doubled to more than $600 million per year, although the number of beneficiaries remained relatively constant. Inpatient care increased from $200 million to almost $500 million in the same 5-year period, and mental health care to children and adolescents in hospitals and residential treatment centers (RTCs) accounted for 3 out of every 4 days of total inpatient mental health care. In 1991, about $305 million were for treatment of children and adolescents, with approximately $164 million being paid to RTCs (Baine, 1992).

CHAMPUS has traditionally provided much more generous coverage of mental health treatment than provider insurance. In 1991, CHAMPUS allowed 45 days of inpatient or hospital care, 150 days of RTC care, and 23 outpatient visits per year. Additional treatment was allowed only under unusual circumstances. Most private insurance does not cover care in an RTC. CHAMPUS also covers about twice as many outpatient visits as many private insurers, and no lifetime benefit or dollar limit is imposed as with other insurers (Baine, 1992). CHAMPUS requires a $150 deductible per person and $300 per family. A co-payment of 20% of allowable charges is required for outpatient services, and a small daily fee or $25 per day, whichever is more, for inpatient services (Office of CHAMPUS, 1992). Prior to 1991, no limitation on the number of covered RTC days existed.

The Department of Defense (DOD) has instituted several cost control procedures during the period covered by this evaluation. At approximately the same time that data collection started for the Fort Bragg Evaluation (October 1990), preadmission authorization for residential care became mandatory in most areas covered by CHAMPUS. It is reported that although total CHAMPUS costs increased in fiscal year 1991, there was a slight (0.26%) reduction in mental health costs; however, RTC costs continued to increase. Under these new cost control procedures, average length of stay in RTCs dropped from 188 days to 136 days, and for acute hospitalization from 23.6 days to 18.6 days from 1990 to 1991. However, the number of hospital admissions increased 17%, the number of RTC admissions went up 13%, and admission for inpatient substance abuse rose 65% during this period (Martin, 1992).

The DOD has responded to the increases in CHAMPUS costs by implementing a coordinated care effort that makes local hospital commanders responsible for limiting expenditures in their catchment area. Under this Gateway to Care Program, more beneficiaries are treated in military hospitals. As of May 1992, the DOD has also authorized payment of partial hospitalization at some sites (Nelson, 1993).

No definitive study has yet been completed that has demonstrated the superiority of the continuum-of-care model to more traditional methods of service delivery. In fact, significant controversy exists about managed care systems in general. The application of a variety of managed care schemes to children's mental health services by CHAMPUS has recently been debated in a congressional hearing (Select Committee, 1992). Furthermore, studies dealing with some CHAMPUS reform initiatives are themselves surrounded with controversy (General Accounting Office, 1992, 1993a, 1993b). These previous evaluations dealt only with cost and utilization, not with the therapeutic effects on those being served. The Fort Bragg Evaluation is the first comprehensive evaluation of a system of care that includes the comprehensive assessment of mental health outcomes.

The Fort Bragg Demonstration Project

In 1986, Lenore Behar, director of children's services for the North Carolina Department of Human Resources, Division of Mental Health, Developmental Disabilities, and Substance Abuse Services (DMH/DD/SAS), and a nationally known consultant on children's mental health services, developed the demonstration concept and by 1987 had gathered a small group to plan a program and an evaluation of a system of care that would be an alternative to traditional CHAMPUS services. Congress requested the Department of the Army, in August 1989, to fund the Fort Bragg Child and Adolescent Mental Health Demonstration Project (the demonstration) and independent evaluation through a contract with the DMH/DD/SAS.

The North Carolina DMH/DD/SAS contracted with Cardinal Mental Health Group, Inc. (Cardinal), a private, not-for-profit corporation located in Fayetteville, North Carolina, to provide a continuum of care for the Fort Bragg catchment area (an approximately 40-mile radius surrounding the army post) involving services to eligible military dependents under the age of 18. Using a closed-system or exclusive provider organization model, families seeking services for their children and adolescents were required to use the demonstration's clinical services, which were free, or to choose to seek and pay for services on their own. The range of services included both community-based nonresidential and residential treatment components. Cardinal contracted with individuals and agencies in the community already providing traditional mental health services, such as outpatient therapy and acute inpatient hospitalization, and itself provided intensive outpatient treatment. Across the country, Cardinal developed services not previously available, including in-home counseling, after-school group treatment services, day treatment services, therapeutic homes, specialized group homes, and 24-hour crisis management teams. All children and adolescents requesting services received a comprehensive intake/assessment to determine the appropriate level of service.

For children using more than outpatient services, the clinical services were coordinated with the other child-serving agencies and practitioners in the community, especially pediatric, educational, and protective services. Services within the continuum and across other agencies were linked through a case management component and interdisciplinary treatment teams led by a doctoral-level staff person. Related services such as transportation and other wraparound services were also provided. All services provided by or through the Rumbaugh Clinic were done without any financial cost to the family.

The services had no financial barriers to the families (i.e., no copayments or deductibles). Moreover, because this project was initiated as a cost reimbursement contract, theoretically no limits were placed on types of services to be offered or the cost of these services. The demonstration was to provide the best possible services that the children required, without the usual limitations placed on providers by either insurance companies or other public agencies. Thus, this was to be a test of the continuum-of-care model without the severe financial limitations or implementation problems usually found when multiple agencies need to collaborate and pool funds. However, Cardinal was well aware of the scrutiny of its operations from the state, the army, and Congress and was under pressure to produce the most cost-effective treatment possible. The cost of the demonstration and the evaluation together was approximately $17 million per year.

The Fort Bragg Evaluation Component

The Center for Mental Health Policy of the Vanderbilt Institute for Public Policy Studies at Vanderbilt University was awarded a

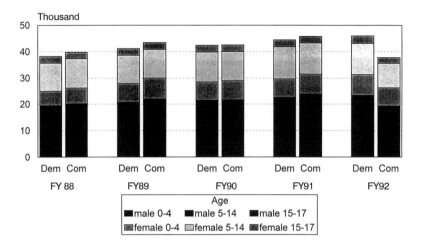

Figure 9.1. Population of Eligible Children: Age and Sex by Site

subcontract by the North Carolina DMH/DD/SAS to conduct an independent evaluation of the demonstration. The study is longitudinal, with the initial baseline data being collected within approximately 30 days of entry into the service system, followed by three additional waves approximately 6 months apart. Extensive and complex recruitment procedures were followed to maximize participation in the evaluation. The sample was weighted toward those receiving the most expensive care, and participation by families was voluntary.

    Although the evaluation was unable to use random assignment of children to different systems of care, two comparison sites were designated by the army at Fort Campbell, Kentucky, and at Fort Stewart, Georgia, where children and adolescents received care traditionally covered by CHAMPUS. Primary consideration was given to the following factors in selecting the comparison sites: geographic location, size of military and dependent populations, types of units assigned and readiness requirements of the major command, and availability of on-post mental health services. For example, Figure 9.1 shows the comparability in age of children in the catchment areas. Finding such equivalence would be very difficult to accomplish in a study of civilian services and makes the quasi-experiment stronger than usual.

Theory Failure

Several program evaluation theorists (Bickman, 1987, 1990; Chen & Rossi, 1992; Lipsey, 1990) differentiate between program theory failure and program implementation failure. In the current study, the theory being tested is that a comprehensive and coordinated system of mental health care is more cost-effective than a fragmented service system with a limited variety of services. The theory can only be tested if the demonstration implements this theory sufficiently well and the evaluation methods are valid. Figure 9.2 shows the evaluators' conceptualization of the theory of the demonstration, indicating several underlying assumptions. Most of these assumptions have been tested in the evaluation.

The Fort Bragg Program Theory

Starting on the left side of Figure 9.2 are the *intake* characteristics of this system. The topmost box indicates that there is a single point of entry into the system. Unlike many nonsystems or more complex systems, the eligible population can receive mental health services only through the Rumbaugh Clinic. As part of their contract, the demonstration had to provide these services at no cost to the client. Thus, there was no co-payment or deductible associated with any service. As noted earlier, families can choose to obtain services outside the system, but they must either pay for those services themselves or pay through another insurer. This single point of entry is important because it allows the Rumbaugh Clinic to control access to services. Moreover, it should be simple for potential clients to know where mental health services can be obtained.

As part of the contract with the army, the state had to ensure that clients would receive an intake and subsequent service promptly. The contract originally called for the diagnosis and assessment to begin within 1 week after a referral for nonemergency cases, and for the assessment to be completed and reviewed by a treatment team within

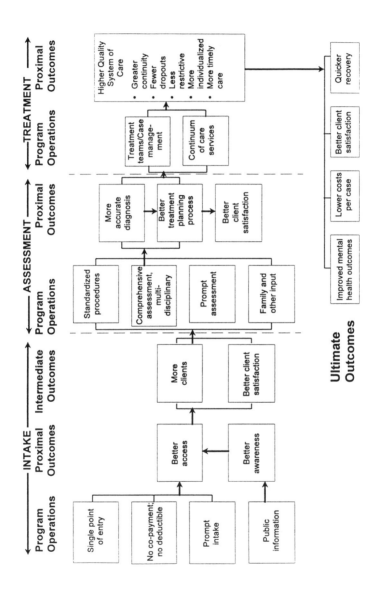

Figure 9.2. Fort Bragg Child and Adolescent Demonstration: Program Theory

2 weeks or less. Because of the unexpected high client flow, this standard for completion of assessment was later amended to 3 weeks instead of 1 week. Standards of timeliness are not part of nonsystems of care. As shown in the bottom-most box in the left-hand column of Figure 9.2, at the start of services the Rumbaugh Clinic was required to engage in a public information or marketing program to inform both the providers and potential clients about the new system of care. These activities are hypothesized to produce a proximal outcome of an increase in access to services. This increased access should result in three intermediate outcomes: increasing the number of clients served, treating more mild and more severe cases, and increasing client satisfaction about the intake process from what one would expect from the traditional CHAMPUS services. The hypothesis related to increasing the number of clients served is obviously based on reducing many barriers to obtaining services. It is expected that when clients know where to receive services and are not charged for them, more will seek out services.

The second main section of this figure illustrates the program operations during the *assessment* process. All families are given a standard intake process. This usually includes comprehensive testing and a review by an interdisciplinary treatment team. Again, the contract sets standards for prompt assessment (within 3 weeks) and input from family and other relevant professionals. These program activities are hypothesized to lead to three proximal outcomes: (a) a more accurate diagnosis that should lead to (b) a better treatment planning process and (c) increased client satisfaction with the assessment process. A more accurate diagnosis should be expected because of the comprehensive assessment process and involvement of the multidisciplinary team. Treatment planning should be improved because of the increased accuracy about the child's strengths and weaknesses. Client satisfaction with the assessment process should be improved because of the involvement of the family and the perceived accuracy of the assessment process.

The actual *treatment* provided by the demonstration includes management of the more complex cases by the treatment team and the clinical case manager and access to the wide variety of services available in the continuum of care. As noted earlier, the services provided by the demonstration include hospitals, residential treatment centers, in-home counseling, after-school treatment services, day treatment services, therapeutic homes, specialized group homes, a 24-hour crisis management team, wraparound services, and intensive outpatient treatment. These program activities should lead to the proximal outcome of more appropriate care provided to the child: that is, a better match between the needs of the child and the family and the treatment provided. Operationally, *appropriateness* can be defined as care that

- Is more individualized
- Has more timely transitions between levels of care
- Has continuity between services
- Occurs in less restrictive settings
- Has fewer dropouts from treatment

The demonstration should lead to the following ultimate outcomes as compared to mental health treatment provided under traditional CHAMPUS: improved mental health, lower costs per case, quicker recovery, and more client satisfaction. The more appropriate services should increase the probability that treatment affects the client. Although the total costs of the demonstration may be higher, primarily because of an increase in the number of clients treated, it is expected that similar cases will cost less at the demonstration than at the comparison sites. However, it is recognized that these last hypotheses may have to be examined together to discern the true effects of the demonstration. That is, it is expected that for similar cases, the demonstration will be more cost-effective than traditional care. This ratio of effectiveness to cost will be the ultimate outcome that is so important to the evaluation.

Implementation Failure

According to the model presented in Figure 9.2, the demonstration must meet these multiple assumptions to be successful. If any one of these assumptions is not met, then the demonstration may fail. Stakeholders are most interested in testing the theory of the demonstration, not just in knowing if the demonstration was well implemented. However, in order to test the theory, the demonstration has to be properly implemented. Thus, it is important for the evaluation to confirm that the demonstration was implemented properly at both the systems and services levels.

Because this theory is testing a systems-level intervention, it is important to differentiate this intervention from a simpler services-level intervention. The systems-level evaluation is concerned with the effectiveness of the organization and delivery of services in contrast to examining the effectiveness of a specific service. It is the complex package of services that is being tested and not individual direct clinical services such as psychotherapy or individual components such as case management.

Thus, it follows that the systems theory can be valid and the evaluation may still show that the demonstration is not more cost-effective unless four assumptions are met:

1. The theory at the systems level must be well implemented.
2. The theory at the services level must be valid.
3. The theory at the services level must be well implemented.
4. The evaluation must be well implemented.

We are simplifying this description a bit here by not questioning the theory of the evaluation—that is, the use of scientific methods to discover truth. But alas, this is also an assumption.

A program failure can occur if the theory at either the systems or services level is not well implemented. Thus, program failure can be divided into two categories: (a) systems failure and (b) services failure. The former is concerned with the systems-level aspects of the demonstration, such as intake/assessment, case management, and the variety of services that are available for treating clients. A services failure deals with the implementation of the direct mental health services that are provided to the clients, such as group therapy. Finally, the theory could be correct and well implemented at both the systems and the services level, but the evaluation could still fail to detect a positive effect on the clients because of the distinct but (it is hoped) rare event of a faulty evaluation.

Systems-Level Implementation

At the systems level, the demonstration needs to put in place the appropriate components of service and ensure that the components are well integrated. These services must be available to clients in a timely manner. The system must also allow timely transitions from one service level to another. That is, the level of service needs of clients must be carefully monitored, and changes in these needs should be responded to quickly. If the demonstration does not implement these critical features of the theory, then the evaluation cannot test the theory. Both the services and the management of these services must be present: That is, an excellent case management system will not affect clinical outcomes unless appropriate direct mental health services are made available. The demonstration management and staff are responsible for the appropriate implementation of the theory at the systems level.

The evaluation is responsible for documenting the implementation of the theory but cannot precisely judge the effectiveness of individual components of the demonstration at the systems level (e.g., intake/assessment, case management, cohesiveness of the system) because assignment of clients to those system components was not random but systematically related to their needs. This is an important limitation of the evaluation in that there are *no* studies with this population of clients that demonstrate that any of the specific components at the systems level (e.g., case management) actually improve the mental health of clients if properly implemented.

The evaluation has assessed the possibility of failure at the systems level by several methods. First, we provide a brief discussion of the evaluation's analysis of the implementation of the demonstration. Next, we describe findings concerning the measurement of the quality of two key systems-level components. Finally, we examine service utilization to test differences between the demonstration and comparison sites that are related to the program theory.

Implementation Analysis

Several steps are needed to examine comprehensively the implementation of a model demonstration program. First, the theories and assumptions underlying the intervention should be explicated, as done above and represented in Figure 9.2. Second, the program as implemented must be compared to the program as planned. Finally, any structural, environmental, and political barriers responsible for diluting full-scale implementation of the program must be documented.

The overall strategy for examining program implementation was based on the theory-driven and component approaches (Bickman, 1985, 1987, 1990; Chen, 1990; Chen & Rossi, 1983) to program evaluation. These evaluators have nominated specific structural and procedural aspects of implementation as foci for each of the major implementation questions posed above. A case study approach (Yin, 1986, 1993) was taken to describe the structure and processes of the demonstration, with a focus on operations during the third year of the demonstration, fiscal year 1992, as an example of the fully functioning system. This case study approach incorporated multiple methods and multiple sources of information. First, the demonstration generated a wealth of documentation that was available for review and analysis, including correspondence, program descriptions, policies and procedures, administrative reports, and committee meeting minutes. Second, a series of semistructured interviews was held with key stakeholders. Third, the evaluation had available a comprehensive set of outcome and utilization data describing participants at the demonstration and comparison sites. Finally, a series of questionnaires and interviews with service providers and service agency representatives from all sites yielded information on the mental health system for children and adolescents and their families at the demonstration and comparison sites. These instruments included responses to scales measuring philosophy of care (Jerrell & Hargreave, 1991), consumer feedback from specially designed satisfaction surveys, and a network analysis. The latter substudy employed the network analysis approach (Marsden, 1990; Morrissey, 1992) to assess the extent to which a coordinated system of care existed at each of the three sites. This approach focused on the organization, structure, and process of mental health service delivery.

From these data to compare the program as implemented to the program as planned, it is evident that the demonstration was implemented consistently with the expectations of the contract and program theory.[1]

1. The demonstration implemented a single point of entry to services for the target population.

2. The demonstration met the terms of the contract regarding participant eligibility: age, beneficiary status, and diagnostic eligibility.

3. The demonstration served three times the number of children originally estimated. Also, on the basis of preliminary data for July 1991 through December 1991, it served 6.1% of the Fort Bragg beneficiary population aged less than 18, representing more than twice the number of children being served before the demonstration was implemented. The 6.1% served does not reflect inappropriately high utilization; this figure remains substantially less than the nationally reported prevalence of serious mental disorders.

4. Clients served at the demonstration showed similar clinical characteristics of at least the same severity as clients served through CHAMPUS at the comparison sites.

5. Client participation at the demonstration site was increased by

   a. Removal of barriers to care, such as co-payment and deductible, for which a parent is responsible under CHAMPUS

   b. Clear community information on where services were available

   c. Positive community impressions about the demonstration project that overcame the stigma of requesting mental health services

6. The continuum-of-care model proposed by the demonstration was implemented according to the expectations of the contract and program service philosophy through the provision of

   a. A comprehensive range of services, including the development of intermediate service levels (intensive outpatient and substance abuse services, in-home crisis stabilization, day treatment, therapeutic home services, and group homes)

   b. Case management and multidisciplinary treatment teams for clients in the most intensive levels of care

   c. A high level of coordination throughout the community of mental health services for military-dependent children and youth. (This finding can be explored in more depth here to provide a concrete picture of the findings from the network analysis.)

The network analysis provided a measure of coordination for the overall mental health service system at each site that indicated a good flow of information and resources among the various agencies despite the "cliques" or subgroups to which agencies were most strongly connected.[2] In network analysis, *coordination* refers to the ability of all agencies to interact with other agencies in the community. If a community network is fragmented, tight subgroups of agencies interact only within their own subgroup. Coordination is the opposite: Despite the presence of tight subgroups, agencies engage with other agencies outside their own subgroup as well. This measure of coordination was at the community level, and similarity between sites regarded the mental health service system for all children, not just military dependents.

Mental health service providers and other community respondents also rated to what extent they thought a coordinated system of mental health services existed for (a) all children, youth, and their families in their communities and (b) military-dependent children, youth, and their families who were served through the demonstration or CHAMPUS at the comparison sites. When general service system coordination was assessed, the Fort Bragg area was rated as only slightly more coordinated than the service system at the Forts Campbell or Stewart areas. The relative equivalence between sites when community-wide service coordination is examined confirmed the general findings of the network analysis discussed above.

However, when community respondents were asked about service system coordination for military-dependent children and youth, the Fort Bragg area received a significantly more positive rating than the comparison sites. Figure 9.3 presents these findings. Therefore, despite very similarly functioning mental health service systems for *all* children and youth in the three sites, the Fort Bragg site was significantly more coordinated in services for *military-dependent children.*

Additional findings of the implementation study indicate that at the demonstration

1. Qualified staff were recruited, hired, and trained.
2. A fully operational quality improvement system was implemented.
3. The effects of the demonstration's coordination of services at the community level on the military-dependent children and youth in the Fort Bragg area included:

   a. Fewer reported systems-level problems
   b. Greater adequacy and quality of mental health services available
   c. Better service system performance
   d. Better adherence to the goals of an ideal service system

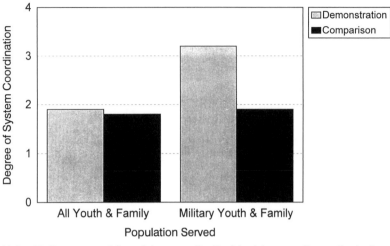

Note: Ratings ranged from 0 (no coordination) to 4 (very well coordinated).

Figure 9.3. Coordination of Systems of Care

In each of these areas, the effects on military-dependent children and youth were rated as having improved over time and as being significantly more positive at Fort Bragg than at the comparison sites of Fort Campbell and Fort Stewart.

In conclusion, the implementation study provided not only a comprehensive description of *how* the demonstration was put in place but also the evidence necessary to conclude that the demonstration was executed with sufficient fidelity, despite barriers, to provide an excellent test of the program theory—the continuum of care.

Quality of Systems-Level Key Components

From the evaluation project's perspective, the quality study[3] and the previously described implementation study were critical not only in describing the substance of the demonstration but in setting the stage for the subsequent cost/utilization and outcome studies. The evaluation project needed to have evidence that the program theory was implemented as planned at the systems level and that the key systems-level components of service were of sufficient quality to have the theoretically predicted effect on mental health.

Quality in relation to mental health services is complex to define (Bickman & Peterson, 1990; McGlynn, Norquist, Wells, & Lieberman, 1988; Peterson & Bickman, 1992; Wells, 1988). Mental health services have many components and dimensions, and the definition of *quality* in this regard may differ by whether the judgments are made by the individual, the health care provider, the payer, or, ultimately, society. Thus, it has been recognized that the definition of *quality* depends on who does the valuing.

As noted earlier, most previous research on services may be described as having a *black box* approach, in that it studies inputs and outcomes, but not what goes on in the box, which is actual service. This study was an initial attempt to systematically represent some workings within the black box. The component theory of evaluation (Bickman, 1985) was developed as a comprehensive means of first describing and then assessing statewide services delivered to preschool children. The logic behind this approach is that evaluations can be designed to examine individual components of a program (or service) rather than the entire program/service. A component is viewed as the largest homogeneous unit of a service. Components, then, serve as the building blocks of services and, although not fully independent of one another, may be studied separately.

At the core of the component method is identification of critical components of a service or program, then the prioritization of those components based on the judgments of experts. The resulting product is an inventory of components. An advantage of the component approach is that it is in tune with a "continuous improvement" theory of quality (Berwick, 1990) that aims at working alongside providers to improve services. The component approach fits well here because it provides an evaluation of key components rather than of the service as a whole. This approach avoids labeling the entire service as good or bad, instead focusing on different aspects of different services.

The quality study assessed the quality of two service system components unique and crucial to the continuum-of-care model: *intake assessment* and *case management.* Intake assessment and case management were chosen as the foci for the quality study because they are especially vital to the effectiveness of the demonstration: That is, they are defined, developed, and implemented differently in the continuum of care than in typical treatment settings. Furthermore, these two components were selected because they encompass the primary activities and philosophies of the program (continuum of care, least restrictive services, etc.).

The instruments used to measure the quality of services for both components were similar. They included (a) an instrument measuring parental satisfaction with the intake assessment, treatment planning, and case management; (b) a semistructured interview administered to staff members performing intake assessment that addressed background, job attitude, and perceptions of the intake process; (c) a scale of the philosophy of care also administered to all Rumbaugh Clinic staff (the Community Program Philosophy Scale); (d) a questionnaire administered to direct service providers outside the Rumbaugh Clinic about the quality of intake assessment at Rumbaugh Clinic; (e) a week-long activity log completed by case managers; (f) an expert review of medical records; and (g) a network analysis examining the interagency coordination of services and the impact of that coordination at both demonstration and comparison sites.

The results of the quality study showed that the intake assessment component was of high quality:

1. Parents were satisfied with the intake assessment service they received, and staff members were pleased with their job.
2. Providers outside the clinic rated the Rumbaugh Clinic intake process as being of high quality.
3. The expert reviewer was able to find documented evidence of quality indicators within the clinical records.
4. The intake assessment at the demonstration was rated as the highest in adequacy and quality of all the support services available.

The data also illustrate considerable faithfulness by the intake assessment staff to the indices of quality identified by the stakeholder groups as well as the philosophy of the demonstration.

The data dealing with the case management component indicated that the case management services at Rumbaugh Clinic were exemplary for most of the clients, with a high degree of fidelity to the values of the stakeholders.

1. There was a strong emphasis on planning and coordination of the treatment plan, which was in keeping with the written expectations of the army contract and the job description for case managers.
2. Careful attention was paid to meeting the standards for treatment reviews and level-of-care criteria.
3. The general positive satisfaction ratings by parents suggested that these activities were carried out in a way that promoted client and family involvement. More details concerning the implementation and quality studies can be found in their respective final reports.

Utilization of Services

An additional and critical form of evidence of the successful implementation of this system difference is showing that different types of services were received by similar clients at the demonstration and comparison sites. Although improving the quality of traditional services may have an effect on mental health outcomes, this is not the primary objective of this demonstration. The key aspect of the theory of the demonstration is the centralized management of traditional services plus provision of nontraditional services that are believed to be more appropriate for the client. As noted earlier, these services include group homes, therapeutic homes, day treatment, and the availability of wraparound or other supportive services. The following are the service utilization data that were obtained from the Rumbaugh Clinic management information system (MIS) and the CHAMPUS claims data set. At this point in the project, preliminary data are available from the period July 1, 1991, to December 31, 1991.

The first important question about services concerns access to care. A significant outcome of the demonstration, as shown in Figure 9.2 depicting the program theory, is to increase access by reducing financial costs to the family, providing a central and single point of intake, and educating the community about the availability of a variety of services.

From July 1, 1991, through December 31, 1991, more than three times as many children were served in the demonstration as in the comparison sites, accounting for approximately 6% of the eligible population in contrast to approximately 2% in the comparison sites. The 6% figure is still considerably less than the 11% to 19% estimates of the percentage of children in the general population who are in need of mental health services. Even with high accessibility and few financial barriers, less than one half to one third of the children estimated to need services were being served at the demonstration, and a much smaller proportion at the comparison sites.

The next two tables are concerned with the utilization of services by children and adolescents. Services in these analyses have been categorized into inpatient hospital, residential treatment center (RTC), intermediate residential and nonresidential, and outpatient services. The intermediate residential category includes services provided in therapeutic group homes, therapeutic foster care, acute care group homes, and a wilderness camp. The intermediate nonresidential category includes day treatment, after-school/evening activities, latency partial hospitalization, in-home services, and clinical case management. Outpatient services include outpatient therapy, inpatient periodic (not overnight) intake/assessment, and evaluation. The intermediate services were available only at the demonstration site, as they were not reimbursable under traditional CHAMPUS benefits at that time. Table 9.1 shows, on the left, the percentage of the treated population who received any treatment in the demonstration or comparison sites during this time period. On the right side, it shows the percentage of children who received their most restrictive level of care in that setting during that time period. Approximately 10% of the children who received treatment in the CHAMPUS-funded comparison sites were hospitalized in contrast to 4% in the demonstration site. Less than 1% of the children at the demonstration received care in an RTC during this period compared to about 5% in the comparison sites. For these two restrictive settings, more than three times as many treated children received care in the more restrictive environments. In contrast, over a third of the children treated in the demonstration received an intermediate level of care that was not available at the comparison sites.

Table 9.1 Percentage of Treated Population Receiving Five Service Levels

	All Services Received[a]		Most Restrictive Service Received	
Type of Service	*Demonstration*	*Comparison*	*Demonstration*	*Comparison*
Hospital	3.9	9.9	3.9	9.9
RTC	0.6	5.1	0.3	4.0
Intermediate residential[b]	2.9	—	1.8	—
Intermediate nonresidential[b]	39.0	—	33.6	—
Outpatient	82.8	89.2	46.6	81.5

NOTE: Demonstration n = 2620, comparison n = 831.
a. These columns may contain duplicated counts because a child is counted once for each service received.
b. In the comparison sites, no intermediate services were available.

Table 9.2 shows the average number of days during this time that children in the treated population spent in a hospital or residential treatment center and the number of outpatient sessions. Interestingly, hospitalized children from both sites spent an average of about 26 days in the hospital during this 6-month period. In contrast, children who received services in a RTC at the comparison site spent an average of approximately 75 days compared to 46 days at the demonstration. However, reversing this trend, the demonstration clients experienced more than twice as many outpatient sessions on the average.

To summarize these utilization trends, the demonstration made available a large number of alternative services. They served three times as many eligible children and served them in less restrictive settings.

In summary, the Fort Bragg Demonstration can be viewed as a very successful implementation of the continuum-of-care theory at the systems level. Data from the implementation and quality studies demonstrate that the model was implemented with great fidelity. Early services utilization data indicate that access to care has more than tripled. Children who were in treatment at the demonstration site were more likely to avoid a hospital stay than children at the comparison sites. These findings indicate that the implementation

Table 9.2 Service Utilization in the Evaluation Sample (Averages)

	Demonstration	Comparison
Hospital days	27	25
RTC days	46	75
Outpatient visits	13	5

failure at the demonstration site is unlikely. The stage is now set to determine if this type of care is better for children and adolescents. In addition, a careful examination of cost-effectiveness is underway.[4]

Services-Level Implementation

The next way a demonstration can appear to fail is at the services level. The demonstration's staff and management may faithfully and completely implement all of the systems-level aspects of the theory, yet the evaluation may show that the demonstration had no effect. This outcome is possible if the direct mental health services (e.g., psychotherapy) are not effective in altering the clients' mental health status. These components of services (e.g., outpatient psychotherapy, hospitalization, day treatment, in-home services, etc.) may fail to be effective for two reasons: (a) They are, in fact, ineffective; and/or (b) the demonstration does not implement them with sufficient quality. As with the systems-level components, the former is a real risk because no previous studies have demonstrated that psychotherapy with children and adolescents is effective in community settings (Weisz & Weiss, 1993), nor is there any clear scientific evidence that the other forms of intervention used in the demonstration are efficacious. Thus, the demonstration theory may be correct (i.e., that a system of care is better), and the demonstration may be adequately implemented at the systems level, yet the evaluation may not show any effects on clients' mental health. That is, the demonstration may be very effectively delivering seemingly appropriate and timely services that are ineffective themselves. This is akin to simply rearranging the chairs on the deck of the Titanic in an attempt to keep it afloat. Finally, the services may be theoretically effective, but the demonstration may not deliver them with sufficient fidelity to have an effect.

The demonstration is responsible for delivering what are currently believed to be the best services available but is not responsible for the actual effectiveness of those services. Like all practitioners in the field, those conducting the demonstration must assume the effectiveness of these direct services. As at the systems level, the evaluation documented the implementation of the continuum-of-care theory and its proximal effects on utilization, but is unable to judge with much precision the effectiveness of individual service components because clients were not randomly assigned to individual components. It is doubtful that statistical adjustment for the strong selection factors that were responsible for clients receiving particular types of patterns of services could be successful.

Quality Improvement Activities

To examine the effectiveness or quality of every direct component of care in a continuum is impossible in any single study. As a pragmatic and economical substitute for studying each component of care, however, extant program resources can often be used to study services-level issues. The evaluation has depended upon the assessment of the demonstration's own quality improvement (QI) activities. According to the stipulations of the Department of the Army contract, the demonstration must follow the requirements of the Joint Commission on Accreditation of Health Care Organizations (JCAHO). Consistent with the JCAHO model (JCAHO, 1991, 1993), QI is a complex management tool, including (a) credentialing and privileging of clinicians, (b) monitoring against indicators of quality programming, (c) clinical care studies, and (d) utilization reviews. Indicators are developed for each service component to reflect issues of quality and to identify areas needing further investigation through clinical care studies. Examples of such indicators are (a) in emergency services, the number of clients moving from telephone interview to face-to-face interview to hospital admission per month; or (b) in diagnostic services, the number of days elapsing between the family's request for services and the scheduled intake assessment. Essentially, in areas where the demonstration planned to implement QI activities, the evaluation assessed the extent to which the demonstration met its own QI criteria and standards. The evaluation team's efforts here were supplemented by a consultant who had extensive experience in this area.

The consultant's report indicated that the Rumbaugh Clinic's QI program complied, in both design and implementation, with JCAHO standards that especially concerned evaluation and monitoring of services. Moreover, it was noted that the staff used the data generated by the QI activities to improve program elements. In general, the consultant had high praise for the QI program at the Rumbaugh Clinic. Furthermore, these findings were supported by Army Health Services Command reviewers of the QI program (Flannery, 1992). The evaluation assumes that a well-designed and implemented QI program ensures that the direct services were also well implemented. Given the data from the implementation and quality studies, this appears to be a reasonable assumption.

Evaluation Failure

Finally, the demonstration may be properly implemented at both the systems and the services level, and the services may also be valid and well implemented, yet there may be a failure in the evaluation.

Measurement Failure

The demonstration will not be seen as effective if the evaluation focused on the wrong outcome measures. For example, if the evaluation examined changes in IQ scores as an important outcome of this study and found none, then the evaluation could report that the demonstration was ineffective. However, because the demonstration did not target intelligence as an outcome and the theory of the demonstration does not predict any changes in IQ, this conclusion would not be fair. Besides possibly selecting the wrong outcome measures, the evaluation may have chosen insensitive measures. Poor measurement is a realistic possibility because the field of child and adolescent mental health measurement and evaluation is in its infancy.

It is unlikely, however, that the evaluation selected inappropriate outcomes, for authorities acting for the army, the state of North Carolina, and the demonstration have reviewed the targeted outcomes and have agreed on their significance.

To help guard against the danger of selecting inappropriate or insensitive measures, several steps were taken in planning the evaluation. First, widely used and accepted outcome measures were used. Second, for the most critical outcome, mental health status, multiple measures were obtained from multiple informants. Not only were checklist types of information obtained from the primary caretaker, the teacher, and the adolescent, but structured clinical interviews were also conducted with both caretaker and child (Heflinger et al., 1991). Third, the evaluation attempted to validate the instruments on the data collected for the project. For example, as noted earlier, it was found that the measures of psychopathology correlated with the level of care that the clients were receiving.

The outcome instrument package developed for this study consists of a combination of structured and semistructured interviews, behavioral checklists, and self-report questionnaires. As noted earlier, most of the instruments have been well standardized and have been used in similar research on child psychopathology. The domain of child psychopathology is measured by the Child Assessment Schedule (CAS; Hodges, Kline, Fitch, McKnew, & Cytryn, 1981; Hodges, Kline, Stern, Cytryn, & McKnew, 1982), including the parallel form, the Parent-CAS (PCAS); selected modules from the revised Diagnostic Interview Schedule for Children (DISC-2.1; Shaffer, Fisher, Piacentini, Schwab-Stone, & Wicks, 1989); the Child Behavioral Checklist (CBCL; Achenbach & Edelbrock, 1983); and the Youth Self-Report (YSR; Achenbach & Edelbrock, 1987) for teenagers. Interview and self-report forms developed at Vanderbilt are used to collect background information, including the child's physical and mental health history, experiences with schools, and contacts with law enforcement and court systems.

To measure social functioning, the Self-Perception Profile (SPP; Harter, 1982) is used. The CBCL and the YSR also include items that measure social competence. In addition, the interviewer completes the Global Level of Functioning Scale (GLOF), a modification of the Child Global Assessment Scale (CGAS; Shaffer et al., 1983), and the Child and Adolescent Functional Assessment Scale (CAFAS; Hodges,

Bickman, Ring-Kurtz, & Reiter, 1991), developed by Kay Hodges in conjunction with this project and modeled after the North Carolina Functional Assessment Scale (NCFAS), which was developed primarily for use with adults.

The domain of family functioning is assessed through several self-report instruments, including the Family Assessment Device (FAD; Epstein, Baldwin, & Bishop, 1983), the Family Inventory of Life Events (FILE; Olson et al., 1982), the Family Resource Scale (FRS; Dunst & Leet, 1987), and the Brief Symptom Inventory (BSI; Derogatis & Spencer, 1982). In addition, Vanderbilt collected information on family members' physical and mental health history.

An additional set of questionnaires was developed at Vanderbilt to measure the level of satisfaction experienced by clients and their families with the services received at the demonstration and comparison sites (Brannman & Heflinger, 1993). Issues addressed include (a) access and convenience, (b) involvement in treatment decision making, (c) relationships with therapists and other staff members, and (d) expectations and effectiveness of services. Additional collateral data were collected from the child's teacher using the Teacher Report Form (Edelbrock & Achenbach, 1984) and from the child's therapist using a survey specially developed for this project.

In the development of this package, each instrument underwent a series of pilot tests and refinements based on feedback received. Several instruments have been adapted for use in this package and altered to eliminate duplication of items among instruments and to enhance readability. The instrumentation package has undergone review by members of a family advocacy organization as well as African American and Hispanic mental health experts for possible cultural biases.

To assure high-quality interview data, all interviewers participated in an intensive 5-day training program and subsequent independent training that took approximately 4 months to complete. To qualify to collect data, each interviewer had to reach criteria (Kappa = .90) in the administration of the CAS to five practice cases. To maintain quality, every interview (with the participant's permission) was recorded on either videotape or audiotape, and a 10% sample of each interviewer's tapes was reviewed by a trained instructor.

Design Failure

The design of an evaluation can also contribute to its ability to detect client improvement. In particular, the statistical power of the design is critical (i.e., the ability of an evaluation to detect an effect that is really there). The evaluation concern for sufficient statistical power is not misplaced. In a review of a large number of meta-analyses of various interventions, Lipsey, Crosse, Dunkle, Pollard, and Stobart (1985) found that evaluations had less than a 50-50 chance of detecting an effect that was really there. In these cases, the underpowered design would result in a finding of no difference when in fact there was a difference between the treatment and control groups.

Several factors contribute to the power of the design, including the strength and integrity of the intervention, the sensitivity of the instruments used to measure outcomes, and the statistical analysis used. However, the clearest and most easily measured variable that contributes to statistical power is sample size (Hedrick, Bickman, & Rog, 1993).

From the initial planning of the Fort Bragg Evaluation, a sufficiently large sample was included to allow the detection of an effect size to be of clinical importance. As more information was available about both the characteristics of the instruments and attrition, an empirical estimate of power based on Monte Carlo modeling (Lambert, 1993) was produced that provided an estimate of the number of clients needed for the study. This number is approximately 950 participants at entry into the study. In a longitudinal study, two factors contribute to sample size—recruitment and attrition.

The obvious first step in having a sufficient sample size for analysis is the recruitment of clients. Although it was relatively easy to access clients at the demonstration from the beginning of the project, no such access existed at the comparison sites. For the comparison sites, three strategies were devised for recruitment: (a) advertisements in army post newspapers asking parents to contact Vanderbilt if their child had received mental health services within the last 2 weeks, (b) cooperation of the agency that reviewed applications for inpatient hospitalization so that they mailed information about the project to parents, requesting them to contact Vanderbilt, and (c) networking with area mental health providers to ask parents whose children were in   red by CHAMPUS if Vanderbilt could contact them. The latter strategy was the most successful but required personal contact with most providers on a weekly basis.

Another factor that affects the number of participants whose data are actually available for analysis is the attrition rate. The current attrition rate for the four waves of data collection is 9% per wave. An approximately additional 2% of the sample withdrew from the study at each wave (i.e., requested that they not be contacted again). If a participant had taken part in a previous wave of data collection, there was a more than 90% chance of collecting data from them on a subsequent wave of data collection. However, if no data were collected from them, then there was only a 50-50 chance of interviewing them on a subsequent wave. These data indicate that it is still worthwhile to follow up on participants who were not interviewed on a previous wave of data collection.

Several procedures have been instituted to control the attrition rate. Three months before a follow-up interview, a "check-in" letter is mailed to remind the child's primary caretaker about the project and ask them to call Vanderbilt if any change in address or telephone number has taken place. A second "follow-up" letter is sent 2 weeks before the next interview target date. One to 2 weeks before the target date for readministration of the interview, the parent is contacted by phone. Should a phone number have been changed, the staff attempt to contact one of the alternate persons who was reported to know the family's location, provided by the parent during the first administration. A phone call to the mental health provider who originally supplied the name may also be attempted, as well as a visit to the place of residence at the last interview. The staff may also use the post and military worldwide locator system, on-line access to a credit reporting service, and state driver's license records to find a family. All reasonable efforts were made to locate participants. In conclusion, we believe that we reduced the possibility of evaluation failure by using appropriate measurement and sufficient statistical power. However, the possibility of a flawed evaluation must be acknowledged. For example, because the design was a quasi-experiment, there may be large initial differences between the participants in the demonstration and those in the comparison group. Although we attempted to recruit similar clients, the field staff had to depend on volunteers. We will check for this and other possible failures in our initial data analyses.

Summary

In summary, it should be clear that many assumptions underlie the seemingly simple concept of a continuum of care. For this theory of service delivery to positively affect the lives of children, the service system must satisfy several difficult criteria. It must implement the system with great fidelity and use systems-level interventions (e.g., case management) of unknown but assumed effectiveness. Finally, it must deliver services of also unknown efficacy in a community setting with the belief that they will do their job. These tasks require important skills and are difficult to accomplish. If they are accomplished, then evaluation methods must also be valid and meet critical assumptions. If these challenges are met, the opportunity exists to determine if and how this systems-level intervention improves mental health outcomes for children and their families in a cost-effective manner.

Notes

1. For a complete description of the methods and findings of the implementation study, see Heflinger (1993a).
2. For information on the network analysis, see Heflinger (1993b).
3. For complete description of the methods and findings of the quality study, see Bickman, Bryant, and Summerfelt (1993).
4. This chapter represents work at the midpoint of the Fort Bragg Evaluation. The studies of outcome and cost-effectiveness were completed in September 1994, but conclusive evaluation results are not yet available.

References

Achenbach, T. M., & Edelbrock, C. (1983). *Manual for the Child Behavior Checklist and Revised Child Behavior Profile.* Burlington, VT: Queen City Printers.

Achenbach, T. M., & Edelbrock, C. (1987). *Manual for the Youth Self-Report and Profile.* Burlington, VT: University of Vermont, Department of Psychology.

Baine, D. P. (1992). Prepared statement to the Select Committee on Children, Youth, and Families. In U.S. House of Representatives (Eds.), *The profits of misery: How inpatient psychiatric treatment bilks the system and betrays our trust* (GPO-1992-52-362; pp. 172-194). Washington, DC: Government Printing Office.

Behar, L. (1985). Changing patterns of state responsibility: A case study of North Carolina. *Journal of Clinical Child Psychology, 14,* 188-195.

Berwick, D. M. (1990). *Curing health care: New strategies for quality improvement.* San Francisco: Jossey-Bass.

Bickman, L. (1985). Improving established statewide programs: A component theory of evaluation. *Evaluation Review, 9,* 189-208.

Bickman, L. (1987). The functions of program theory. In L. Bickman (Ed.), *Using program theory in evaluation* (pp. 5-18). San Francisco: Jossey-Bass.

Bickman, L. (Ed.). (1990). *Advances in program theory.* San Francisco: Jossey-Bass.

Bickman, L., Bryant, D., & Summerfelt, W. T. (1993). *The final report of the quality study of the Fort Bragg Evaluation Project.* Unpublished manuscript, Vanderbilt University, Center for Mental Health Policy, Nashville, TN.

Bickman, L., & Dokecki, P. (1989). The for-profit delivery of mental health services. *American Psychologist, 44,* 1133-1137.

Bickman, L. B., & Peterson, K. A. (1990). Using program theory to describe and measure program quality. In L. Bickman (Ed.), *Advances in program theory* (pp. 61-72). San Francisco: Jossey-Bass.

Brannan, A. M., & Heflinger, C. A. (1993, October). *Client satisfaction with mental health services.* Paper presented at the 21st annual meeting of the American Public Health Association, San Francisco.

Burns, B. J. (1990). Mental health service use by adolescents in the 1970s and 1980s. In A. A. Algarin & R. M. Friedman (Eds.), *A system of care for children's mental health: Expanding the research base. Third annual research conference proceedings* (pp. 3-19). Tampa: Florida Mental Health Institute.

Chen, H. (1990). *Theory driven evaluations.* Beverly Hills, CA: Sage.

Chen, H., & Rossi, P. (1983). Evaluating with sense: The theory driven approach. *Evaluation Review, 7,* 283-302.

Chen, H., & Rossi, P. (Eds.). (1992). *Theory driven evaluations in analyzing policies and programs.* Westport, CT: Greenwood.

Derogatis, L. R., & Spencer, P. (1982). *Brief Symptom Inventory.* Baltimore: Johns Hopkins University, Clinical Psychometric Research.

Dorwart, R. A., Schlesinger, M., Davidson, H., Epstein, S., & Hoover, C. (1991). A national study of psychiatric hospital care. *American Journal of Psychiatry, 148,* 204-210.

Dunst, C. J., & Leet, H. E. (1987). Measuring the adequacy of resources in households with young children. *Child Care, Health and Development, 13,* 111-125.

Edelbrock, C. S., & Achenbach, T. A. (1984). The teacher version of the Child Behavior Profile: I. Boys aged 6-11. *Journal of Consulting and Clinical Psychology, 52,* 207-217.

Epstein, N. B., Baldwin, L. M., & Bishop, D. S. (1983). The McMaster Family Assessment Device. *Journal of Marital and Family Therapy, 9,* 171-180.

Flannery, D. (1992, October). *Report of the review of quality assurance mechanisms at the Fort Bragg Child and Adolescent Mental Health Demonstration.* Unpublished manuscript, U.S. Army Health Services Command, San Antonio, TX.

General Accounting Office. (1992). *Defense health care: CHAMPUS mental health demonstration project in Virginia* (GAO/HRD 95-93). Washington, DC: Author.

General Accounting Office. (1993a). *Defense health care: Additional improvements needed in CHAMPUS' mental health program* (GAO/HRD 93-94). Washington, DC: Author.

General Accounting Office. (1993b). *Psychiatric fraud and abuse: Increased scrutiny of hospital stays is needed for federal health programs* (GAO/HRD 93-92). Washington, DC: Author.

Harter, S. (1982). The perceived competence scale for children. *Child Development, 53,* 87-97.

Hedrick, T. E., Bickman, L., & Rog, D. J. (1993). *Planning applied social research.* Newbury Park, CA: Sage.

Heflinger, C. A. (1993a). *An interorganizational network approach to evaluating the implementation of the Fort Bragg Child and Adolescent Mental Health Demonstration Project.* Unpublished manuscript, Vanderbilt University, Center for Mental Health Policy, Nashville, TN.

Heflinger, C. A. (1993b). *The final report of the implementation study of the Fort Bragg Evaluation Project.* Unpublished manuscript, Vanderbilt University, Center for Mental Health Policy, Nashville, TN.

Heflinger, C. A., Bickman, L. B., Lane, T. W., Keeton, W. P., Hodges, V. K., & Behar, L. (1991). The Fort Bragg Child and Adolescent Demonstration: Implementing and evaluating a continuum of care. In A. Algarin & R. M. Friedman (Eds.), *A system of care for children's mental health: Expanding the research base. Fourth annual research conference proceedings* (pp. 83-96). Tampa: Florida Mental Health Institute.

Hobbs, N. (1982). *The troubled and troubling child.* San Francisco: Jossey-Bass.

Hodges, K., Bickman, L., Ring-Kurtz, S., & Reiter, M. (1991). A multi-dimensional measure of level of functioning in children and adolescents. In A. Algarin & R. M. Friedman (Eds.), *A system of care for children's mental health: Expanding the research base. Fourth annual research conference proceedings* (pp. 149-154). Tampa: Florida Mental Health Institute.

Hodges, K., Kline, J., Fitch, P., McKnew, D., & Cytryn, L. (1981). The Child Assessment Scale: A diagnostic interview for research and clinical use. *Catalog of Selected Documents in Psychology, 11,* 56.

Hodges, K., Kline, J., Stern, L., Cytryn, L., & McKnew, D. (1982). The development of a child assessment schedule for research and clinical use. *Journal of Abnormal Child Psychology, 10,* 173-189.

Inouye, D. (1988). Children's mental health issues. *American Psychologist, 43,* 813-816.

Jerrell, P., & Hargreave, W. A. (1991). *The operating philosophy of community programs* (Working Paper Series No. 18). Berkeley, CA: Institute for Mental Health Services Research.

Joint Commission on Accreditation of Health Care Organizations (JCAHO). (1991). *Consolidated standards manual.* Oakbrook, IL: Author.

Joint Commission on Accreditation of Health Care Organizations (JCAHO). (1993). *Mental health accreditation manual.* Oakbrook, IL: Author.

Kiesler, C. A., & Simpkins, C. G. (1991). Changes in psychiatric inpatient treatment of children and youth in general hospitals, 1980-85. *Hospital and Community Psychiatry, 42,* 601-604.

Kiesler, C. A., & Simpkins, C. G. (1993). *The unnoticed majority in psychiatric inpatient care.* New York: Plenum.

Knitzer, J. (1982). *Unclaimed children: The failure of public responsibility to children and adolescents in need of mental health services.* Washington, DC: National Academy Press.

Lambert, W. (1993). *Power analysis of the Ft. Bragg Evaluation Project: Technical details of a practical Monte Carlo power analysis.* Unpublished manuscript, Vanderbilt University, Center for Mental Health Policy, Nashville, TN.

Lipsey, M. W. (1990). *Design sensitivity: Statistical power for experimental research.* Newbury Park, CA: Sage.

Lipsey, M. W., Crosse, S., Dunkle, J., Pollard, J., & Stobart, G. (1985). Evaluation: The state of the art and the sorry state of the science. In D. S. Cordray (Ed.), *Utilizing prior research in evaluation planning* (pp. 7-28). San Francisco: Jossey-Bass.

Marsden, P. V. (1990). Network data and measurement. *Annual Review of Sociology, 16,* 435-463.

Martin, E. (1992, April). Prepared statement to the Select Committee on Children, Youth, and Families. In U.S. House of Representatives (Eds.), *The profits of misery: How inpatient psychiatric treatment bilks the system and betrays our trust* (GPO 1992-58-362; pp. 215-249). Washington, DC: Government Printing Office.

McGlynn, E. A., Norquist, G. S., Wells, K. B., & Lieberman, R. P. (1988). Quality of care research in mental health. *Inquiry, 25,* 157-168.

Morrissey, J. (1992). An interorganizational network approach to evaluating children's mental health service systems. In L. Bickman & D. Rog (Eds.), *Evaluating mental health services for children* (pp. 85-98). San Francisco: Jossey-Bass.

Nelson, S. S. (1993, October 11). Benefit available . . . partially. *Army Times,* 25-26.

Office of the Civilian Health and Medical Program of the Uniformed Services (CHAMPUS). (1992). *CHAMPUS handbook* (1992-675-578). Washington, DC: Government Printing Office.

Olson, D. H., McCubbin, H. I., Barnes, H., Larsen, A., Muxen, M., & Wilson, M. (1982). *Family inventories.* (Available from the Department of Family Social Science, 290 McNeal Hall, University of Minnesota, St. Paul, MN 55108)

Peterson, K. A., & Bickman, L. (1992). Normative theory and program quality in mental health services. In H. Chen & P. Rossi (Eds.), *Theory-driven evaluations in analyzing policies and programs* (pp. 165-176). Westwood, MA: Greenwood.

Saxe, L., Cross, T., & Silverman, N. (1988). Children's mental health: The gap between what we know and what we do. *American Psychologist, 43,* 800-807.

Saxe, L., Cross, T., Silverman, N., Batchelor, W. F., & Dougherty, D. (1987). *Children's mental health: Problems and services.* Durham, NC: Duke University Press.

Select Committee on Children, Youth, and Families, U.S. House of Representatives (Eds.). (1992, April). *The profits of misery: How inpatient psychiatric treatment bilks the system and betrays our trust* (GPO-1992-58-362). Washington, DC: Government Printing Office.

Shaffer, D., Fisher, P., Piacentini, J., Schwab-Stone, M., & Wicks, J. (1989). *Diagnostic Interview Schedule for Children: DISC-2.1C, child version.* Unpublished manuscript, New York State Psychiatric Institute, Department of Child and Adolescent Psychiatry.

Shaffer, D., Gould, M. S., Brasie, J., Ambrosini, P., Fisher, P., Bird, H., & Aluwahlia, S. (1983). A Children's Global Assessment Scale (CGAS). *Archives of General Psychiatry, 40,* 1228-1231.

Silver, A. A. (1984). Children in classes for the severely emotionally handicapped. *Journal of Developmental and Behavioral Pediatrics, 5,* 49-54.

Soler, M., & Shaffer, C. (1990). Fighting fragmentation: Coordination of services for children and families. *Nebraska Law Review, 69,* 278-297.

Stroul, B. A., & Friedman, R. M. (1986). *A system of care for severely emotionally disturbed children and youth.* Washington, DC: Georgetown University Child Development Center.

Weisz, J. R., & Weiss, B. (1993). *Effects of psychotherapy with children and adolescents.* Newbury Park, CA: Sage.

Weithorn, L. A. (1988). Mental hospitalization of troublesome youth: An analysis of skyrocketing admission rates. *Stanford Law Review, 40,* 773-838.

Wells, K. B. (1988). Quality-of-care in mental health: Policy and personal perspectives. *Focus on Mental Health Services Research, 3*(1), 1.

Yin, R. (1986). *Case study research.* Newbury Park, CA: Sage.

Yin, R. (1993). *Application of case study research.* Newbury Park, CA: Sage.

Zeigler-Dendy, C. (1989). *Invisible Children Project.* Alexandria, VA: National Mental Health Association.

Evaluation of the
Mental Health Services Program
for Youth:

Examining Rhetoric in Action

LEONARD SAXE
THEODORE P. CROSS
GRETCHEN S. LOVAS
JUDITH K. GARDNER

Children's mental health care has long languished as a stepchild of adult mental health care, itself a neglected and resource-starved sibling to general health care. In tandem with recognition of a general crisis in how we provide health care (see Starr, 1992), increased concern is emerging about the health problems of children (see, e.g., National Commission on Children, 1991), with mental health care in the forefront of efforts to reform how we provide services to children and families in need. Changes to the children's mental health system have focused on the provision of better coordinated and more comprehensive services (see Saxe, Cross, Silverman, & Batchelor, 1987; Stroul & Friedman, 1986), efforts stimulated by the government's Child and Adolescent Service System Program (CASSP; see Day & Roberts, 1991; Schlenger, Etheridge, Hansen, Fairbanks, & Onken, 1992). The Mental Health Services Program for Youth (MHSPY), begun in 1989 by the Robert Wood Johnson Foundation (RWJF;

Beachler, 1990), is the first major privately funded extension of CASSP. MHSPY is designed to demonstrate the feasibility and effectiveness of comprehensive and coordinated services for children with severe emotional disturbances. The present chapter describes the evaluation of this program.

The raison d'être of attempts to reform the system of care for children with serious mental health problems is clear. Children are being served poorly, and the need for mental health services far outstrips demand (Saxe et al., 1987; Saxe, Cross, & Silverman, 1988). According to Saxe et al. (1987), it is conservatively estimated that 12% of children (approximately 7.5 million children) have a diagnosable mental disorder, half of whom (6%) are estimated to have a serious mental disorder. Yet the vast majority of children are inadequately served, and many of those who receive such services receive them inappropriately. Our traditional system of care directs the majority of resources to a small number of children who are placed in residential settings (see Knitzer, 1982; Saxe et al., 1987). There is a growing belief that hospitals are costly and inefficient settings and that community-based care, offered in alliance with families, can be developed to provide better, and perhaps less expensive, care. Community-based care is designed to improve the quality, appropriateness, and availability of services.

Unfortunately, accepted ideas about reform have, for the most part, remained untested (see Institute of Medicine, 1989; Rog, 1992). MHSPY begins to fill this gap and is designed to demonstrate the feasibility of integrating services for seriously disturbed children across child-serving public agencies (including mental health, child welfare, education, and juvenile justice). The initiative is supported by nearly $25 million in funding from RWJF, most of which is provided as grants to selected states. The evaluation is designed to test the precepts of the demonstration and to facilitate replication and extension of the program models developed at each of the sites.

MHSPY Demonstration

The underlying premise of the demonstration is that provision of comprehensive and coordinated mental health care is more effective and efficient than the current limited and fragmented systems of care for children with severe emotional disturbances (SED). The hypothesis is that organizational and financial changes to the structure of the service system will enable more comprehensive and better organized provision of care.

The demonstration was implemented at sites in eight states[1] (see Table 10.1) that represent diverse geographic and demographic areas. All of the projects involve collaborations among mental health, child welfare, education, and with one exception (Oregon), juvenile justice.[2] In some states, other agencies participate as well—for example, drug and alcohol and mental retardation (Pennsylvania) and public health (California). In each of the projects, some mix of advocacy, provider, and community groups have been important participants, either in an advisory capacity or in planning and decision making. All the projects have also expressed commitment to some level of parent participation in planning and policy making.

Responsibility for the projects generally rests with interagency groups, in some cases newly created. State-level management of each project resides in the mental health agency. At the local level, most projects are also managed from within mental health, although one is based in a child welfare agency (Wisconsin), and two are in standalone agencies or offices that were created expressly for MHSPY (California, Pennsylvania).

All of the projects include a case management component. Case managers have primary responsibility for ensuring that children receive the services that they need, and combine direct intervention with clients with the coordination of services. Some sites use a managed care model that includes case manager monitoring of costs; others leave the monitoring of costs to project financial managers. The Oregon and Wisconsin models emphasize case manager monitoring of the clinical content of care across agencies. Caseload ratios range from 1:4-12 to 1:20, and most consider their model to be "intensive," with the expectation of extensive face-to-face contact with both children and families.

All of the MHSPY projects are implementing a complement of alternative community-based services, including crisis services, in-home services, therapeutic foster care, school-based treatment, and respite services. Most projects emphasize the provision of "wrap-

Table 10.1 Features of Demonstration Sites at Baseline

Feature	CA	KY	NC	OH	OR	PA	VT	WI
Sociodemographic								
Target area	San Francisco	Bluegrass region	Smoky Mountain and Blue Ridge areas	Inner-city Cleveland and East Cleveland	Portland and Centennial Sch. Dists., Multnomah County	Delaware County, including city of Chester	State of Vermont	Dane County, including city of Madison
Size	city/county	17 counties	11 counties	part of city	part of county	county	state	county
Population under 18	90,000	144,670	84,467	85,000	129,500	150,000	154,000	not available
Minority population	45.0%	not available	13.0%	77.0%	11.3%	11.0% Chester 79.0%	<1.0%	<10.0%
Poverty rate (late 1980s)	13.7%	19.0%	50.0%	54.3%	11.4%	7.4% Chester 25.0%	12.1%	9.7%
Interagency Structures of Overall System of Care								
CASSP awarded	1988	1985	1988	1984	1988	1985	1985	1984
Structures created	1990	1989		1984-87	1989	1980	1988	1990

(continued)

Table 10.1 (Continued)

Feature	CA	KY	NC	OH	OR	PA	VT	WI
Interagency Structures of Overall System of Care (Continued)								
At state and local levels		●		●			●	●
At state level only	●				●	●		
Interdependent Functions of Interagency Groups								
Program development at state and local levels		●		●		●	●	
Case review at state and local levels		●		●			●	
Project Management								
State level: mental health	●	●	●	●	●	●	●	●
Local level: mental health		●	●	●	●		●	
Local level: child welfare								●

Feature	CA	KY	NC	OH	OR	PA	VT	WI
Project Management (continued)								
Local level: stand-alone agency or office	•					•		
Case Management								
Caseload ratios Year 1	1:20	1:8-24	1:20	1:15	1:17	1:15	1:4-12	1:13
Case managers monitor costs as well as services		•			•		•	
Case managers monitor clinical content of care					•			•
Emphasis on wraparound services	•	•		•			•	•
Emphasis on culturally competent services	•			•				
Implementation Goals								
Total planned services	12	15	10	11	9	11	10	11

(continued)

Table 10.1 (Continued)

Feature	CA	KY	NC	OH	OR	PA	VT	WI
Implementation Goals (continued)								
Number new to system	6	4	2	2	2	4	5	0
Financial Strategies								
Medicaid expansions	•	•	•		•	•	•	•
Medicaid capitation plans	•	•	•	•				•
EPSDT expansions	•			•		•	•	
Title IV-E expansions	•	•	•	•		•	•	
Reallocations of state hospital funds	•	•	•	•		•		•
Blended funding pools	•	•		•	•	•	•	
Tradeoffs among agency funding streams	•	•	•					
Private, nonprofit "entities" to hold funds					•			•

212

around" services (individualized services that cannot be purchased through traditional funding mechanisms). The California and Ohio projects have placed special emphasis on the provision of culturally competent services.

A wide range of financial change strategies have been employed by MHSPY sites. To accommodate individualized service planning, each site has tried to create a system in which funds can be used flexibly. Six of the sites have created blended funding pools from multiple agencies on state and/or local levels, and most of the projects expected to expand their use of Medicaid by (a) adding services to their state Medicaid plans, (b) obtaining waivers to restrictions on billing for home- and community-based services, or (c) creating a capitated payment plan (an alternative to billing per service unit). Pennsylvania billed for mental health services through Medicaid's Early and Periodic Screening, Diagnosis, and Treatment Program (EPSDT). Many projects considered various reallocations of funds— for example, moving state hospital funds to the local community for alternative services.

Although there is conceptual unity to projects supported by this initiative, the eight sites differ dramatically. They represent a range of urban, suburban, and rural environments, and vary in size from inner-city Cleveland/East Cleveland to the state of Vermont. Ethnic composition varies substantially as well: Vermont's population is less than 1% minority, whereas inner-city Cleveland/East Cleveland's is 74% African American, and San Francisco's is a diverse mix of white, Asian, African American, and Hispanic. None of the sites began the project with adequate capacity to address the needs of their clients. The large urban centers, however, have many public and private service providers offering a variety of services, whereas the more rural sites have shortages of providers and less variety in services.

The sites also have varied histories of service system reform. Some have a 20-year history of legislative and state-level system change; others have a strong history of grassroots collaboration among local agencies. CASSP has had a particularly striking impact on several of these sites. Changes in organizational structures, planning, and policy making initiated under CASSP appear to have facilitated further system change under MHSPY. Three sites with early (1984-1985)

CASSP awards (Ohio, Pennsylvania, and Vermont) had interagency planning and policy-making structures at both state and local levels before proposals were developed for MHSPY. Kentucky and Wisconsin, also early CASSP recipients, were implementing such structures during the MHSPY proposal process. In all of these states, MHSPY projects were conceived as part of a larger process of system reform. In other states, particularly in California and Oregon, planning and implementation under MHSPY have proceeded concurrently with policy making, program development, and the creation of interagency structures. The sites thus began MHSPY at very different stages of system development.

Evaluation Goals

The primary goal of the evaluation is to test the hypothesis that changes in the organization and financing of mental health care can improve the care provided to children with SED. The primary unit of analysis is the system of care, and research questions focus on how the system functions. The evaluation is thus concerned not only with individual programs and treatments but also with the administrative and financial structures and processes that support the delivery of care. A second goal of the evaluation is to describe the diversity of forms that an effective system of care can take and to show how implementation of systems of care varies across sites in response to differences in population, geography, financing, administrative and legal structures, and local history. The evaluation has been designed to provide policy-relevant feedback to the funders of the demonstration, the sites, and, most important, other communities attempting to restructure their systems of care for children.

Logic Model

For evaluation purposes, a logic model has been developed to represent how MHSPY is expected to lead to change in the nature of care (see Figure 10.1). The model identifies key constructs, their operationalization, and the variables being measured (see also Table 10.2).

The logic model has been used to select and design measures and to guide data analysis. At the heart of the model are the explicit themes of the MHSPY demonstration: *comprehensiveness* and *coordination* of services. A comprehensive system has available a broad array of community-based services, in addition to inpatient and outpatient services, and a wide range of clinical interventions. A coordinated system integrates treatment planning and services across child-serving agencies. Comprehensiveness and coordination are necessary but not sufficient conditions for program success. The logic model also depicts the role of *appropriateness*, closely related to comprehensiveness and coordinated care. Appropriate services are based on an understanding of the child in his or her environment, are informed by sound clinical judgments, are minimally restrictive, and preserve children's and families' dignity. The model highlights the context in which the demonstration is being conducted, the processes by which sites are implementing changes, and the anticipated outcomes of the demonstration. It includes three separate domains—organizations, finances, and clients—expected to change as a result of this initiative.

Context

The first section of the logic model depicts the influence of context on the MHSPY demonstration. Although the principles guiding MHSPY (see Stroul & Friedman, 1986) are consistent, four contextual factors affect each site: history of system change, characteristics of the existing service system, sociodemographic environment, and extent of community and family involvement. The expectation is that differences among the sites on these contextual variables will shape the process and outcome of change.

Process

The process component of the logic model concerns the means by which sites are developing and implementing comprehensive, coordinated, and appropriate systems of care. Our initial assessments indicate that the sites are primarily adopting two broad approaches to change. First, to create more comprehensive systems, they are adding, enhancing, or otherwise expanding the services or resources

216

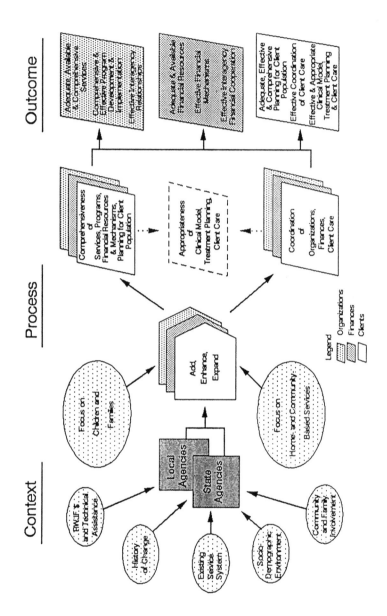

Figure 10.1. Logic Model for Evaluation of RWJF Mental Health Services Program for Youth

Table 10.2 Logic Model Dimensions

Dimensions	Domains	Context (History, Environment, Baseline)	Process (Additions, Enhancements, Expansions)	Outcome (Adequacy, Availability, Effectiveness)
Comprehensiveness				
	Organizations	Service range, capacity, and delivery		
		Program development and implementation		
	Finances	Financial resources, mechanisms, and innovations		
		Service costs		
	Clients	Population profile, needs, and access to services		
		Service/need match		
↓ ↓ ↓				
Appropriateness				
	Clients	Clinical model, treatment planning, client care		
↑ ↑ ↑				
Coordination				
	Organizations	Structure of the service system		
		Interagency relationships and coordination		
		Parent and community involvement		
	Finances	Interagency financial cooperation		
	Clients	Service coordination and innovations		
		Parent involvement		

being provided to children with SED. Second, sites are increasing the coordination of services with the establishment of interagency organizational structures at the state and/or local level, the negotiation of interagency agreements, and the establishment of case management to enhance interagency coordination on the client level. States are also increasing financial coordination through the use of blended funding or interagency strategies designed to maximize available funds.

Outcome

The outcomes to be assessed by the evaluation of MHSPY are the key constructs—comprehensiveness, coordination, and appropriateness of care—as reflected in organizational, financial, and client-level changes. Comprehensiveness, for example, may be manifest in the degree to which a continuum of care is established (organizations), the availability of adequate funds for the provision of services (finances), or the degree to which the system has services available to meet a particular child's needs (clients). Coordination may be manifest in interagency financial and programmatic planning (organizations/finances) or in the degree to which multiple service providers are able to develop coherent treatment plans (clients). Appropriateness may be seen as the provision of expert clinical judgment and intervention in individual cases (clients).

Methods

To test the systems-change hypothesis underlying the demonstration, the evaluation employs a quasi-experimental design. Because the eight sites are each implementing distinct change plans, sites are compared to each other to assess the effects of the implementation of different changes. Sites are assessed longitudinally with data collected at baseline and at mid- and end-project. The baseline assessment was designed to describe sites prior to MHSPY implementation. The midproject assessment is designed to portray systems change in process, and the end-project assessment aims to measure the progress of change efforts and their effects on care.

Given that the evaluation is focused on the effects of organizational and financial restructuring on the nature of care, the design integrates data from multiple sources and levels of analysis. In developing the design, the challenge was to find practical ways to collect data essential to the assessment of organizational and financial change, service delivery, and the quality of client care. Three methods of data collection were developed for the evaluation. Whenever possible, these methods rely on data collection and dissemination that are already occurring as part of project administration and clinical assessment and monitoring. Several types of data are being collected: (a) organi-zational/financial data (relying on document review, interviews, ob-servation, and surveys), (b) case-specific data (information extracted from the project management information systems), and (c) clinical assessment data (client diagnostic and quality-of-care data from clinical case conferences).

Organizational/Financial Data

To understand how organizational and financial change is associ-ated with the development of systems of care, data collection focuses on how sites chose to finance and deliver care and how organiza-tional and financial structures and processes change over time. This component of the evaluation, labeled the *organizational/financial as-sessment*, involves understanding the organizational structure used to serve children with SED. MHSPY sites attempted to implement broad changes; the goal is to understand the behavior of service agen-cies as well as clinical interactions with clients. Evaluating MHSPY has required measuring entire service systems to represent both the preexisting and new system structures and processes related to the quality of care. These data had to be collected separately for each site, given the large differences in the sites prior to MHSPY and the var-iation in the change efforts by site. Case studies of each site were developed, and significant similarities and differences among sites were examined using a cross-site analysis of case study data.

The organizational/financial assessment initially relied on docu-ment review and on interviews with key informants (administrators, managers, treatment staff, parents) to compile baseline descriptions of each project (see Table 10.3). Baseline assessments set the frame-work for the evaluation by describing the structure of the service system, the services available in the continuum of care, major strate-gies used in the financing of services, and significant characteristics of the target population.[3] They also described the history of states' attempts to improve and enhance services to children and adoles-cents with SED, as well as their change goals and implementation plans. The problems and successes that accompanied the early stages of the project were also documented.

Table 10.3 Methodology for Organizational/Financial Assessments

Component	Baseline	Midproject	End-Project
Data Source			
Document review[a]	●		
Key informant interviews	● (~16/site)	● (~2/site)	
Group observations		● (~3/site)	
Group interviews		● (~3/site)	
Surveys			
Analysis			
Focus	Qualitative descriptions of history, context, goals, structures, implementation plans, financial strategies, perceptions of problems, barriers, strengths	Qualitative analysis of project principles and policies as reflected in process of implementation across all dimensions and levels of project	
	Quantitative descriptions of target populations, services, projected revenues and expenses		
Products	Individual baseline assessments	Cross-site/cross-level analysis of selected issues	
	Cross-site baseline assessment		

a. Documents included proposals to Robert Wood Johnson Foundation; planning and program materials developed by agencies, providers, and advocacy groups; and federal and state legislation and regulations.

At midproject, the assessment focused on the process of implementation: describing changes in goals and strategies; assessing progress in implementing changes in structures, finances, and service delivery; and documenting problems and successes arising during the demonstration. Methods consisted of observations of key working groups within the system, as well as group and individual interviews. The type of meetings observed varied by site, but included treatment team meetings, along with local, regional, and state administrative meetings. Group interviews followed each observation, and key informant interviews were conducted with state and local project managers. This procedure allowed for the collection of data that were not accessible through other means, particularly about the coordination of care. Thus, for example, it was possible to assess such variables as the participation of multiple agencies in decision making, the degree of inclusion of parent representatives in the coordination of care, and the degree of coordination among the levels of the system.

In later stages, the same array of data collection procedures will be used to focus on system change (e.g., number and range of services in place at project end, interagency structures implemented). The evaluation will also analyze participant perceptions of success or failure (e.g., whether new structures improve service coordination) and the perceived level of comprehensiveness, coordination, and appropriateness of organizations, finances, and client care (e.g., degree to which treatment plans and services meet children's needs).

Case-Specific Data

Although changes in the organization and financing of care may indicate system change, a key indicator of whether a system of care has been effectively implemented is whether the quality of care changes. Assessing change in care requires collecting data on which services were delivered to which clients. The second component of data collection, case-specific data, obtains a standard set of client background and service data (see Table 10.4) obtained from record-keeping and data collection systems used by each site. These data are being compiled in a computerized database on clients and the services they receive.

The development of the client database was facilitated by the MHSPY National Program Office (NPO), which encouraged sites to use a management information system (MIS) to maintain program

Table 10.4 Revised Case-Specific Variables in Data Set, Linked by Client ID

Referral Variables	Plan of Care Variables	Progress Report Variables	Annual Variables
Sex	Diagnosis	Plan of care	Date
Referral source	Axis	edition	General health
Birthdate	Plan of care edi-	Progress report	Education status:
Ethnicity	tion number	date	grade
Living arrange-	Plan of care date	Report period	Grade level
ment	Authorization	From:	Special Ed:
Special ed. eligible	period	To:	yes no
Special ed. place-	From:	Service code	School attendance
ment	To:	On plan of care	Juvenile justice
Grade	Issue code	Recipient	status custody
Grade level	Goal code	Relationship to	Foster care
Major problems (3)	Service code	client (if not client)	Placement
Medication at re-	Service recipient	Provider	Number of place-
ferral	Relationship to	Public system	ments
Accepted to pro-	client (if not	Unit description	Therapeutic foster
gram	client)	Number of units	care
Date:	Provider		Day care services
Discharge from	Public system		Incidents of abuse
program	Unit description		How long
Date: Reason:	Units authorized		

records (see Cole, 1992; Cross, Gardner, & Friedman, in press). With the input of professionals from the sites and in conjunction with a software development firm, the NPO developed software that was intended to support the coordinated provision of mental health care for children with SED (Cole, 1992). The software, CareTrack, encompassed a set of client-specific data elements that were identified as important for assessing the provision of care to children with SED. In several sites, staff designated as information specialists have used CareTrack for data entry for the evaluation, and other sites (in general, those with MIS experience) have implemented alternate data management programs. The evaluation has capitalized on the implementation of MISs, and a computerized client database for the evaluation is being gathered.

To collect case-specific data, each project has been asked to incorporate a set of common data elements in its computerized record-keeping procedures and to forward copies of the data periodically to the evaluators. The case-specific data provide information in several domains that are essential to evaluate a system of care: (a) child and family background and diagnostic data, (b) the client's plan of care, and (c) services delivered to the client. An additional section collects data on clients' mental health, physical health, educational, child welfare, and juvenile justice status. Plan of care and service data are updated at least every 3 months.

The case-specific data allow us to assess what services were planned and then actually delivered for which clients over the course of the program. The system permits measurement of the history of service use for each client during the program and will help provide a picture of changes in patterns of agency participation, service delivery, and costs during the course of the demonstration. Analyses of the case-specific data are being conducted throughout the evaluation and provide both a quantitative assessment of client outcomes (e.g., diagnostic and functional status, service use) and, when integrated with data obtained from the organizational/financial assessment and/or the clinical assessment conference, an assessment of the link between the service system and the child and family (e.g., adequacy of services/needs match, impact of structural and financial changes on service use patterns). Case-specific data will be used, for example, to examine how plans of care match services to clients' needs and whether services planned for clients were actually delivered. Also, these data will show the range of services utilized in each site and will help examine interagency coordination and the continuum of care. Case-specific data will thus provide a measure of how changes in the system of care are related to the services provided to individual clients.

Clinical Assessment Data

The evaluation must also consider the clinical appropriateness of the care children receive. It is possible to develop a system that provides a full continuum of services, that effectively finances and coordinates care, but that does not provide appropriate care. The care that children receive must be based on an accurate assessment of the child and must provide the most effective treatment possible for a particular child given the current state of clinical knowledge.

The third component of data collection, the *clinical assessment conference*, provides evaluative data on the clinical care given to project clients. Developed and implemented by clinicians and researchers at the Yale Child Study Center (see Fallon, Adnopoz, & Solnit, 1993) in collaboration with the Brandeis evaluation team, case conferences assess the nature and quality of care for a sample of clients served by each project. Each conference is a microcosm, at the level of client care, of the larger project. An important aspect of this methodology is that expert clinicians bring a developmentally informed clinical perspective to bear on data on the care of individual children (Fallon et al., 1993).

In a clinical assessment conference, members of an individual child's service team present that child's case history and course of treatment. The Yale clinician-evaluators then facilitate a discussion of the case designed to assess the choice of treatments (including what treatments were preferable but not available) and the treatment process. Patterns of service utilization and their relationship to the child's and family's needs are examined. Interventions with the child are evaluated in terms of their impact on the child's current mental health and developmental trajectory. Immediately following the conference, the evaluators form consensus judgments of care on several dimensions: the resources available, the coordination of services, the flexibility of the system, the planning of treatment for the expected length of the emotional disturbance, the actual treatment and care of the child, the treatment alliances between the service providers and the child or the child's family, the monitoring of the child's care and, finally, the process of achieving consensus during the conference among the members of the treatment team (Fallon et al., 1993). These assessments yield a qualitative evaluation of the nature of the child and the quality of clinical evaluation and intervention. The resulting data will be used to understand how efforts to provide a system of care for children with SED are related to the quality of clinical care in individual cases.

Midproject Findings

As of early 1993, the MHSPY demonstration has passed its mid-point. Each of the sites has been fully operational for at least 1 year, and substantial data are now available. In terms of the evaluation, baseline assessments of each site and a preliminary cross-site base-line analysis have been completed, and a midpoint assessment is now being developed. The array of evaluation methodology has been im-plemented to varying degrees. At this point, the progress of the evaluation can be assessed, and the eight sites implementing systems of care can be described and compared.

Assessment of Evaluation Methodology

Because the organizational/financial assessment, case-specific data, and the clinical assessment conference were all new tools in children's mental health services research, one type of learning has been how these have been implemented. Each of these data collection methods has produced valuable data, although each has limitations and has required modification.

The most accessible data at midproject are the organizational/financial assessment data, and we have relied on these data to de-scribe how systems of care are being implemented in each site (see above). The organizational/financial assessment has been produc-tive because, as detailed below, it has measured variables that appear to be related to the range and availability of services for children and the ability of agencies to coordinate efforts. Examining service sys-tems as the unit of analysis has provided greater understanding of how sites are creating different types of systems of care.

The organizational/financial assessment has been demanding be-cause of the wealth of information available and the lack of initial clarity about which variables were central to explaining the develop-ment of systems of care. The logic model identified important factors such as organizational and financing structures, history of inter-agency collaboration, legislation and regulations, and client care regulations and procedures. Each of these had to be understood within the context of each state's system of care. Analysis focused on identifying essential system information and reducing data to key variables that illuminate system change. For both baseline and mid-project assessments, data were organized into categories under the dimensions of the logic model. Several iterations of this process have reduced the organizational and financial data to a manageable set of variables on which sites can be qualitatively described and compared (see Lovas, 1993).

The implementation of case-specific data has been slower than expected because collection of this data was dependent on implementation or adaptation of new technology. Almost all sites continue to have difficulties with entering information about their clients into the relational database that has been customized for MHSPY and/or with downloading automated data from existing mainframe computers or other sources. Nevertheless, all but one site have been able to provide data to the evaluators. Data records are often incomplete, however, and do not reflect the total number of clients served by the sites. It is sometimes possible to reconstruct records, and each month the percentage of usable data improves.

To cope with this case-specific data collection problem, an original version of the data set was pared down to a set of principal variables that will be common across sites (see Table 10.4). Decisions about what to exclude were made on both practical and substantive grounds. For example, data on the education, marital status, and documented problems of family members, background client events, diagnostic testing information, and cost and revenue sources for services were eliminated because all were difficult to collect in a uniform way. Information about plans of care and progress reports of services provided were, however, retained, even though most sites are not yet providing this information in computerized form. The latter data are essential to the evaluation, and a variety of strategies (including use of hard-copy documentation) will be used to obtain this information on every child served. Programs are being developed to import site data into a standardized format that will be used to generate analysis of the essential variables. These analyses will be used in conjunction with other evaluative data to compare progress across sites, as well as to assess progress within individual sites.

The clinical assessment conferences have yielded important insights not available through any other method. Conference-generated data have enabled us to evaluate clinical decision making of service providers at the sites and thus to address issues concerning quality of care that are distinct from issues such as the availability of services or degree of interagency coordination. An additional benefit of the clinical assessment conferences is that they generate hypotheses that can be tested by other evaluation data sources.

The size of the sample is limited, primarily because each case demands considerable time and preparation. As of the beginning of 1993, evaluation clinicians had made 13 site visits to conduct clinical assessment conferences—8 initial visits and 5 second visits. At each case conference, a new child (and family) was discussed and, during second visits, follow-up assessments were also conducted. A third set of case conferences will be conducted during the final year of the project. The last set of conferences will examine clinical care during the final stages of the program, at a time when many planned changes in the organization and financing of care are expected to have been implemented. Because the final round will include follow-ups as well as new cases, a clinical picture of at least three children per site over a 2- or 3-year period will be obtained.

The clinical assessment conferences have highlighted both the nature of effective care and crucial obstacles to optimal care. This was apparent in the ways in which service providers have responded to children's needs. In one conference, for example, the local interagency team's presentation of a case demonstrated a sophisticated understanding of both the child and effective care; nevertheless, care was compromised because the child needed residential treatment following inpatient care and no appropriate setting was available. A gap in the continuum of care compromised the quality of treatment. In another case, the interagency group creatively used a team of foster families to prevent institutionalized care for two brothers, but lacked the input of medical professionals about the boys' biological conditions. Case conference data will provide rich qualitative data to supplement the primarily quantitative case-specific data analysis.

Program Results

At midproject, the evaluation has assessed the initial status of the MHSPY projects at baseline and has begun to analyze data collected at midpoint on the process of implementation. Our baseline evaluation identified a number of common elements that seem central to implementing a system of care. Each project is seeking to develop a more comprehensive and coordinated system of care, in which the needs of individual children are paramount and services are provided in the community whenever possible. Each has (a) developed or built upon significant collaborative relationships among participating agencies; (b) created or designated already existing interagency structures for planning and decision making; (c) incorporated parents, advocates, and community representatives in the planning and policy-making process; (d) developed a strong interagency case management program; (e) implemented new or expanded community-based services as alternatives to inpatient care; and (f) developed financial strategies that will allow greater flexibility in the use of service dollars.

Despite these commonalities, a cross-site analysis of the baseline data (see Lovas, 1993) has made it clear that there are multiple ways to organize systems of care. Each site must implement system changes within the context of its own environment. Individual adaptations to varying environments and conditions result in somewhat different program "models." Although the impact of many contextual variables can only be fully evaluated at later stages of the project, the impact, or potential impact, of others was apparent at baseline. Thus, for example, contextual sociodemographic variables are expected to affect the makeup of each site's client population. Other variables, such as the participation of various child-serving agencies or discrepancies in access, may also affect the demographics of the client pool. At the Oregon site, for example, African American youth are significantly overrepresented in the juvenile justice system, but because juvenile justice withdrew from the project, may be underrepresented in the client pool.

Contextual variables may affect MHSPY implementation as well. The number and type of services in place at baseline and the order in which services are implemented may affect the success of planned implementations. Implementation may be more or less problematic depending on how many services are already in place, which varies considerably between sites. Of the 11 services targeted for implementation in Dane County, Wisconsin, for example, none were new to the system of care; in both California and Vermont, half the planned services did not yet exist. Crisis and respite services may need to be present before other services can function effectively; only California, Ohio, and Oregon had adequate mobile crisis units at the beginning of implementation. Some of the sites without such services planned to implement them early; others did not plan to have fully functional crisis units in place until late in the project. Issues of access can be exacerbated by poverty or by distance, and both urban and rural sites will need to address lack of access. Language barriers and other cultural issues may inhibit the effectiveness of services. In San Francisco, for example, Asians are underrepresented in mental health caseloads, but when they do seek services, appear to have more severe problems. In addition, staff at several projects have expressed concern about overreliance on conduct disorder diagnoses for African American youth, and at least one site (San Francisco) planned to specially evaluate any child with the sole diagnosis of conduct disorder. Sociodemographic issues can also affect decisions about ancillary services. Families in areas with high unemployment face different problems and need different services than families in more affluent areas.

In addition, the structure of the service system may limit the ability of systems to implement change. When power is centralized, the system may have a greater ability to respond quickly to calls for reorganization. The integration of services in a decentralized system may necessitate a more protracted developmental process. North Carolina, for example, has traditionally encouraged interagency collaboration by local providers, with little centralization of authority, and the Wisconsin site operates in a decentralized county-based system. Finally, the amount of control the mental health authority has over programmatic change may be limited by the structure of the state's health and social welfare systems. Negotiations with private nonprofit providers may need to be supplemented with financial incentives that are not necessary when community mental health centers are the providers; California, Ohio, Oregon, and Wisconsin all purchase services from private nonprofit providers.

The history of service system change plays an important role in shaping these projects. The cross-site analysis makes it clear that each project starts from a different developmental point, imbedded within whatever change plans already exist in the state and locality, and building upon the planning and policy making that have already occurred and the interagency structures and relationships that already exist. There appears to be a strong correlation, for example, between CASSP award dates and the existence at baseline of formal interagency structures for planning and policy making (see Table 10.1). Of the many interagency structures in each of the eight states, some are advisory or management committees specific to CASSP or MHSPY. Others oversee CASSP and MHSPY but have been created as structures that are larger than any one project or program and belong to the state's overall interagency system of care for children and adolescents with SED. States with early CASSP awards were generally further along in establishing structures at both state and local levels than later recipients.

Contextual and historical factors often interact, however. Differences among the states that had early CASSP awards can be traced to contextual differences in the structure of the service system. In Kentucky, Ohio, and Vermont, statewide multilevel structures were legislatively mandated, with interdependent sets of responsibilities laid out for each level of the system of care. In Wisconsin, which, as noted above, has an autonomous county-based system of mental health care, the process was slower, and county participation remains voluntary. Pennsylvania's interagency structure was created in 1980, well before its CASSP award. CASSP added a loosely connected set of committees at both state and local levels, but local CASSP projects have considerable autonomy. In the states with later CASSP awards, there were also differences. California and Oregon had only state-level interagency structures in place at baseline, whereas North Carolina, in which state-level leadership for system change is in the mental health system, had no overall interagency structures in place.

Differences among the sites at baseline in the development of interagency structures can also be seen in the assigned responsibilities of interagency groups (see Table 10.1). In Kentucky, Ohio, and Vermont, levels of the system are quite interdependent. Although they each have a mechanism to elicit local input into planning and program development, and the local sites have considerable responsibility for implementation, the state level has taken on (or has been legally assigned) responsibility for making final decisions on program standards and services. Another example of interdependence between levels is reflected in how cases are reviewed. In each of these same states (Kentucky, Ohio, Vermont), case review is a step-by-step process that can lead to review by a state-level interagency group if problems are not resolved at lower levels.

In Pennsylvania, where the CASSP systems are more autonomous, the local group in Delaware County developed its own program guidelines and standards, and case review does not move beyond the local level even though Pennsylvania's state-level CASSP committee has responsibility for the overall system of care. California, North Carolina, Oregon, and Wisconsin have few formally defined responsibilities for program development at the state level. None of these states have case review at the state level, and only Wisconsin has a formal structure for case review at the local level.

A final example of the impact of previous system change can be seen by examining the readiness of the MHSPY sites for program implementation. In Pennsylvania and Vermont, in particular, detailed program guidelines and standards had been developed prior to MHSPY implementation, and Kentucky was establishing similar guidelines and standards. In contrast, California and Oregon had to manage program development and program implementation concurrently. Other contextual issues can intervene in implementation: Program development can be faulty or inadequate, or unforeseen barriers can arise. But at baseline, sites that had already done preparatory work were more focused and better prepared for implementation.

Although no assumption is made that there is a "right" way to go about system change, or even that system change by itself is a requisite for better outcomes for individual children, these data imply a developmental process in system change. Sites that started the process earlier or imbedded the process within formal structures seem further along and better able to galvanize their resources for the implementation of further goals.

What is less clear from the baseline data is how that developmental process unfolds and what the crucial elements are, both contextual and historical, that allow one site to move quickly through the process while another flounders. Although there may be no "right" model, there may be elements that must be present in order for efforts at system change to be successful. As evaluation of the organization and financing elements of the MHSPY demonstration continues, we hope to understand better the process of system change and the characteristics that facilitate it.

At the midprogram point, the clinical assessment conferences have also generated initial insights about the nature of care within MHSPY (Fallon et al., 1993). According to the clinical evaluators, strengths of MHSPY interventions include the creativity, commitment, and enthusiasm of service providers from multiple fields, particularly special educators, social workers, and case managers, as well as the effective involvement of parents and foster parents in treatment planning in most cases. Often their involvement effected a substantial improvement in children's environments—residential, educational, and social. Support of the MHSPY program has helped to sustain interagency involvement, coordination, and flexibility. Nevertheless, there is a deficit of involvement of nurses, physicians, and psychologists in MHSPY, with associated difficulties with providing appropriate psychopharmacological interventions and deficits in the amount of psychotherapeutic assessment, treatment, and supervision. As the MHSPY program evolves, the clinical team is continuing to track these factors related to the quality of care.

Conclusion

The National Commission on Children (1991) titled its final report on the state of our nation's children *Beyond Rhetoric*. Indeed, there is widespread agreement that the time for rhetoric has passed in the development of systems of care for children with mental disorders. The RWJF initiative is evidence that we are ready to put into action our ideas about improving care. MHSPY is also evidence of our willingness to allow such demonstrations to be carefully assessed. Although providing more services (being comprehensive) and undoing the fragmentation of the present mental health, child welfare, education, and juvenile justice systems (implementing coordination) are clearly the direction in which to move, how to do so effectively and efficiently remains unclear (see Rog, 1992). The present evaluation is designed to identify the features of comprehensive and coordinated care and to understand the relationship of these features of new systems of care to the outcomes of children.

What is clear from the available data about MHSPY is that the program idea takes diverse forms. Each system "looks" different, and one of our principal challenges is to determine whether there are common active ingredients to these systems. This problem is made even more difficult by the nature of the problems faced by each of the systems: Not only is each child and family unique, but the types of problems and needs of each community are somewhat different. As depicted in the logic model, however (see Figure 10.1), two key ideas drive MHSPY projects: child-focused services and community-based interventions. MHSPY's underlying program model can thus be viewed as an antidote to finance-driven health and social services that provides a new focus on needs-driven services (see Cross & Saxe, in press). For several decades, health and social services have increasingly been influenced by financing concerns and, to some extent, the needs of large, self-regulating service agencies (see Starr, 1992). The needs of clients—in our case, children with emotional disorders and their families—have been lost. As money has distorted clinical decision making (e.g., encouraging unnecessary psychiatric hospitalization of children) and the maintenance of organizations has become more important than the services they provide, the gap between children's needs and services has grown wider. All of the MHSPY sites have in common their focus on designing services around the needs of children—regardless of how they accomplish this goal.

Understanding how society can better aid children and families faced with serious mental illness is still in a formative stage. The goal of the present evaluation is to increase what we know about how to change systems, being respectful to the complexity of the problem and the needs of both those responsible for these systems and those served by these systems. Our findings, it is hoped, will enable communities to expand and experiment with new ways of delivering services and will lead, in addition, to new research that can systematically test the effectiveness of clearly articulated alternative interventions.

Notes

1. One of the eight sites—Delaware County, Pennsylvania—withdrew from the demonstration at the end of the second year of implementation.

2. In Oregon, juvenile justice was involved during planning for MHSPY, but withdrew from the project during the first year of implementation.
3. Individual monographs of the baseline assessments of each site are available from the authors.

References

Beachler, M. (1990). The mental health services program for youth. *Journal of Mental Health Administration, 17,* 115-121.

Cole, R. (1992). *Case management to assure quality care in multi-agency systems: Building standards of practice into an automated clinical record.* Unpublished manuscript, Mental Health Services Program for Youth, National Program Office, Washington, DC.

Cross, T. P., Gardner, J. K., & Friedman, C. (in press). Implementation of a management information system for children's mental health care: Lessons from a national demonstration. *Research and Evaluation in Group Care.*

Cross, T. P., & Saxe, L. (in press). Children's mental health: An ineffective and inefficient system. In G. Melton (Ed.), *Following the money: Economics and regulation of children's services.*

Day, C., & Roberts, M. C. (1991). Activities of the Child and Adolescent Service System Program for improving mental health services for children and families. *Journal of Clinical Child Psychology, 20,* 340-350.

Fallon, T., Adnopoz, J., & Solnit, A. (1993, May). *Evaluation of multi-agency programs for emotionally disturbed children: The Clinical Assessment Conference.* Paper presented at the 70th annual meeting of the American Orthopsychiatric Association, San Francisco.

Institute of Medicine. (1989). *Research on children and adolescents with mental, behavioral, and developmental disorders: Mobilizing a national initiative. Report of a study by a committee of the Institute of Medicine, Division of Mental Health and Behavioral Medicine.* Washington, DC: National Academy Press.

Knitzer, J. (1982). *Unclaimed children: The failure of public responsibility to children and adolescents in need of mental health services.* Washington, DC: Children's Defense Fund.

Lovas, G. S. (1993, March). Evaluation of the Mental Health Services Program for Youth: Preliminary cross-site baseline analysis. In J. K. Gardner, L. Saxe, G. S. Lovas, & A. Glass, *Evaluation of the Robert Wood Johnson Foundation Mental Health Services Program for Youth at mid-project.* Symposium conducted at the Sixth Annual Research Conference on a System of Care for Children's Mental Health: Expanding the Research Base, Tampa, FL.

National Commission on Children. (1991). *Beyond rhetoric: A new American agenda for children and families: Final report of the National Commission on Children.* Washington, DC: Government Printing Office.

Rog, D. J. (1992). Child and adolescent mental health services: Evaluative challenges. In L. Bickman & D. J. Rog (Eds.), *Evaluating children's mental health services: Methodological issues* (pp. 5-16). San Francisco: Jossey-Bass.

Saxe, L., Cross, T. P., & Silverman, N., with Batchelor, W. (1987). *Children's mental health: Problems and services.* Durham, NC: Duke University Press.

Saxe, L., Cross, T. P., & Silverman, N. (1988). Children's mental health: The gap between what we know and what we do. *American Psychologist, 43,* 800-807.

Schlenger, W. E., Etheridge, R. M., Hansen, D. J., Fairbank, D. W., & Onken, J. (1992). Evaluation of state efforts to improve systems of care for children and adolescents with severe emotional disturbances: The CASSP initial cohort study. *Journal of Mental Health Administration, 19*(2), 131-142.

Starr, P. (1992). *The logic of health care reform: Transforming American medicine for the better.* Knoxville, TN: Whittle Direct Books.

Stroul, B. A., & Friedman, R. M. (1986). *A system of care for severely emotionally disturbed children and youth.* Washington, DC: Child and Adolescent Service System Program Technical Assistance Center.

Service Systems for Youth With Severe Emotional Disorder:

System-of-Care Research in California

C. CLIFFORD ATTKISSON

KARYN L. DRESSER

ABRAM ROSENBLATT

Advocates for child mental health services have been handicapped by a dearth of scientific knowledge to guide and structure advocacy. Historically, public advocacy on behalf of children's needs has been

AUTHORS' NOTE: The Child Services Research Group of the Institute for Mental Health Services Research conducts services research on systems of care for children and adolescents with severe emotional disorders. The Institute for Mental Health Services Research is funded, in part, by a Center Grant from the Division of Epidemiology and Services Research of the National Institute for Mental Health. An earlier version of this chapter was presented as invited testimony to the U.S. House of Representatives, Select Committee on Children, Youth, and Families, by Clifford Attkisson, Ph.D., on April 29, 1991. Research presented in this chapter reflects more recent data available on or before April 1, 1993, and was supported by research and training grants from the Division of Epidemiology and Services Research of the National Institute of Mental Health (MH46122, MH43694, and MH18261); by evaluation research contracts from the California State Department of Mental Health (89-70225, 90-70195, and 91-71106); and by a Robert Wood Johnson Foundation Mental Health Services for Youth Initiative Grant to the California State Department of Mental Health and the San Francisco Department of Public Health, Family Mosaic Project (CM 25-01-008A). We also acknowledge the many contributions of our colleagues and associates: Harold Baize, Lasse Bergman, Abner Boles, Donna Dahl, Justine Desmarais, Albert Fernandez, Rachel Guerrero, Curtis Henke, Teh-wei Hu, Pat Jordan, June Madsen, Nancy Mills, Lonnie Snowden, Sue Tico, and Norm Wyman. The views expressed in this chapter represent those of the authors only.

based primarily upon appeals decrying (a) neglect of youth by makers of public policy, (b) disproportionate allocation of public funds in favor of other population groups or to adult acute care facilities, and (c) the apparent failure of institutional approaches in meeting the needs of youth with serious disorder. Although classic efforts (Joint Commission on the Mental Health of Children, 1970; Knitzer, 1982; Knitzer, Steinberg, & Fleisch, 1991; see also Day & Roberts, 1991, for a brief history) have played an essential role in bringing children's unmet needs to national attention, the era of moral advocacy has been mostly unsuccessful in mitigating the plight of the imperiled population of youth at risk. Recently, however, a new era emphasizing services research findings as a basis for public policy has been initiated. Governmental agencies and private foundations now encourage research to study methods of organizing and financing effective systems of care that can be disseminated to communities through knowledge transfer. The importance of this policy shift cannot be emphasized too strongly. Evidence is mounting that the current generation of American youth is much worse off than the preceding generation along several important dimensions—including their mental, physical, and emotional well-being (Fuchs & Reklis, 1992).

Recent government publications have signaled a shift from sole reliance on moral advocacy in mental health policy development (National Advisory Mental Health Council, 1988a, 1988b; National Institute of Mental Health [NIMH], 1991a; Taube, Mechanic, & Hohmann, 1989). In the child field, related publications emphasize services research as a more reliable long-range strategy to forge services and service systems sound enough to stimulate sufficient and sustainable public and legislative support (Burns & Friedman, 1990; Dougherty, 1988; Dougherty, Saxe, Cross, & Silverman, 1987; Inouye, 1988; Institute of Medicine, 1989; National Advisory Mental Health Council, 1990; Saxe, Cross, & Silverman, 1988; Stroul, 1990). Reliance upon services research as a principal foundation of public policy will be further consolidated with NIMH's plan to provide funding for research centers devoted to the study of services and systems of care for youth (Commonwealth Institute for Child and Family Studies, 1990; NIMH, 1991b, 1991c, 1991d, 1992).

In this chapter we present current findings from four service system research projects designed to study and evaluate the implementation and effectiveness of the California system-of-care model for children (Attkisson, Dresser, & Rosenblatt, 1991; Attkisson, Rosenblatt, & Dresser, 1990; Children's Mental Health Services Act of 1987). For each investigation, we present important aspects of the study design, including the services research methods and measures employed in the data collection effort. Empirical findings are presented from the initial phase of each investigation. The service system changes that have occurred as a result of the research activities are also documented.

Imperical Studies of the Child, Research Group Services

Four longitudinal system-of-care research projects have been planned and implemented by the Child Services Research Group since its inception 4 years ago. These projects are now nearing maturity and, viewed together, form a nucleus of complementary investigations. The projects constitute a multifaceted study of the implementation of the California system-of-care model for children. Data analyzed in the research included secondary analyses of state-wide information and primary data collection from four California counties. The California system-of-care model is a comprehensive system-of-care concept focused on children and adolescents with serious emotional disorder. The model was derived from pioneering efforts in Ventura County, California. The model system of care is designed to integrate four service sectors that are critical to youth with severe emotional disorder: mental health care, social services, educational programs, and juvenile justice programs (Feltman & Essex, 1989; Jordan & Hernandez, 1990; Ventura County Children's Mental Health Services Demonstration Project, 1988).

Following initial demonstrations in Ventura County, alternatives to fragmented, discontinuous, and uncoordinated care for children with the most severe emotional disorder are now being implemented in other California counties. Legislation enabling the replication and expansion of the California system-of-care model for children (Assembly Bill 377, Children's Mental Health Services Act of 1987) stipulates (a) that public sector resources are to be expended on behalf of youth with the most severe disorder who are at risk of out-of-home placement (estimated to average 1% to 2% of the child population in the demonstration counties, with variation dependent upon population demography and associated risk factors) and (b) that services for youth are to be integrated across component agencies through joint service plans and continuous case management. The fundamental goal of the model system is to provide comprehensive, coordinated, and integrated care to each child and adolescent. Resource conservation, reliance on least restrictive levels of care, ongoing program evaluation, and a focus on outcomes further characterize the model care systems.

In the California system-of-care model for children, a series of planning steps is followed to create individualized plans of care and case management procedures (see Rosenblatt & Attkisson, 1992, for a more extended description). Administrative structures are also created to allow coordination and monitoring of services provided to children and adolescents in the target population. In the integrated care system, an emphasis is placed on reduction of reliance on restrictive levels of care through effective and coordinated community-based care. The desired system and client outcomes are achieved through emphasis on prevention of out-of-home placement to restrictive care settings such as state psychiatric hospitals, local acute care hospitals, and group homes; maintenance of progressive educational achievement; and reduction of recidivism in the juvenile justice system. Cost containment and cost avoidance are also primary goals of the integrated approach to delivery of services to this most-in-need population of youth.

A description of the model system of care and results from the original Ventura demonstration are presented in Jordan and Hernandez (1990). The model care system was designed as a set of five planning steps that could be followed to implement an effective system of care in a community. The five steps are as follows:

1. Defining the target population (in this case, youth with severe emotional disturbance who are most in need of public services)
2. Establishing the system-of-care goals (in this case, higher benefits for youth, families, and the community as well as wiser use of tax dollars reflected in cost offsets and avoidances)
3. Building interagency coalitions (in this case, between the different sectors, such as juvenile justice, social services, mental health, and education, that serve the target population)
4. Designing services and building in standards for quality, continuity, and client centeredness
5. Monitoring the system for client benefits and public agency costs

Recently, the model incorporated the development of cultural competence among providers within the system of care as a sixth planning goal (M. Hernandez, personal communication, August 1991).

The California AB377 Evaluation Project

Overview

The AB377 Evaluation Project is a multiyear, collaborative mental health services research effort between the University of California, San Francisco, the Institute for Mental Health Services Research, and the California State Department of Mental Health (DMH). It is funded by a California DMH contract, was initiated in October 1989, and is now completing its fourth year of operation. It is anticipated to be a 5-year study, with some indications that it may extend to a 10-year time frame with the addition of more California counties and increased scope focusing on statewide data analyses. The California AB377 Evaluation Project is best conceived as evaluation research designed to document and assess the California integrated system of care for children and adolescents with serious and persistent mental disorder.

The California system-of-care model was designed and its methods were initially assessed in Ventura County, California, during the mid-1980s. Subsequently, the model has been formally disseminated to three additional California counties (San Mateo, Santa Cruz, and Riverside) by enabling legislation (Assembly Bill 377, Children's Mental Health Services Act, 1987). The AB377 legislation in 1987 included an evaluation component, and these state funds, under contract with the California DMH, support this aspect of our research program.

The long-term, central goal of the AB377 Evaluation Project is to determine the costs and effectiveness of the model system in the three counties. Ongoing project objectives include assisting the California DMH in the establishment of system-of-care performance criteria, assisting the counties in their data collection efforts, monitoring program performance through analysis of data related to the performance criteria, and collecting and integrating data from multiple state and county sources. In the study, secondary data, provided by the counties and several state agencies, are collected and analyzed.

The available data sets contain individual-level data, diagnostic and demographic data, and excellent cost and service utilization variables. Individual clinical outcome data are not available from these sources, and the collection of such data is discussed in the next major section of this chapter, "Clinical Epidemiology in Three Systems of Care for Youth," which describes an epidemiologic and service system outcome study funded by NIMH.

The California AB377 Demonstration Counties

In 1989, three counties were awarded state DMH contracts and were enabled by the AB377 legislation to implement the model system-of-care strategy. The three counties, Riverside, San Mateo, and Santa Cruz, were selected on the basis of a competitive application process. The three counties are substantially different in size and composition. Their descriptive characteristics and information about the initial implementation process have been published (Rosenblatt & Attkisson, 1992).

Riverside is the largest of the three counties (population 1,170,413; under-18 population 333,261) and is the fastest growing county in the state of California. The county is huge and extends from eastern Los Angeles to the California/Arizona border. It has sparsely populated desert areas as well as more densely populated areas such as the city of Riverside, which contains a campus of the University of California. Riverside has a substantial Hispanic population (26.7% total, 35.7% under age 18), as well as a significant African American population (5% total, 6% under age 18).

Santa Cruz County is the smallest of the three counties (population 229,734; under-18 population 54,704) and has experienced only moderate increases in population. The county is relatively small and extends along the coast and slightly inland just south of the San Francisco Bay area. It is mostly rural, with the highest population in the city of Santa Cruz, which is a popular vacation destination and also contains a campus of the University of California. The county has a substantial Hispanic population (20% total, 31% under 18), many of whom work in the farming communities in the southern portion of the county. Santa Cruz suffered the most extensive damage of any California county following the highly publicized Loma Prieta earthquake of 1989.

San Mateo County is directly north of Santa Cruz County and extends along the western end of the San Francisco Bay until it joins the city and county of San Francisco. It falls in between the two other counties in terms of both its population (649,623, with 142,486 under age 18) and its suburban character. The county does not have a dominant population center, but does contain the communities of Redwood City and San Mateo. It has substantial Asian (16.2%, 19.6% under 18), Hispanic (17.7%, 25.3% under 18), and African American (5.2%, 6.5% under 18) populations.

Goals of the Evaluation of AB377

The AB377 Evaluation Project follows the legislative mandate to collect data regarding four important system-of-care performance criteria: (a) to ensure that the target population is being served as intended, (b) to reduce reliance on restrictive levels of care, especially reliance on state hospital and group home admissions, (c) to reduce the likelihood of rearrests for youth in the target population who are involved in the juvenile justice system, and (d) to improve the educational performance of target population youth in school settings. Data collection efforts began in October 1989, and useful information is now available for selected variables related to the AB377 performance criteria (Rosenblatt & Attkisson, 1992, 1993b; Rosenblatt, Attkisson, & Fernandez, 1992). For other variables of interest—primarily educational, acute and long-term hospital care, and juvenile justice variables—data will not be available for another year due to the longitudinal nature of the study and the fact that educational achievement scores, recidivism rates, and state hospital use rates must, by their nature, be collected and analyzed at the end of the investigation's Phase 1 data collection cycle in 1993.

AB377 Evaluation Project Findings to Date

Characteristics of Youth Served

Data are being collected to determine if the AB377 counties are serving the designated target population of youth with severe emotional disorder who are either in out-of-home placement or judged to be at risk for out-of-home placement. In prior research, risk for out-of-home placement has also been associated with several other factors, including especially (a) ethnic minority status; (b) history of abuse and neglect; (c) having a primary language other than English; and (d) having a clinical diagnosis of affective disorder, conduct disorder, or attention deficit disorder (Barber, Rosenblatt, Harris, & Attkisson, 1992). In the AB377 Evaluation Project, we are collecting data on the clinical diagnosis and ethnicity of youth served by the AB377 programs (see Rosenblatt & Attkisson, 1992, for details). Data on language spoken and history of abuse and neglect will be collected in our other projects to supplement what can be collected with available state funds.

Ethnicity. In Santa Cruz County, 70% of the youth caseload is Anglo-American, compared to 74% of the county's total population under age 18. Another 22% of the youth caseload is Latino American, close to the 17% of the population under age 18. An additional 3% of the youth caseload is African American, matching the 3% of the total population under age 18. In short, the ethnic breakdowns of the youth served in Santa Cruz are virtually identical to the ethnic breakdowns of the general population under 18.

In San Mateo County, the youth served by the AB377 programs are less reflective of the total population characteristics. The proportion of Anglo-Americans served by the programs and the proportion of Anglo-Americans under 18 in the county are roughly equivalent (45% for the youth served; 48% for the under-18 population). However, African Americans are overrepresented in the target population, representing 20% of those being served but only 6% of the general population under 18. Asian Americans, on the other hand, are underrepresented in the target population, representing only 4% of the target population but 20% of the population under 18. Latino Americans are slightly underrepresented in the target population (20% for the youth served; 25% for the population under 18).

Finally, 61% of the youth caseload in Riverside is Anglo-American compared to 54% of the general population under age 18. Latino American youth constitute the second largest proportion at 24% (less than the 36% found in the general population under 18). Conversely, the African American caseload is overrepresented at 11%, compared to the 6% of the population under age 18 in the county that is African

American. Only 2% of the youth caseload is of Asian American/ Pacific Islander descent, and only 0.25% of the youth caseload served is of Native American descent (compared to 4% and 0.3% respectively of the general population under age 18).

In Santa Cruz, the service population closely mirrors the population as a whole. This is probably because the population is mostly Latino American and Anglo-American, two groups that usually receive mental health services in proportion to their numbers in the general population. In San Mateo, the service population is characterized by an underrepresentation of Asian Americans and an overrepresentation of African Americans, a trend commonly found in studies of mental health services utilization (Snowden, 1987; Sue, 1977). African Americans are similarly overrepresented in Riverside, although Latino Americans are underrepresented. In general, the youth in the services program in San Mateo are the most ethnically diverse, with over half being of ethnic minority origin.

These results indicate that caseloads in all three counties reflect roughly the ethnocultural profile of their overall population. In the absence of population epidemiologic information for mental disorder, we cannot assume that this is optimal. We can only speculate that there are no major barriers to access that pertain to ethnocultural origin. However, if distributions of disorder are not the same across ethnocultural groups when socioeconomic status is controlled, then the lack of apparent differences in our data could mask a problem of access to care.

Clinical Diagnoses. In all the system-of-care counties, the treating clinician or caseworker reports *DSM-III-R* diagnoses upon admission to programs within the county. These diagnoses are made "in the field" by the clinical service providers and do not utilize standardized diagnostic instruments. Clinicians in our study counties are diverse in disciplinary background, amount and type of formal clinical training, and years of experience. They also have varying views in regard to the use of diagnostic systems, the value of diagnosis in clinical work, and level of specific training in psychodiagnostic procedures. Therefore, "clinical diagnoses" are subject to a variety of biases, administrative contexts, and systemic pressures. Nonetheless, these clinician-generated diagnoses provide important information regarding how clinicians view and assess the at-risk youth in their counties. The limitations of clinical diagnoses, however, were a primary factor in our plan to collect research diagnostic data on a random sample of the county system-of-care enrollees—a plan described in the next major section of this chapter, "Clinical Epidemiology in Three Systems of Care for Youth."

Distributions of Clinical Diagnoses. Within the AB377 system-of-care counties, the distributions of clinical diagnoses upon admission to the programs were remarkably similar for all three counties (see Table 11.1). Disruptive behavior disorders were the most prevalent diagnoses in all the counties (29% of the youth served in San Mateo, 48% of the youth served in Santa Cruz, and 34% of the youth served in Riverside). The second most prevalent diagnoses in all three counties were the affective disorders (16% in San Mateo, 24% in Santa Cruz, 26% in Riverside). Adjustment disorders were the third most prevalent in Riverside (17%) and San Mateo (14%) but not in Santa Cruz (only 5%). Anxiety disorders were the third most prevalent group in Santa Cruz (7%) and the fourth most prevalent in San Mateo (10%) and Riverside (10%).

Therefore, the rates and proportions of the clinical diagnoses given to youth upon their most recent admission to a program in the system of care are remarkably similar across counties. Given that the counties are treating the more "severe" youth, we would expect higher frequencies of severe diagnoses such as schizophrenia or other psychotic disorders (in our study counties, these proportions range from 1.6% to 2.3%). Instead, most youth receive clinical diagnoses of behavior disorders, affective disorders, or adjustment disorders. These findings are consistent with those reported by Brandenburg, Friedman, and Silver (1990), and suggest that the severity and persistence of disorder among youth may be less related to diagnosis than to other factors such as level of family disruption or presence of abuse or historical adequacy of the total system of care.

Reliance on Restrictive Levels of Care

Group Homes. The analysis of group home expenditures has been the most central task of the evaluation to date (see Rosenblatt et al., 1992,

Table 11.1 Targeted Youth Populations in AB377 Counties

| | County | | | | | | | |
| | Riverside | | San Mateo | | Santa Cruz | | Total | |
	N	%	N	%	N	%	N	%
Ethnicity								
Anglo-American	3,186	61.02	1,178	44.96	699	70.39	5,063	57.31
African American	592	11.34	516	19.69	28	2.82	1,136	12.86
Latino American	1,246	23.87	534	20.38	219	22.05	1,999	22.63
Asian American	88	1.69	113	4.31	20	2.01	221	2.50
American Indian	13	0.25	11	0.42	4	0.40	28	0.32
Other/mixed	11	0.21	131	5.00	20	2.01	162	1.83
Unknown	85	1.63	137	5.23	3	0.30	225	2.55
Total	**5,221**	**100.00**	**2,620**	**100.00**	**993**	**100.00**	**8,834**	**100.00**
Diagnoses								
Schiz./psychoses	119	2.28	42	1.60	19	1.91	180	2.04
Mood disorders	1,378	26.39	426	16.26	237	23.87	2,041	23.10
Developmental disorders	27	0.52	48	1.83	9	0.91	84	0.95
Anxiety disorders	504	9.65	250	9.54	68	6.85	822	9.30
Personality disorders	4	0.08	23	0.88	6	0.60	33	0.37
Substance abuse	36	0.69	18	0.69	7	0.70	61	0.69
Adjustment disorders	893	17.10	369	14.08	49	4.93	1,311	14.84
Disruptive behavior	1,787	34.23	757	28.89	479	48.24	3,023	34.22
Diagnoses deferred	143	2.74	197	7.52	9	0.91	349	3.95
Other	204	3.91	460	17.56	101	10.17	765	8.66
Unknown	126	2.41	30	1.15	9	0.91	165	1.87
Total	**5,221**	**100.00**	**2,620**	**100.00**	**993**	**100.00**	**8,834**	**100.00**

for details). There are two primary reasons for this focus: (a) the alarming rise of costs associated with group home placements of youth in California and (b) the focus of the initial Ventura demonstration and the AB377 model system demonstration counties on reducing group home placements and costs as a central element of the newly organized systems of care.

A recent publication summarizes the significance of group home placements and costs in the state of California (County Welfare Directors Association, 1990). In fiscal year 1988-1989, more dollars were spent on group home placements than any other out-of-home placement option ($347 million). These funds amounted to almost half of the $728 million spent on out-of-home placements in California. Furthermore, group home costs are rising at an alarming rate when viewed at the statewide aggregate cost level. Group home costs in 1992-1993 are estimated to be in excess of $500 million. As a comparison, the total cost of placing youth in California state hospitals was $29 million in fiscal year 1988-1989, less than 10% of the total amount expended on group homes. In fact, group home placement is second only to state hospital admission as the most costly alternative when children are placed out of home. The average annual group home cost per child per year in 1988-1989 was $31,100 compared with $106,200 per child per year in the state psychiatric hospital. These costs are much higher today. We do not yet have cost per episode data for group homes or for the state psychiatric hospitals. These data, when available, will greatly facilitate our analysis of cost and potential cost avoidances.

Group home facilities themselves vary tremendously, from those that are relatively small (4-10 beds) to large structures (more than 100 beds) that physically resemble psychiatric hospitals. The facilities are defined by the Department of Social Services as "a nonsecure, privately operated residential home of any capacity, including a private child care institution, that provides services in a group setting to children in need of care and supervision, and which is licensed as a community care facility by the department" (County Welfare Directors Association, 1990, p. 5). Through fiscal year 1990, group homes were classified according to four models:

1. *Family*—primarily designed to provide socialization for children who do not display age-appropriate social and relationship skills. Few or no psychiatric and psychological services are provided.
2. *Psychiatric*—primarily designed to treat children with diagnosed psychiatric problems. Full-time staff provide direct psychiatric services to all children in the facility.
3. *Psychological*—intended to treat underlying emotional and psychological problems of children and families and to address behavioral issues. Part-time staff provide direct psychological services to all children.
4. *Social*—meant to treat children who are exhibiting social behavioral problems but who do not evidence marked emotional problems. Part-time staff provide direct psychological services to some children.

Beginning with the 1990-1991 fiscal year, the group home system in California has been composed of 14 rate classification levels. Group homes are assigned to these levels by a system in which points are calculated by a formula that includes the hours of services provided per child weighted by the training and/or professional level of the individual providing the service and incorporating the licensed bed capacity of the home. The system has therefore evolved from a descriptive classification system to a more formula-driven method that is structured more precisely to the costs of care provided to the youth.

The implications of these changes are currently unclear and will need to be tracked over time. Some social services administrators believe that these changes will reduce the cost burden to the state by allowing for more refinement in the reimbursement process. They argue that under the less precise "descriptive" system, homes could be reimbursed at higher rates than truly necessary, given their actual mix of providers and services. The new system also gives more levels of control to the state to determine what levels of care group homes should be providing. For example, under the old system it was unlikely that an entire class of group homes (such as "psychiatric") would be eliminated. However, the state is currently considering the elimination of all Level 14 (the highest level of psychiatric service) group homes.

Group homes, as they exist in California, are unusual in terms of both their size and their availability of psychiatric services. In many other states, residential treatment centers (RTCs) provide the types of services found in the higher-level California group homes. Typically, RTCs are considered larger and more "medically" oriented than group homes. They are also funded through different mechanisms (the availability of CHAMPUS funds have made RTCs a more popular treatment option in recent years). However, in California the higher-level group homes provide many of the same "medical and psychiatric" services as RTCs. Unlike RTCs, group homes are funded largely by Aid to Families With Dependent Children-Foster Care (AFDC-FC), are administered by departments of social services, and serve only youth who are abused, neglected, or wards of the court. In the public sector in California, group homes far exceed residential treatment centers in popularity. In large part, this is due to the relative accessibility of AFDC-FC funds.

Surprisingly little is known about the youth who reside in these group homes. The vast majority (approximately 70%) of youth are placed because of parental neglect, incapacity, or absence. The remainder are placed because of sexual or physical abuse. The underlying reasons for these placements are not known, and we do not know, in the scientific meaning of *know,* what proportion of youth have diagnosable psychological or psychiatric disorders. However, in 1987, 70% of the children placed in group homes resided in either the "psychiatric" or the "psychological" homes, which are designed to provide some type of mental health services. Furthermore, "psychiatric" and "psychological" types of homes constituted 89% of the newly licensed programs in 1987. Finally, it was estimated that only 10% of all children in group homes receive services from local departments of mental health. In essence, the group home program in California represents a de facto mental health system, outside of the formal mental health apparatus, for youth who primarily suffer from parental absence, abuse, and/or neglect.

Group Home Expenditures. The cost data we have collected encompass the combination of all four types of group homes funded within the state. The data we have analyzed represent funds expended through the AFDC-FC program, and the data are provided by the California Department of Social Services. The amounts currently available for analysis reflect only these expenditures and therefore are not inclusive of total group home costs. We estimate, however, that approximately 90% of public expenditures for group home placements are now captured by our analyses. The largest proportion of noncaptured costs resides in expenditure contributions made through the mental health sector, where we now know that approximately 7% of the children in group homes receive supplemental funding through a mental health "patch."

The AFDC-FC costs for the AB377 counties were analyzed by comparing them to the aggregate AFDC-FC costs for the state of California. The use of California as a comparison provides a baseline against which to judge progress of the AB377 counties in achieving programmatic and cost-saving and cost-avoidance goals. To compare counties with each other and with the state, the county costs and the state costs are adjusted for the number of youth residing in the appropriate geographic areas. Therefore, the comparison data are expressed as per capita amounts. The per capita costs were calculated by dividing the group home costs in each county by the number of youth in each county (defined as persons under 18 years of age). The same calculation was performed for the state of California as a whole, by dividing the total costs for California by the number of youth in the state. When these comparisons are made, the AB377 counties, taken together, have progressively achieved lower per capita expenditures and a lower rate of increase in per capita cost over time than the state aggregate per capita costs.

Figure 11.1 illustrates these trends in inflation-adjusted dollars and also displays placements into group homes per 10,000 population under age 18. It displays expenditures and placements for both California and the AB377 counties across a 10-year period beginning in 1982. The figure indicates that the annualized combined expenditures per capita for children and youth in the AB377 counties (at $26.12 per capita [inflation adjusted], as of December 1991) is lower than the combined expenditures per capita for the total state of California (at $43.51 per capita, as of December 1991). It illustrates that the group home per capita expenditures for the AB377 counties and the state were roughly the same until the middle of 1986. July 1986 is approximately 1 year after the Ventura demonstration project began. As discussed in Rosenblatt et al. (1992), on a county-by-county

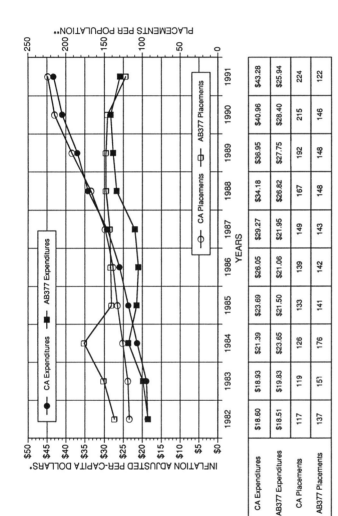

	1982	1983	1984	1985	1986	1987	1988	1989	1990	1991
CA Expenditures	$18.60	$18.93	$21.39	$23.69	$26.05	$29.27	$34.18	$36.95	$40.96	$43.28
AB377 Expenditures	$18.51	$19.83	$23.65	$21.50	$21.06	$21.95	$26.82	$27.75	$28.40	$25.94
CA Placements	117	119	126	133	139	149	167	192	215	224
AB377 Placements	137	151	176	141	142	143	148	148	146	122

*based on the CPI, populations under 18
**per 10,000 population under 18

Figure 11.1. Annual AFDC-FC Group Home Expenditures and Placements, State of California and Combined AB377 Counties

basis, there is substantial external evidence to demonstrate that the AB377 counties had already begun to implement the system of care modeled in Ventura County by the middle of 1986. This shift undoubtedly made these counties highly competitive in the state competition for AB377 system-of-care funding awards.

In addition to group home expenditures, Figure 11.1 also depicts data on group home utilization (placements) in the AB377 study counties. These data give the number of group home placements per 10,000 population under 18 in each county and reflect only the number of placements in group homes, not unduplicated counts of youth. So, for example, a youth who had two group home placements in the course of a reporting period would be counted twice. These data can be used to help understand whether the lower per capita expenditures in the AB377 counties relative to the state expenditures reflect a controlling of the aggregate total number of placements or, alternatively, a controlling of the aggregate expenditure per placement. This analysis helps in specifying whether the AB377 counties are controlling the *number* of placement episodes or the *expenditures per placement episode.*

Figure 11.1 also demonstrates per capita patterns of group home placements, per 10,000 population under 18, that appear virtually identical to the per capita expenditure patterns. This finding is what can be expected if the number of placements drives expenditures. Although the cost per placement has steadily increased since 1980, the study counties have been able to decrease their total expenditures by decreasing the number of placements. Of course, this may not account completely for the total expenditure findings, but it does seem that a significant portion of the ability of the AB377 counties to reduce expenditures on group homes is due to their ability to reduce the number of placements. This is a critical finding because placement frequencies are a controllable element in county service systems.

Estimated Cost Savings. The AB377 counties are showing lower per capita group home expenditure and placement rates than the state of California. Precisely stating the amount of cost savings represented in these lower per capita expenditure rates remains a topic for further investigation. Nonetheless, a rough estimate can be provided given the following assumptions: (a) California per capita rates represent an accurate standard against which to judge the performance of the counties, (b) changes in per capita rates of group home expenditure in the AB377 counties are due to the innovative interventions and began in February 1989, (c) other counties in California can realize similar decreases in group home expenditures if they implement the innovative system of care, and (d) costs of the interventions are *not* included in the analysis.

Given these assumptions, the AB377 counties taken together expended a total of $32.10 per capita under 18 less than the state of California over the 30 months from February 1989 to July 1991. The per capita dollar differences between the AB377 counties and the state of California can be converted to overall dollar differences by multiplying by the population in the state. This calculation shows the amount of money the state could have saved if the state were able to spend per capita amounts at the per capita rate demonstrated by the AB377 study counties.

For the 2 years running from February 1989 to July 1991, the state of California might have saved a total (in actual, non-inflation-adjusted dollars) of $244,725,978 in group home costs if it had followed the trend of the AB377 counties instead of the existing trend in the state. Furthermore, the savings have, in general, been increasing from month to month over the past 2 years. It is important to note, however, that these estimated cost-saving totals do not calculate the costs that go into providing alternative forms of care for the youth. However, given that group home placements are second only to hospitalizations in costs per placement, it is sensible to assume that other forms of care provided to the youth would not completely offset these savings. Nonetheless, this issue will require further investigation. Finally, because the figures we present are per capita and inflation adjusted, these results do not seem to be due to changes in population or the value of money.

Impact on Juvenile Justice Recidivism and Rearrests

To assess the impact of the systems of care on AB377 target population youth who have contact with the juvenile justice system, the rate of rearrests for these youth is being measured, as is the severity of the crime in the instance of a rearrest. These variables are being monitored for the year preceding incarceration and the year following incarceration for each individual. These data must be originally collected by the counties (e.g., they do not reside in existing information systems). At this time, only one county, Santa Cruz, has made rearrest data available. The other two larger counties are still working on collecting the required information. The Santa Cruz data are in raw form, and base rates for rearrests in the county must be determined before the available data can be interpreted.

Impact on School Attendance and Achievement

Data on school attendance and academic achievement test scores are being collected to assess the impact of the system of care on the school performance of youth in the target population who are being served in school-based programs. Information about school attendance and achievement involves original data collection on the part of the counties and is not yet available.

Clinical Epidemiology in
Three Systems of Care for Youth

Overview

Once the AB377 Evaluation Project contract with California DMH was implemented, we sought NIMH support for a longitudinal study of clinical incidence and prevalence of mental disorder, service utilization, and cost outcomes within two of the AB377 counties and a control county. The control county (San Francisco County) was selected because it was geographically contiguous to two of the AB377 study counties. The third AB377 study county, Riverside, was not selected due to the significant impact its inclusion would have on the overall cost of the research project and due to its vastly larger geographic size. Travel costs and relative inaccessibility of potential subjects for field interviews made the selection of Riverside County infeasible at this stage of our research efforts. Riverside continues to participate in the AB377 evaluation effort, and Riverside data will be useful in interpreting the overall results of the NIMH-funded study.

The NIMH-funded research project includes original, individual-level data collection on diagnosis, clinical status and outcome, utilization of services, and cost of care. Whereas the AB377 Evaluation Project focuses attention on outcomes of greatest currency to a community, such as containing the high costs associated with out-of-home placements, tracking school attendance and performance, and decreasing juvenile justice recidivism, the NIMH-funded project focuses on the sociodemographic and clinical profiles of at-risk youth identified by system-of-care counties through a longitudinal study of the clinical incidence and prevalence of mental disorder among this population. With this grant we also examine service utilization and cost outcomes in relation to research-derived diagnoses and the systematic collection of original data on the children's social and familial backgrounds.

Preliminary Research Findings

Preliminary investigations conducted by members of our services research team focused on at-risk youth who have multiple residential placements over time coupled with a high rate of use of restrictive levels of mental health care. Findings from these studies of San Francisco children and adolescents indicate that "multiple-placement" youth (those having high rates of out-of-home placements and changes in residential location) are likely to come from ethnic minority backgrounds, to be non-English-speaking, to be male, to have experienced early separation from their parents, to have experienced physical abuse as well as sexual abuse and neglect, to have lower language achievement scores, and to have been given a clinical diagnosis of personality disorder or pervasive developmental disorder (Barber et al., 1992). Similar results were found when predicting number of inpatient admissions, except that clinical diagnoses tended to be more severe, including most frequently psychotic disorders and major affective disorders. When inpatient psychiatric admissions were excluded from the number of total placement changes, several variables assumed special prominence in predicting a high rate of out-of-home placement: the presence of physical abuse, clinical diagnosis of affective disorders, early separation from a caretaker, a high overall symptom count, and male gender.

Federal Grant Research Goals and Design

The pilot research findings of Barber et al. (1992), based on data abstracted from service program records and databases, inspired the development of a prospective design that allows control of a number of additional variables and more precise measurement of variables of interest. Specifically, we included multiple county sites, a representative sample of youth from all sectors of the total system of services, research diagnostic interviews, assessment of socioeconomic status, assessment of clinical status and functional and social adaptation, documentation of history of abuse and neglect, and recording of service use history across the spectrum of services.

The NIMH-funded study encompasses a comparative analysis of three county systems of mental health and related services for severely emotionally disturbed youth and their families. Study sites initially included two of the AB377 counties (San Mateo and Santa Cruz), and we also planned to include San Francisco as a control county. Developments within the control site have since resulted in the inclusion of a subsample of youth who are now part of San Francisco's own system-of-care efforts, entitled the Family Mosaic Project and funded by the Robert Wood Johnson (RWJ) Service Program for Youth Initiative. Only a small portion of the eligible subject population in San Francisco is being served by the Family Mosaic Project during the time frame of our research. The emergence of this change in San Francisco has made it possible for us to plan two comparisons with the experimental counties. Although this development makes our study more complex, the opportunity to include Family Mosaic Project enrollees was a significant opportunity. Thus, our control county now allows inclusion and comparison of youth in the Family Mosaic service demonstration project in addition to our planned comparison with youth in the wider, more traditional, categorically based service delivery system of San Francisco County.

This modification to our original design presents both opportunities and challenges. First, as detailed later in this chapter, the Family Mosaic Project differs in important ways from the system-of-care interventions in both Santa Cruz and San Mateo. Most notably, the Family Mosaic Project is serving a predominantly African American population and focuses on developing strategies for an effective managed care system funded under a capitated rate. The opportunity to study this important intervention in the context of our total system-of-care study represents an exciting enrichment of our research efforts. Although this opportunity reduces slightly the total number of youth who can be included as control subjects, the Family Mosaic Project will serve less than 10% of the total at-risk population in San Francisco. We estimate that the remaining subjects will provide an ample population from which to draw a sample for our control county.

Consequently, the Family Mosaic Project is highly distinguishable from the San Francisco DMH. Although it is hoped that, over time, the innovations promulgated by the project will instigate change in the care provided in San Francisco, such a modification of the fundamental structure of the services provided within San Francisco County clearly has not yet occurred. It is therefore anticipated that diffusion of Family Mosaic Project intervention into the control sites in San Francisco will not create a fatal confounding of the "innovative care system" and "standard care" control sites.

Eligibility Criteria for Research Subjects

The youth population in the research includes those children and adolescents with serious emotional and behavioral problems who have been or will be identified by the counties' services systems as being currently in an out-of-home placement or at risk of being placed in an out-of-home setting. These criteria make these youth eligible for enrollment in a system of care built upon the principles embodied in the California system-of-care model. The children in the research sample are representative of those receiving care in the county system at the time or who have been identified as eligible for enrollment into the system of care.

Figure 11.2 presents the project time line and the multiple segments of data collection to achieve our goal of measuring clinical prevalence and incidence in the context of assessing the efficacy of innovative systems of care for at-risk youth. The central task of the research will be the collection of data from two random samples of children and youth within each county system: (a) *prevalence samples*—measuring the rates and distributions of disorders among eligible youth throughout the service systems, and (b) *incidence samples*—measuring the rate of identification of new cases, those newly identified to be at risk. Portions of both of these samples will be reinterviewed for further clinical assessment during a follow-up sampling phase, and all the youth will be traced on utilization and cost variables over time. The two types of sampling, incidence and prevalence, will allow an assessment of the distributions of disorders among those who are newly at risk of out-of-home placement or exposure to restrictive levels of care (incidence of new cases during a fixed time frame) and those who are known to be at risk at a fixed point in time (prevalence). The planned follow-up of the incidence and prevalence samples (along with a new incidence sample after 2 years) will allow a sensitive assessment of the effects of system change on the youth being served. In addition, small samples from a broader net (the "discovery points" in the community where signs of serious emotional disturbance often first becomes evident) will be screened.

Each prevalence and incidence measurement period will last approximately 6 months, and it is anticipated the project will take 5 years to complete. The project is currently in the fourth year of implementation, and collection of follow-up data is now in progress, with Wave 1 initial data collection nearing completion. To date, over 500 children and youth have been enrolled into the research, with a goal of enrolling 750 individuals and their families or family surrogates as well as their teachers. Because separate interviews are carried out with the child and the family, we have conducted more than 1,000 interviews to date, using structured diagnostic and social functioning measures. Extensive demographic and family structure and history data are also being collected on each case. We aim to enroll at least 250 cases per study county and expect to enroll more than 300 in one and possibly two of the counties. Follow-up data, Wave 2, will include random samples of 150 or more cases per county.

To summarize, the research is a study of the *clinical epidemiology* of children and youth in treatment. Sampling occurs among those already identified as being in need of service and meeting criteria for entry into a service delivery system. This is distinguished from *population epidemiology*, which involves community random sampling of youth and their families and yields rates of disorder in a given region. The gap between population estimates and the rates generated

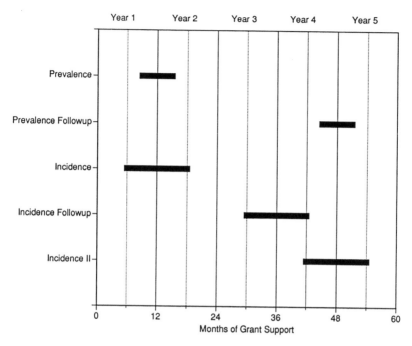

Figure 11.2. Project Time Line

through clinical epidemiology can be considered to represent potential unmet need in a community. Although the method does not provide for estimates of rates of disorder within an entire region, it does
allow researchers to address questions important to understanding
and improving the human service system. The primary research
questions addressed by the Clinical Epidemiology in Three Systems
of Care research project are:

- What are the prevalence, incidence, and distribution of mental disorders among children and adolescents served by the major child-serving
  agencies (mental health, child welfare, juvenile justice, and special education)?
- What are the important variables that account for costs of care within
  service systems for children and adolescents?

- To what extent are the study counties successful in making the dramatic shift from service-agency-driven systems to client-oriented systems of care?

- As service systems are restructured to optimize, coordinate, and integrate resources, is there a shift in the relative importance of variables that account for costs of care and outcomes of care?

- How do the following social and economic forces affect systems of care and efforts to restructure them: (a) shifting demographic and clinical profiles of youth entering care, (b) increased entitlement and demand for services, (c) budget constraints, and (d) inflationary pressures?

The Data Collection Protocol

The study is focused on the collection of diagnostic and social functioning information, using structured diagnostic interviews and standardized functional assessment instruments. Information is gathered in separate interviews with youth and their parents or parental surrogates. These interviews are conducted by master's-level, trained interviewers, and all participants are reimbursed for their time. Supplementary clinical and social functioning information is gathered from those human service professionals most involved with the child's care at the time. Altogether a complete data collection cycle takes an average of 8 hours for an experienced interviewer, approximately 3 to 4 hours spent with the parent and 3 to 4 hours with the child.

The data collection protocol comprises four modules: I. Background Module, II. Behavior and Symptom Checklists, III. Diagnostic Assessment, and IV. Supplementary Measures.

Module I. The Background Module was developed and piloted by the Child Services Research Group. It includes a brief time line (life event history) and inquires about the child's demographic and family (parental) background, current family composition and structure, residential history, education, health, global ratings of health and happiness, immigration status, use and satisfaction with services, and self-reports about the child's relationships with parent figures. Additional information on service use, contemporaneous and historical clinical diagnoses, and family background is gathered through chart reviews.

Module II. Behavior and symptom rating scales are completed by both the parent and child. Parents complete the Child Behavior Checklist, and youth age 11 and above fill out the comparable Youth Self Report (Achenbach & Edelbrock, 1983, 1986; Achenbach, Edelbrock, & Howell, 1987; Achenbach, McConaughy, & Howell, 1987). In addition, younger children (below age 10) complete the Children's Depression Inventory (Kovacs, 1991) with assistance from the interviewer, and youth age 10 and above complete the Beck Depression Inventory (Beck, Ward, Mendelsohn, Mock, & Erbaugh, 1961).

Module III. The Diagnostic Assessment is a thorough survey of the presence of childhood psychiatric symptomatology over the past 6 months. The older age group is administered the Diagnostic Interview Schedule for Children (DISC Version 2.1; Shaffer, Fisher, Piacentini, Schwab-Stone, & Wicks, 1989), and the younger children are given the Kiddies Schedule for Affective Disorders and Schizophrenia (K-SADS; Costello, 1989; Costello, Edelbrock, & Costello, 1985; Costello, Edelbrock, Dulcan, & Kalas, 1984; see also Cohen, O'Conner, Lewis, Velez, & Malachowski, 1987). These standardized instruments yield *DSM-III-R* (American Psychiatric Association, 1987) diagnoses on Axis I, encompassing anxiety and affective disorders, psychotic disorders, and disruptive behavior disorders. Additional modules have been developed and piloted as part of our research efforts. These include modules on post traumatic stress disorder (Fisher, 1991), pervasive developmental disorder, and alcohol and substance abuse. Children are assessed for their level of cognitive abilities using the Kaufman Brief Intelligence Test (K-BIT; Kaufman & Kaufman, 1990).

Module IV. Additional ratings are made by the clinical interviewers upon completion of the parent- and child-structured interviews. Data are also collected from human service professionals involved with the child's treatment, case management, or education. The clinical interviewers complete a brief questionnaire in which they rate the interviews and document substantive and procedural topics to be discussed with supervising staff. They also complete a Children's Global Assessment of Functioning (C-GAS) rating (Shaffer, Gould, Brasic, et al., 1983), provide their own summary diagnoses, and make comments on all five *DSM-III-R* axes—drawing upon information gathered throughout the entire data collection cycle. Social workers, mental health workers, and probation officers are asked to complete functional ratings (C-GAS), and the Teacher's Report Form (TRF; Achenbach & Edelbrock, 1986) is completed by the child's most recent teacher.

Each completed protocol offers a rich survey of the child's history, service use, and clinical profile. Such data will offer an opportunity for the development of quantitative analyses and qualitative narratives about children and youth served in public systems, as well as quantitative analyses documenting themes and patterns regarding the risk factors, protective factors, and vulnerabilities of seriously disturbed youth as viewed over time and system change.

The data set also will allow focus on methodological problems in the field of child psychiatry and epidemiology. One set of problems involves the reliability of clinical and research diagnoses. Comparisons can be made among clinical diagnoses, including (a) diagnoses made by practitioners working closely with children over time, yet compromised by uneven training and the biases that beset in vivo clinical judgment; (b) research-derived diagnoses generated by computer algorithm from a standardized administration; and (c) diagnoses provided by the clinical interviewers based upon lengthy information gathering, as well as the experience of administering a structured diagnostic interview.

Creation of the Sampling Frame

The sampling frame for selecting youth into the prevalence samples is generated from the counties' management information systems, in which numerical client identifiers and additional demographic and service information are encoded for each youth. These databases include information on 562 youth in San Mateo and 516 youth in Santa Cruz, representing 0.39% and 0.94% of these counties' youth populations, respectively. (For comparison purposes, the percentage in Riverside County is 1.4%.) These numbers reflect the counties' historic AB377 caseloads up to December 31, 1991. A sampling pool of youth meeting criteria for entry into the RWJ Family Mosaic Project was created by the study team for San Francisco and includes information on a total of 1,223 youth (Dresser, 1990). These eligibility criteria are identical to the California system-of-care model and focus on youth who have severe emotional disorder and who are currently in an out-of-home placement or are at risk for such a placement. This baseline data set makes possible the development of a comparable sampling frame for San Francisco and represents 1.04% of the child population of this county. Initial data collection plans included collection of the full interview protocol on 250 cases within each of the three counties for a total sample of 750 youth and their families. This goal will be met or exceeded in the two intervention counties, and 200 cases are now projected as feasible in the control county.

For sampling purposes, a unique random list was generated for each of four groupings: ethnic minority males, ethnic minority females, Anglo males, and Anglo females. This strategy of stratified random sampling is designed to maximize the likelihood of creating adequate numbers of youth in each grouping, as will be necessary for making cross-group comparisons. In addition, because recruiting of participants proceeds down each randomly generated list, an attempt is being made to include all females, and all youths under age 11, due to the relatively low numbers of these youth in the client populations. Oversampling of ethnic youth in some counties may also be undertaken to create an opportunity for comparisons among ethnic subgroups. With the completion of the data set, prevalence estimates can be generated, with the assignment of numerical weights for each subgroup in proportion to the numbers of like youth in the study populations.

The incidence sample is generated through the implementation of recruiting efforts when new clients are interviewed and assessed by the counties' mental health teams for entry into the service system. "New" cases include those opened for the first time into the integrated service delivery system within a standardized time frame, regardless of their prior history in categorically based services. Periodic review of updated database information from each study county allows the research team to cross-check this recruitment effort to protect the integrity of the incidence portion of the sample.

Additional Data Collection Activities and Ministudies

As part of this program of research, we plan to focus attention on a select few additional data collection activities and ministudies. On the top of this list are two projects essential to the interpretation of project data and clarification of complementary research issues. First, available county database information on youth in public sector care makes possible a comparison of study sample youth to all youth in mental health care in the counties at the time. Second, we plan to gather data from a sample of youth who, though not enrolled in the systems of care, are receiving a variety of other human services in which dysfunction may first become evident.

Some of these youth may be suffering from severe emotional disorder even though they have not been targeted for treatment by the care systems. For example, some youth receiving primary medical care or in regular foster care may not have been enrolled in the care system even though they actually have severe disorder and qualify for inclusion in the target population. Such youth may not come to the attention of the care system for a number of reasons, ranging from a specific lack of appropriate referral and screening mechanisms to generalized limits on the resources of the care system to embrace all youth who suffer from severe emotional disturbance. In other cases, youth may come to the attention of the service system but be inappropriately assessed as not meeting target population criteria. This study, by collecting data on youth who either are not recognized by the service system or are rejected from inclusion in the service system, is designed to assess the degree of unmet need among youth who receive human services but who have not been designated as part of the target population served by the system-of-care interventions.

Robert Wood Johnson Foundation
Mental Health Services Program for Youth

Concurrent with submission for the NIMH research award and the initial phase of the AB377 Evaluation Contract, our research team (Dresser, 1990) also consulted with San Francisco County and the California DMH regarding the California DMH grant application to the national competition for the Robert Wood Johnson Foundation (RWJ) initiative entitled the Mental Health Services Program for Youth. Subsequently, California was awarded a 1-year development grant. The Child Services Research Group will participate in the ongoing development of this major innovation by developing the core information system of the project, consulting on the evolution of organizational structure and financing methodology, and providing program evaluation and research expertise in the process of planned change.

During implementation, the Child Services Research Group will be responsible for the installation of a relational database system and a computing network that will be the primary administrative information system, clinical database, and planning system for the project (Attkisson, Hager, Rosenblatt, Smith, Dresser, & Strizich, 1993). The RWJ initiative in San Francisco is called the Family Mosaic Project (Smith, Attkisson, Dresser, & Boles, 1993).

The Family Mosaic Project (FMP) is one of eight national demonstration sites funded to provide comprehensive services to youth with serious emotional disorder. The FMP reflects the AB377 model care system goals and aspires to chart new territory in financing care through capitation methods for youth with serious disorders. Although the FMP began with an emphasis on stimulating and enhancing interagency collaboration through intensive case management, the project is rapidly moving toward a capitated financing strategy to implement its goals. Through March 1, 1993, the FMP had served 143 families containing 246 youth. Client families are primarily African American, as are the majority of high-risk youth. In addition, most youth served are male, and 40% are over the age of 13. The project emphasizes cultural competence in the provision of services; interacts with family members as collaborators in the intervention process; fosters interdisciplinary coordination of professional response to need; ensures stable foster care placements by providing ongoing clinical support; specializes in in-home care and strives to bring care to the home, the classroom, and other nontraditional settings; and uses intensive case management to provide a structure for comprehensive care and advocacy.

Smith et al. (1993) discussed the major challenges faced by implementers of the Family Mosaic Project over its initial 3 years. These challenges include training and maintenance of a committed staff, ensuring cultural competence of service programs and providers, dealing with the inflexibility of categorical funding streams, establishing funding sources for a capitated financing system and setting accurate capitation rates, and establishing a productive services research and program evaluation capability. In addition, the Family Mosaic Project has struggled with the challenges of being a research and clinical services training site. All of these challenges have been faced in the context of defining the relationship of the Family Mosaic Project to all other San Francisco child-serving agencies and administrative bodies.

California CASSP Evaluation Project

The Child and Adolescent Service System Program (CASSP) has been funded in the state of California for the past 4 years by NIMH. The NIMH CASSP was established to assist states and communities in their efforts to improve child and adolescent service systems (Day & Roberts, 1991; NIMH, 1983). CASSP has several special areas of emphasis, including the development of (a) systems of care for children and their families, (b) community-based service approaches, (c) cultural competence, (d) services for special populations of high-risk youth, and (e) strategies for financing services.

CASSP promotes the development of systems of care that are child centered and family focused, with the needs of the child and family dictating the types and mix of services provided. Accordingly, systems of care should also be community based, maximizing the use of services that are within or close to a child's community. As outlined by the CASSP model, systems of care should be characterized by the components listed below:

1. Comprehensive services to address the child's physical, emotional, social, and educational needs
2. Individualized services in accordance with the unique needs and potential of each child
3. Services provided within the least restrictive, most normal environment
4. Full participation of families
5. Integration with other child-caring agencies and programs
6. Coordination through case management mechanisms
7. Early identification and intervention

8. Smooth transitions to the adult service system
9. Protection of children's rights and effective advocacy
10. Cultural sensitivity and nondiscrimination

The system of care promoted by CASSP includes a range of non-residential services (such as outpatient, day treatment, home-based, and crisis services) and a range of residential services (such as therapeutic foster care, group homes, residential treatment, and inpatient services).

In California, the CASSP, for which funding began in July 1989, is administered by the California DMH. A retrospective evaluation of the CASSP in California has been conducted by our research group.

The major objectives of the CASSP research project were (a) evaluation of CASSP system-of-care demonstrations; (b) evaluation of CASSP efforts to develop interagency and interdepartmental coordination and collaboration; (c) evaluation of CASSP efforts to develop family participation and advocacy related to services for children and adolescents with emotional disorder; (d) evaluation of CASSP efforts to promulgate cultural competency in systems of care for children and adolescents; (e) evaluation of CASSP efforts to enhance allocation of resources to children's services and systems statewide; and (f) evaluation of CASSP efforts to develop more effective data collection and research related to services and systems of care for children and youth with emotional disorder.

These objectives were met through a variety of research methodologies. Throughout a representative sample of the 58 urban, suburban, and rural counties in California, face-to-face interviews with management and program staff in state- and county-level departments of mental health, social services, juvenile justice, and education, as well as with state legislators, state and local parent leaders, and mental health advocates, were conducted. Telephone interviews were conducted with a random sample of members of a statewide network of parents of severely emotionally disordered children and adolescents. In addition, an extensive review of relevant documents, including recent state legislation, departmental and organizational policy statements, and minutes of various state and local councils and committees, was implemented. Secondary data analyses of state-collected mental health treatment cost and utilization data, as well as demographic, diagnostic, and utilization data from 2 years of state psychiatric hospital data, were completed.

A technical report describing this project and presenting initial findings has been provided to the California DMH (Madsen, Dresser, Rosenblatt, & Attkisson, 1994).

Challenges and Obstacles
Encountered in Conducting the Research Program

The conduct of child services research in our setting is challenged by many factors that militate against optimal implementation of our research goals. We struggle to meet these challenges, and coping with barriers often consumes as much time for the project directors as does the direct scientific activity. On many occasions we sigh with relief when we can sit as a research team and focus without distraction on scientific tasks. Happily, these moments have become more frequent as the major research projects have taken shape and the research team has gained experience and cohesion.

Leadership Challenges

The Role Mix for Project Leaders

Leadership in child services research requires breadth of scientific skills and capacity to understand and manage a variety of human factors that greatly influence quality of the research and level of re-search goal attainment. Project leaders must be able to negotiate and plan with governmental and administrative personnel, understand the agendas and frames of reference of service program adminis-trators and service providers, supervise technical research staff and data collectors, train interviewers and support them in the field, and be able to see the research from the perspective of the service recipient and family members. In addition, project leaders must have, in com-posite, skills in biostatistics, computing, and research design. The mixture of these roles and skill areas presents a formidable challenge to leaders of child services research projects.

Communication of Project
Goals to Staff and Collaborators

Above all, it has helped enormously for us to convey effectively the goals and intellectual context of the research to the research staff and to our clinical and administrative collaborators. When we fail to communicate these goals and meanings to staff and colleagues, the process itself and our productivity suffer. It is not difficult to fail in this regard, and considerable emphasis must constantly be placed on the quality and timing of communications. Because budgets to support the research efforts are thinly stretched and are not ample to begin with, we often have to rely on young, bright, and inexperienced support staff. These individuals often possess excellent motivation and the fundamental verbal and quantitative skills. Nevertheless, they are inexperienced in research and often are distracted by social and developmental themes within their individual lives. This reality, in combination with initial lack of understanding of the overall research objective, creates special demands in the supervisory process. In response, project leaders must be attuned to their responsibilities as supervisors, role models, and articulators of research goals. Idealism combined with academic achievement and strong intellectual abilities provides a powerful base for creative action. With time, however, idealism must give way to acknowledgment of the limits and defects of the research project, given all the realities that must be faced. Project leaders must cope with this challenge in their own right while enabling the less experienced to make the transition. Not all arrive on the other side of the mountain.

Organizational Challenges

1. *Child services research is limited by the readiness of collaborating organizations to function as a system of care.* Readiness to function as a system of care proceeds from the awareness of the need for an organized system of services and progresses to the establishment of mechanisms required (a) to actualize a comprehensive approach to integrating types and levels of care, (b) to finance the essential organizational structures in order to manage consumer access and flow,

and (c) to plan and evaluate through information and control systems. Without such mechanisms, systems of care cannot form, exist, and flourish. Fragmented systems pull for chaos in the data collection process.

2. *System-of-care research is limited by the readiness of the system to collaborate in research.* The systems of care with which we have collaborated have demonstrated a range of readiness to actually participate in the research. Although eagerness is not highly correlated with readiness, it is an essential component of readiness. A careful assessment of readiness is a requirement before launching into a research project. Systems must also make tangible contributions to the research process in terms of funding, personnel, and space to conduct the work. Systems also must demonstrate the capacity to cope with presence of research personnel and integrate such individuals into the fabric of the system of care. In addition, research results are often not available for immediate use, and tolerance of this fact is an essential capacity for successful collaboration.

Methodological Challenges

Availability and Adequacy of Measures

Measures available for child and adolescent services research are generally lacking in depth of psychometric research and normative base. In addition, measures do not sufficiently allow assessment of the developmental components of disorder and dysfunction. Consequently, investigators must construct novel approaches and/or adopt measures for which there is limited consensus. Progress at this time must tolerate the study of the adequacy of measures in the context of collection of basic data. Although there are irrationalities in this approach, no progress at all will be made on basic questions if all resources are allocated to measurement development. The likelihood of the latter approach is highly remote. Whenever possible, we have attempted to construct observable indices of functioning about which there is a high level of measurement reliability and consensus about validity and utility as outcomes of service intervention. These indices, in combination with standard protocols and measures, bolster the overall utility of the research.

Multiple Respondents, Requiring
Complex Communication Networks

Research standards now include emphasis on the importance of obtaining data from a range of respondents (the respondent domain) reflecting multiple perspectives on symptoms, syndromes, and level of functioning. Our project includes measures requiring data collection from youth, their family members, their teachers, and their service providers. These measures address a broad range of measurement domains and social contexts. This measurement effort requires maintenance of a complex communication net across the respondent domain (Rosenblatt & Attkisson, 1993a). The challenge for us has been to staff and manage the complex process of identifying the respondents, recruiting them to participate, and exchanging information with respondents in person, by telecommunications, and by facsimile. When these tasks are multiplied by hundreds of subjects across several counties in a large geographic region, research activities become detailed and dynamic with regard to level of coordination required, communication styles that must be accommodated, and modes of communication that must be integrated.

Maintaining Consistent Project
Time Frames and Sequences

A priori research designs are orderly and rational plans. Unfortunately, implementation patterns of research designs often do not mirror the aspired level of order and rationality. Time frames are challenged at almost every step of project implementation. Considerable effort must be expended in synchronizing the initial planning phase, the interviewer training phase, and the assembly of the final measurement package. In our case, we also had to cope with the most powerful earthquake since 1906 in northern California—the Loma Prieta quake, which occurred in the initial phase of our work.

Maintaining an Adequate Supply of
Qualified and Motivated Interviewers

Due to cost constraints, we have relied upon relatively young persons with backgrounds in the social sciences who were able to work on a per-case contract basis. Most of these individuals have master's degrees and have had good training and experience as interviewers. Typically, the work opportunity is attractive as a way of attaining experience prior to further graduate study or until more lucrative salaried employment can be secured. Consequently, there is a need to replace interviewers lost to other employment or graduate study. In addition, the demands of field data collection in homes and service institutions are not acceptable for some individuals even when they are talented interviewers. Turnover requires constant training of new personnel and continuous monitoring and supervision of interviewers to identify and resolve problems or add skills that may affect interviewer effectiveness and resiliency.

Subject Identification and Recruitment

In service systems research, merely identifying the potential subjects to be included in the study can pose major challenges. Service systems often do not maintain high-quality records, and building an adequate subject pool from inadequate records can be a frustrating process. Fortunately, we have found, somewhat diagnostically, that the better organized systems tend to keep better records. In the most ideal settings, these records are computerized and readily available. This has, for the most part, been the case in at least two of our study counties. However, once youth are identified, finding the youth can prove difficult. Many of these families frequently change residences, further complicating the process of contacting families directly.

Once subjects are identified, the recruitment itself is an art, reflecting a dynamic process that requires judgment and basic clinical skills. There is extensive individual variability in the exercise of these skills. Subjects must be informed and must feel comfortable to choose or not to choose to be participants. When incentives are too high, or the individual sense of power and choice is too low, subjects can be enrolled without freedom of choice. A skillful recruiter provides as much objective information as the potential subject requires or can handle. The skillful recruiter knows how to ask questions and how to answer questions and solicit questions as a part of the decision-making process. The skillful recruiter knows when to withdraw and when to gently press for a decision. In the written literature it sounds as if a cold or impersonal process takes place in the recruitment of subjects. Indeed, some would urge that enrollment of subjects always occurs as a cool, rational, and linear process that does not involve a meaningful and a personal exchange. We feel that if this were the case, little or no research in the child field would ever be conducted.

Regulatory and Legal Challenges

Human Subjects Approval Process

The nature of child services research requires the investigator to be interested in and to collect data across multiple components of the child services delivery system. Of special interest as service system components are the mental health sector, the social services sector, the juvenile justice system, and the educational system. Frequently, when information about the adaptation and social functioning of youth within all of the domains of the child's life is needed, data are required from providers and administrators across all of these sectors. Usually, each sector requires its own individual review of the human subjects protocol. On occasion, even individual institutions that are within a single sector of care (such as psychiatric hospitals) require an independent review of the protocol. This often requires, in addition to a formal process, the informal presentation of study goals and objectives to groups of providers and administrators and an active process of engaging these individuals in the goals and objectives of the research project. This activity can be highly supportive of the ultimate goals of conducting the research, yet multiple reviews can frequently be redundant and overlapping processes. As long as services to children and youth are provided primarily within categorical streams of services, it is highly unlikely that anything can really be done about the degree of redundancy and overlap in the review process. One could argue that these requirements encourage critical scrutiny and provide the context for the necessary oversight that precludes the implementation of superficial studies or protocols that could potentially be invasive or harmful.

Legal Requirements for
Reporting Child Abuse and Neglect

In several instances in our research activities, it has been necessary to report child abuse or neglect that, to the best of our knowledge, was not previously identified or reported. Although the legal requirement for such reports is clear, care must be taken in how such reports are made. All the youth interviewed during the course of our research either are currently in treatment or were recently in treatment. In all cases of potential abuse or neglect, we try to work with the treating clinician to make the report in a way that minimizes potential damage to the therapeutic relationship between the family and the clinician. We do not proceed with a report until we have had the opportunity to speak with the clinician of record. In most instances, the clinician knows of the potential abuse and/or neglect and has already filed a report. In other instances, our discussion with the clinician is a piece of information that leads the clinician to file a report.

As a result of this process, in only a few cases has it been necessary for our research team to file such reports. In all cases of potential abuse or neglect, interviewers are required to receive supervision from senior members of the research team. All persons participating in the research are informed in the consent process of the need to break confidentiality should previously undisclosed abuse or neglect be found. Even with such safeguards, each potential report of abuse or neglect raises significant tensions for the research team. Respect for the parents and families must be balanced against the need to protect the child. Abuse and neglect are rarely obvious in the course of a research interview, so a judgment concerning the veracity of the claim virtually always needs to be made. An unnecessary report can lead to significant strains for the family, and a needed report not made can result in harm to the child. Either event can irrevocably damage the credibility of the research project.

Control of Confidential Data, Storage of Individual-Identified
Materials, and the Challenges of Electronic Media

Our research activities require the maintenance and control of large volumes of patient-identified confidential data. In most cases, within electronic media, such data are coded exclusively with unique subject numbers. However, in some cases during intermediate phases of the research, name-identified data are essential to allow for the creation of unique identifiers or integration of multiple data sets where there is no single unique identifier. Fortunately, most software programs currently allow for password protection of such files, and we use such measures on all confidential data. Nonetheless, such protection is not foolproof; therefore, in all of these situations, we are challenged to work speedily and effectively to reduce risks and at the same time prevent any activity that could minimize the immediate and long-term value of the data for current and sometimes unplanned purposes. Nonprofessional personnel have to be constantly apprised of the risk and enlisted in the effort to create security and protect confidentiality.

Fiscal Challenges

Cost Per Interview

The cost of enrolling subjects in child services research projects is formidable. The cost of each interview reflects the cost of personnel, training and supervision, supplies and services to maintain the interview process, subject recruitment, transportation, and ongoing recruitment of interviewers. The actual cost per interview varies by the complexity of the interviewer's task, the challenge of locating subjects for interview, the number of measures included, and the number of follow-up interviews. Our solution to controlling interview costs and ensuring efficiency in resource conservation has been to contract with interviewers on a per-case basis. This approach has allowed us to continue effective interviewers, discontinue less effective interviewers, avoid payment of hours not spent in the interview process, and modulate the level of effort as needed. The cost tradeoff has been in training expenses and loss of overall level of effort on several occasions.

Cost of Paper, Supplies, and Communication

Child services research projects are people and "paper" intensive. Documentation and communication require considerable resource allocation to consumable supplies, telephone and facsimile services, and photocopy services. In our projects we have gradually learned how to batch purchase large blocks of supplies to concentrate effort and to reduce per unit costs. This is a constant challenge, and fragmented purchasing often cannot be easily avoided.

Recruiting, Selecting, Training, and Sustaining Interviewers and Data Collection Personnel

These tasks have been ongoing and demanding challenges. Our project could not afford the inefficiency of full-time personnel, and subcontracting the interview and data collection protocols was not feasible due to the requirements of the collaborating systems of care and the advantages of having direct knowledge of the data collection process. Our choice to use contracts with individuals and to pay on the basis of completed interviews or blocks of effort has worked very well. Training costs may be a bit higher with this strategy, but the overall cost per case is considerably lower, the process is much more efficient, and the relative flexibility to eliminate ineffective personnel is incomparable.

Generalizing the Findings

Our studies focus on system-of-care demonstrations in four California counties. However, our findings should be generalizable not only to the state of California but to the nation as a whole. With respect to California, the counties participating in our studies include rural, suburban, and urban areas in both the northern and southern portions of the state. There is tremendous geographic, social, and ethnic diversity within these counties, ranging from coastal regions to deserts, from cities to farms, from some of most affluent regions in the state to some of the poorest. The model care system will be implemented in additional California counties during 1993-1994, with statewide implementation being the stated goal of the California DMH. It is hoped that study findings will play an important part in shaping statewide implementation of the model that began in Ventura County.

With respect to generalizing our findings to the nation as a whole, we argue that the change efforts underway in California are in response to the types of problems found in many other states as well as the entire country. In fact, models of care based on, or similar to, the original Ventura model are being implemented in many communities across the United States.

Finally, California is the largest and arguably most culturally and ethnically diverse state in the nation. Many of the pressures faced by the state today are likely to be faced by other states in the future. Developments in California are not unlike trends across the nation. In fact, California currently stands at the leading edge of both the potential problems and the potential solutions of treating the children and youth who suffer from serious emotional disorder.

References

Achenbach, T. M., & Edelbrock, C. S. (1983). *Manual for the Child Behavior Checklist and Revised Child Behavior Profile*. Burlington, VT: University of Vermont, Department of Psychiatry.

Achenbach, T. M., & Edelbrock, C. S. (1986). *Manual for the Teacher's Report Form and Teacher Version of the Child Behavior Profile*. Burlington, VT: University of Vermont, Department of Psychiatry.

Achenbach, T. M., Edelbrock, C., & Howell, C. T. (1987). Empirically based assessment of the behavioral/emotional problems of 2 and 3 year old children. *Journal of Abnormal Child Psychology, 15,* 629-650.

Achenbach, T. M., McConaughy, S. H., & Howell, C. T. (1987). Child/adolescent behavioral and emotional problems: Implications of cross-informant correlations for situational specificity. *Psychological Bulletin, 101,* 213-232.

American Psychiatric Association. (1987). *Diagnostic and statistical manual of mental disorders* (3rd ed., Rev.). Washington, DC: Author.

Attkisson, C. C., Dresser, K., & Rosenblatt, A. (1991, April 29). Service systems for youth with severe emotional disorder: Systems of care research in California. In *Close to home: Community-based mental health services for children, Hearing Before the Select Committee on Children, Youth, and Families, U.S. House of Representatives* (pp. 96-130). Washington, DC: Government Printing Office.

Attkisson, C. C., Hager, J., Rosenblatt, A., Smith, L. R., Dresser, K. L., & Strizich, M. (1993). *Informatics in child services research*. Unpublished manuscript, University of California, San Francisco.

Attkisson, C. C., Rosenblatt, A., & Dresser, K. L. (1990). *Assessing systems of care for severely emotionally disturbed youth in three California counties*. Paper presented at the annual meeting of the American Public Health Association sponsored by the Mental Health Section of APHA, New York City.

Barber, C. C., Rosenblatt, A. B., Harris, L., & Attkisson, C. C. (1992). Use of mental health services among severely emotionally disturbed children and adolescents in San Francisco. *Journal of Child and Family Studies, 1*, 183-207.

Beck, A. T., Ward, C. H., Mendelsohn, M., Mock, J. E., & Erbaugh, J. K. (1961). An inventory for measuring depression. *Archives of General Psychiatry, 4*, 561-571.

Brandenburg, N. A., Friedman, R. M., & Silver, S. E. (1990). The epidemiology of childhood psychiatric disorders: Prevalence findings from recent studies. *Journal of the American Academy of Child and Adolescent Psychiatry, 29*, 76-83.

Burns, B. J., & Friedman, R. M. (1990). Examining the research base for child mental health services and policy. *Journal of Mental Health Administration, 17*, 87-98.

Children's Mental Health Services Act of 1987, California Welfare and Institutions Code 5565.10-5565.40.

Cohen, P., O'Conner, P., Lewis, S., Velez, N., & Malachowski, B. (1987). Comparison of DISC and K-SADS-P interviews of an epidemiological sample of children. *Journal of the American Academy of Child and Adolescent Psychiatry, 26*, 662-667.

Commonwealth Institute for Child and Family Studies, Virginia Commonwealth University, and Florida Mental Health Institute, Research and Training Center for Children's Mental Health. (1990). *Report of the NIMH Child Mental Health Services Research Planning Workshop*. Richmond, VA: Author.

Costello, A. J., Edelbrock, C. S., Dulcan, M. K., & Kalas, R. (1984). *Testing of the NIMH Diagnostic Interview Schedule for Children (DISC) in a clinical population*. Rockville, MD: National Institute for Mental Health, Center for Epidemiologic Studies.

Costello, E. J. (1989). Developments in child psychiatric epidemiology. *Journal of the American Academy of Child and Adolescent Psychiatry, 28*, 836-841.

Costello, E. J., Edelbrock, C. S., & Costello, A. J. (1985). Validity of the NIMH Diagnostic Interview Schedule for Children: A comparison between psychiatric and pediatric referrals. *Journal of Abnormal and Child Psychology, 13*, 579-595.

County Welfare Directors Association of California, Chief Probation Officers Association of California, and the California Mental Health Directors Association. (1990, Spring). *Ten reasons to invest in the families of California: Reasons to invest in services which prevent out-of-home placement and preserve families*. Sacramento: Author.

Day, C., & Roberts, M. C. (1991). Activities of the Child and Adolescent Service System Program for improving mental health services for children and families. *Journal of Clinical Child Psychology, 20*, 340-350.

Dougherty, D. (1988). Children's mental health problems and services: Current federal efforts and policy implications. *American Psychologist, 43*, 808-812.

Dougherty, D., Saxe, L. M., Cross, T., & Silverman, N. (1987). *Children's mental health: Problems and services*. Durham, NC: Duke University Press.

Dresser, K. L. (1990). *The Robert Wood Johnson target population in San Francisco*. San Francisco: Child Services Research Group.

Feltman, R., & Essex, D. (1989). *The Ventura model: Presentation package*. (Available from: Randall Feltman, Director, Ventura County Mental Health Services, 300 Hillmont Avenue, Ventura, CA 93003)

Fisher, P. W. (1991). *Post-Traumatic Stress Disorder Module for the DISC 2.1*. (Available from the College of Physicians and Surgeons of Columbia University, 722 West 168th Street, New York, NY)

Fuchs, V. R., & Reklis, D. M. (1992). America's children: Economic perspectives and policy options. *Science, 255*, 41-46.

Inouye, D. K. (1988). Children's mental health issues. *American Psychologist, 43*, 813-816.

Institute of Medicine. (1989). *Research on children and adolescents with mental, behavioral, and developmental disorders.* Washington, DC: National Academy Press.

Joint Commission on the Mental Health of Children. (1970). *Crisis in child mental health: Challenge for the 1970s.* New York: Harper & Row.

Jordan, D. D., & Hernandez, M. (1990). The Ventura planning model: A proposal for mental health reform. *Journal of Mental Health Administration, 17*, 26-47.

Kaufman, A. S., & Kaufman, N. L. (1990). *Kaufman Brief Intelligence Test, Manual.* Circle Pines, MN: American Guidance Service.

Knitzer, J. (1982). *Unclaimed children: The failure of public responsibility to children and adolescents in need of mental health services.* Washington, DC: Children's Defense Fund.

Knitzer, J., Steinberg, Z., & Fleisch, B. (1991). Schools, children's mental health, and the advocacy challenge. *Journal of Clinical Child Psychology, 20*, 102-111.

Kovacs, M. (1991). *The Children's Depression Inventory.* North Tonawanda, NY: Multi-Health Systems.

Madsen, J., Dresser, K. L., Rosenblatt, A., & Attkisson, C. C. (1994). *Evaluation of the California implementation of the Child and Adolescent Service System Program.* San Francisco: University of California, San Francisco, Department of Psychiatry, Child Services Research.

National Advisory Mental Health Council. (1988a). *Approaching the 21st century: Opportunities for NIMH neuroscience research* (DHHS Publication No. ADM 88-1580). Rockville, MD: National Institute of Mental Health.

National Advisory Mental Health Council. (1988b). *A national plan for schizophrenia research* (DHHS Publication No. ADM 88-1571). Rockville, MD: National Institute of Mental Health.

National Advisory Mental Health Council. (1990). *National plan for research on child and adolescent mental disorders* (DHHS Publication No. ADM 90-1683). Rockville, MD: National Institute of Mental Health.

National Institute of Mental Health (NIMH). (1983). *Program announcement: Child and Adolescent Service System Program.* Rockville, MD: Author.

National Institute of Mental Health (NIMH). (1991a). *Caring for people with severe mental disorders: A national plan of research to improve services* (DHHS Publication No. ADM 9-1762). Washington, DC: Government Printing Office.

National Institute of Mental Health (NIMH). (1991b). *Child and adolescent mental health service system research demonstration grants* (Program Announcement 91-40). Rockville, MD: Author.

National Institute of Mental Health (NIMH). (1991c). *Implementation of the national plan for research on child and adolescent mental disorders* (Program Announcement 91-46). Rockville, MD: Author.

National Institute of Mental Health (NIMH). (1991d). *Research on hospitalization of adolescents for mental disorders* (Program Announcement 91-58). Rockville, MD: Author.

National Institute of Mental Health (NIMH). (1992). *Centers for research on mental health services for children and adolescents* (Program Announcement 92-20). Rockville, MD: Author.

Rosenblatt, A., & Attkisson, C. C. (1992). Integrating systems of care in California for youth with severe emotional disturbance—I: A descriptive overview of the California AB377 Evaluation Project. *Journal of Child and Family Studies, 1*, 93-113.

Rosenblatt, A., & Attkisson, C. C. (1993a). Assessing outcomes for sufferers of severe mental disorder: A review and conceptual framework. *Evaluation and Program Planning, 6,* 347-363.

Rosenblatt, A., & Attkisson, C. C. (1993b). Integrating systems of care in California for youth with severe emotional disturbance—III: Answers that lead to questions about out-of-home placements and the California AB377 evaluation project. *Journal of Child and Family Studies, 2,* 119-141.

Rosenblatt, A., Attkisson, C. C., & Fernandez, A. (1992). Integrating systems of care in California for youth with severe emotional disturbance—II: Initial group home utilization and expenditure findings from the California AB377 Evaluation Project. *Journal of Child and Family Studies, 1,* 263-286.

Saxe, L., Cross, T., & Silverman, N. (1988). Children's mental health: The gap between what we know and what we do. *American Psychologist, 43,* 800-807.

Shaffer, D., Fisher, P., Piacentini, J., Schwab-Stone, M., & Wicks, J. (1989). *Diagnostic Interview Schedule for Children (DISC-2.1).* New York: New York State Psychiatric Institute.

Shaffer, D., Gould, M. S., Brasic, J., et al. (1983). A Children's Global Assessment Scale (CGAS). *Archives of General Psychiatry, 40,* 1228-1231.

Smith, L. R., Attkisson, C. C., Dresser, K. L., & Boles, A. J., III. (1993). Implementation of the Robert Wood Johnson San Francisco Family Mosaic Project. In K. Kutash, C. J. Liberton, A. Algarin, & R. M. Friedman (Eds.), *A system of care for children's mental health: Organizing the research base. Sixth annual research conference proceedings.* Tampa: Florida Mental Health Institute.

Snowden, L. (1987). *Reaching the underserved: Mental health needs of neglected populations.* Beverly Hills, CA: Sage.

Stroul, B. A. (Ed.). (1990). *Child and Adolescent Service System Program Technical Assistance Research meeting.* Washington, DC: Child and Adolescent Service System Program Technical Assistance Center, Georgetown University Child Development Center.

Sue, S. (1977). Community mental health services to minority groups: Some optimism, some pessimism. *American Psychologist, 32,* 616-624.

Taube, C. A., Mechanic, D., & Hohmann, A. (Eds.). (1989). *The future of mental health services research* (DHHS Publication No. ADM 89160). Washington, DC: Government Printing Office.

Ventura County Children's Mental Health Services Demonstration Project. (1988). *Final report on the Ventura County Children's Mental Health Demonstration Project: A 3-year update and addendum to the 2-year report on the Ventura model for interagency children's mental health services.* (Available from Randall Feltman, Director, Ventura County Mental Health Services, 300 Hillmont Avenue, Ventura, CA 93003)

Index

About the Editors

Leonard Bickman is Director of the Center for Mental Health Policy at Vanderbilt University. He is a Professor of Psychology and Public Policy at George Peabody College, and a Professor of Psychiatry at the Vanderbilt School of Medicine, as well as Director of the Social Psychology Graduate Program at Peabody College. He has conducted major evaluation studies for foundations and federal and state governments. He is currently directing a large-scale evaluation of an innovative children's mental health system that is supported by a grant from the National Institute of Mental Health and a contract from the U.S. Army. He is coeditor of the Applied Social Research Methods Series, and on the editorial board of New Directions in Evaluation. He is past president of the Society for the Psychological Study of Social Issues, and a fellow of the American Psychological Association. His fellowships and awards include the City College of New York Distinguished Alumni Award for Outstanding Contributions to the Advancement of Psychology; Forchheimer Visiting Professor, The Hebrew University of Jerusalem; American Psychological Association Award for Distinguished Contributions to Education and Training in Psychology; and the Peabody Faculty Excellence Award.

Debra J. Rog, Ph.D., directs the Washington Office of the Vanderbilt University Center for Mental Health Policy and holds a Research Assistant Professorship in the Department of Public Policy. She currently is Principal Investigator of an evaluation of the Robert Wood Johnson Foundation/Department of Housing and Urban Development Homeless Families Program, a nine-city demonstration focused on establishing comprehensive service systems for homeless families with multiple problems. Other current areas of research involve services-enriched housing, children's mental health, and knowledge dissemination. Prior to joining Vanderbilt, she served as the Associate Director in the National Institute of Mental Health Office of Programs for the Homeless Mentally Ill, where she was responsible for developing and implementing research and evaluation activities. One area of focus was the development and evaluation of comprehensive systems of care for homeless, mentally ill individuals. She also is a recognized research methodologist, with publications and papers in the areas of applied social research and program evaluation, and has served as coeditor of the Applied Social Research Methods Series since its inception in 1984.

About the Contributors

C. Clifford Attkisson, Ph.D., is Professor of Psychology in the Department of Psychiatry at the University of California, San Francisco, and is Dean of Graduate Studies and Associate Vice Chancellor for Student Academic Affairs on the San Francisco campus. Previously, he served for 10 years as the Associate Dean of the Graduate Division and has been a member of the psychology faculty at UCSF for 23 years. He earned the Ph.D. degree in 1970 at the University of Tennessee, and his undergraduate work was completed at the University of Richmond in Virginia, his home state. He is a frequent contributor to the scientific literature in his field and is senior editor of three widely cited volumes: *Evaluation of Human Service Programs, Patient Satisfaction in Health and Mental Health Services,* and *Depression in Primary Care.* In addition, he has published numerous articles and book chapters in the mental health services research and the service system research fields. His teaching activities and research projects have focused on human services program evaluation, information systems for the human services, clinical services research, and service systems research. His current research program is a study of innovative systems of care for children and adolescents who suffer from serious emotional disorder.

Lenore B. Behar, Ph.D., is a clinical psychologist who is Head of the Child and Families Services Branch in the North Carolina Division of Mental Health, Developmental Disabilities, and Substance Abuse Services. She has been responsible for the development and oversight of child mental health services in North Carolina for 23 years.

289

Her experience in a progressive state, known for its leadership among the states in developing services for children, has equipped her well to serve as an adviser to other states and to federal agencies.

Theodore P. Cross is a Senior Research Associate at the Family and Children's Policy Center, Heller School for Social Welfare, Brandeis University. He is Principal Co-Investigator of the evaluation of the Robert Wood Johnson Foundation's Mental Health Services Program for Youth, and is currently a staff member of the Technical Assistance Center on Evaluation of Children's Mental Health Systems. His research examines systemic interventions in the areas of children's mental health and child abuse. Trained as a clinical psychologist, he maintains a private practice in child and family therapy.

Karyn L. Dresser, Ph.D., is a social psychologist trained in children's services research. She currently serves as the Research and Evaluation Coordinator for the Family Mosaic Project in San Francisco, teaches at Bay Area colleges, and consults to human service organizations regarding implementing comprehensive integrated systems of care for emotionally disturbed children and youth.

Mary E. Evans, Ph.D., is a Principal Research Scientist and the Assistant Director of the Bureau of Evaluation and Services Research at the New York State Office of Mental Health. She is also an Adjunct Associate Professor in the School of Public Health, State University of New York at Albany.

Robert M. Friedman, Ph.D., is a clinical psychologist who has specialized in research and policy analysis for children and families. He received his B.A. from Brooklyn College and his M.S. and Ph.D. from Florida State University. He is currently Professor and Chair of the Department of Child and Family Studies at the Florida Mental Health Institute, University of South Florida, and he also serves as Director of the Research and Training Center for Children's Mental Health. He is a researcher, author, policy analyst, and consultant on issues such as clinical services for children and families, the development and evaluation of community-based systems of care, collaborations between mental health and child welfare systems, and prevalence of emotional disorders. He has published and presented more than 125 papers and articles. He is coauthor with Beth Stroul of *A System of Care for Severely Emotionally Disturbed Children and Youth*, which has been widely used across the country to plan services for children with emotional disorders and their families. He is also coeditor of a special edition of the *Journal of Mental Health Administration* on children's mental health services, and coeditor of a book titled *Advocacy on Behalf of Children With Serious Emotional Problems*. He has consulted with more than 40 states and several federal agencies, has testified before congressional committees, and has been either a grant recipient or an adviser to several major private foundations. His current research includes multisite systems evaluations, longitudinal epidemiological studies, and analyses of the service needs of children in child welfare, mental health, education, and juvenile justice systems.

Judith K. Gardner was Associate Research Professor at the Heller School of Brandeis University and a Lecturer at Harvard University. She died in November 1994, shortly before publication of this chapter. She was a developmental psychologist and devoted her career to understanding and promoting research to aid children and families. She was a core member of the Children and Family Policy Research Center at Brandeis and was Principal Co-Investigator of the evaluation of the Robert Wood Johnson Foundation's Mental Health Services Program for Youth.

Craig Anne Heflinger, Ph.D., is a licensed clinical psychologist and Research Associate Professor at the Vanderbilt Institute for Public Policy Studies, Center for Mental Health Policy. She managed the start-up of the Fort Bragg Evaluation Project and the study of program implementation for that project. Her current projects include research on family issues in children's mental health services and policy and evaluation of state services to reduce the use of restrictive institutional mental health settings for children and youth.

Kathleen V. Hoover-Dempsey is Associate Professor, Department of Psychology and Human Development, Peabody College of Vanderbilt University. Her major research is on family-school relationships, particularly the role of parents' involvement in children's education.

She has examined, for example, the role of parents' sense of efficacy in involvement choices, strategies, and actions, and the influence of parents' involvement activities on perceptions of personal and parental functioning. Her scholarly publications have appeared in such journals as *American Educational Research Journal, Elementary School Journal*, and *Journal of Educational Research*. Long concerned with the mutually influential roles of families, schools, and child care programs in children's development, she is coauthor, with Nicholas Hobbs and others, of *Strengthening Families: Strategies for Care and Parent Education* (1984). She teaches courses in educational psychology and child, adolescent, and life span development; she has served as consultant to numerous early childhood, elementary, and secondary education programs.

Chris Koyanagi has more than 20 years of experience representing both mental health advocacy and provider associations in Washington. Currently she is an analyst of public policy issues for the Brazelon Center for Mental Health Law, a legal advocacy organization concerned about the rights of persons with severe mental illness. Her particular areas of responsibilities are health care reform and children's mental health services. She acts as chair of several Washington coalitions on mental health issues and provides leadership for coordinated lobbying strategies by the mental health community on major federal policy issues. She also provides technical assistance to congressional committees, members of congress and their staff as they develop legislative proposals; and she works closely with key federal executive branch agencies responsible for mental health services and rights of persons with mental illness. She has authored several publications and journal articles concerning mental health public policy.

Gretchen S. Lovas, M.A., is currently a doctoral candidate in the Department of Psychology at the University of California at Davis. She headed the organizational assessment component of the evaluation of the Robert Wood Johnson Foundation's Mental Health Services Program for Youth; she also studied the effects of the Child and Adolescent Service System Program on systems of care through a grant from the federal Center for Mental Health Services. Her current research interests concern infant social and emotional development, the attachment system in both infants and adults, and the intersections between early development and gender.

Kathleen A. Maloy, J.D., Ph.D., is a Research Associate and Deputy Director at the Center for Mental Health Policy. She has expertise in child and adult mental health policy and services research, state policy making, health care policy and financing, and health policy issues related to the co-occurrence of mental and substance abuse disorders. She has been working closely with state officials in Tennessee to develop collaborative evaluation plans for the Children's Plan, Tennessee's effort to reorganize and refinance the delivery of services for children. She recently completed a case study of the first 2 years of the Children's Plan, funded by the Annie E. Casey Foundation. Her other professional experience includes being a Senior Policy Analyst with the Mental Health Policy Resource Center in Washington, DC, where she was responsible for secondary research and evaluation, policy analysis, and legislative review. As Chief Legal Counsel for the Tennessee Department of Mental Health, Mental Retardation, Alcohol and Drugs, she was responsible for all legal aspects of department policy making and procedures, including operation of four state mental hospitals and three facilities for the mentally retarded. She participated in policy making on a range of issues including privatization, Medicaid financing, interagency relationships, and service delivery in the community. As an Assistant Attorney General in Tennessee, she represented the Departments of Mental Health, Education, and Labor in federal and state civil litigation, reviewed agency rule making and policy making, and advised the legislature on issues related to the constitutionality and legality of state laws and agency procedures.

Barry Nurcombe, M.D., graduated in medicine from the University of Queensland in 1955. He completed residency training in child psychiatry at the Children's Hospital Medical Center and Harvard Medical School, Boston. Subsequently, he has been the Director of Child and Adolescent Psychiatry at the University of New South Wales, Sydney, Australia, and the University of Vermont, Burlington, Vermont, and Medical Director, Emma Pendleton Bradley Hospital, East

Providence, Rhode Island. Since 1989 he has been Director of Child
and Adolescent Psychiatry and Professor of Psychiatry, Vanderbilt
University School of Medicine, Nashville, Tennessee. His publications have been in the following areas: psychosomatic medicine, the
preschool education of culturally disadvantaged Australian aborigi-
nal children, intervention with mothers of low-birth-weight babies,
hypothetico-deductive reasoning during the diagnostic process, the
hospitalization of adolescents, depression in childhood and adolescence, posttraumatic stress disorder and dissociative disorder in adolescence, and forensic child psychiatry. He has authored the following books: *Children of the Dispossessed: The Clinical Process in Psychiatry*
(with R. M. Gallagher), *Child and Adolescent Mental Health Consultation in Hospitals, Schools and Courts* (with G. Fritz, R. Mattison, and
A. Spirito), and *Child Mental Health and the Law* (with D. F. Partlett).

Sarah E. Ring-Kurtz, M.S., received her Bachelor's degree from the
University of California at Berkeley. She worked for 4 years at the
Center for Mental Health Policy at Vanderbilt University, training
and managing lay interviewers for the Child and Family Services
Project. Recently she completed her Master's degree in child clinical
psychology at Eastern Michigan University. Her clinical endeavors
include psychological assessment and psychotherapy with children
and adolescents from foster care and residential treatment settings.
Her research has focused on the assessment of psychopathology in
children, structured interviewing techniques in the diagnosis of
childhood mental disorders, and depression in college students.

Abram Rosenblatt is Assistant Adjunct Professor at the University
of California, San Francisco, Co-Investigator with a National Institute of Mental Health funded Center for the Study of the Organization and Financing of Services to the Severely Mentally Ill in Berkeley,
California, and Director of Research for the Child Services Research
Group. He earned the B.A. degree in psychology from the University
of California, San Diego, and M.A. and Ph.D. degrees in clinical psychology from the University of Arizona. His current research interests are in the area of mental health services and policy research, with
an emphasis on services to children with severe emotional disturbance. He is an associate editor of the *Journal of Child and Family*

Studies, and is a member of several national committees pertaining to children's mental health services evaluation and research. His recent scholarly contributions include book chapters and articles in peer-reviewed journals on depression, program evaluation, research methods, quality assurance, juvenile delinquency, outcomes research, integrations of economics and psychology in health services research, and children's mental health services research.

Leonard Saxe is Professor of Psychology at the Graduate School and University Center of the City University of New York. He is a social psychologist whose work focuses on the evaluation of social interventions and policy analysis. He has served as a Congressional Science Fellow at the Office of Technology Assessment (OTA). He was senior author of OTA's 1986 study, *Children's Mental Health,* and has been Principal Investigator of the evaluation of the Robert Wood Johnson Foundation's children's mental health initiative. He is the coauthor of a research text (*Social Experiments*) and numerous articles and chapters on the conduct of mental health research. He received a 1989 prize from the American Psychological Association for Distinguished Contributions to Psychology in the Public Interest (Early Career).

Diane L. Sondheimer is Deputy Chief, Child, Adolescent, and Family Branch, Federal Center for Mental Health Services. She also directs a portfolio of research demonstration grants that test the effectiveness of innovative models of organizing, delivering, and financing children's mental health systems.

Susan Sonnichsen is a student in the doctoral program of psychology and human development at Peabody, Vanderbilt University. She received her B.A. in psychology in 1989 from the University of Virginia, and her M.S. in psychology from Vanderbilt in 1994. She has participated in the Fort Bragg Evaluation Project since 1990, specifically addressing the issue of parental involvement in children's mental health services, in addition to other issues related to families. Currently, she is Data Manager for the Family Empowerment Project, an evaluation of an intervention program designed to enable parents to more effectively navigate the mental health service system for their children. Her clinical training program has included the provision of individual and group therapy in the public schools of Metro Nashville. Prior to coming to Vanderbilt, Susan was a Research Assistant in the Office of Programs for the Homeless Mentally Ill at the National Institute of Mental Health.

Mark L. Wolraich, M.D., graduated medical school and did his internship at the State University of New York Syracuse Health Science Center. He completed his residency at the University of Oklahoma Health Sciences Center and did a 2-year fellowship in developmental pediatrics at the University of Oregon Health Sciences Center. He is a Professor of Pediatrics at Vanderbilt University and is the Chief of the Division of Child Development in the Department of Pediatrics. He is also the Director of the Junior League Center for Chronic Illness and Disabilities of Children and the Greater Nashville Regional Program of the Tennessee Early Intervention System. He chairs the American Academy of Pediatrics Task Force on Coding Mental Health in Children, and he is the President of the Society for Behavioral Pediatrics.